ECONOMIC COMMISSION FOR EUROPE
Committee on Environmental Policy

ENVIRONMENTAL
PERFORMANCE REVIEWS

LITHUANIA

UNITED NATIONS
New York and Geneva, 1999

Environmental Performance Reviews Series No. 4

NOTE

Symbols of United Nations documents are composed of capital letters combined with figures. Mention of such a symbol indicates a reference to a United Nations document.

The designations employed and the presentation of the material in this publication do not imply the expression of any opinion whatsoever on the part of the Secretariat of the United Nations concerning the legal status of any country, territory, city of area, or of its authorities, or concerning the delimitation of its frontiers or boundaries.

UNITED NATIONS PUBLICATION
Sales No. E.99.II.E.7
ISBN 92-1-116709-4
ISSN 1020-4563

Preface

The ECE Committee on Environmental Policy included the Environmental Performance Review of Lithuania in its work programme in January 1997. In February of the same year, the preparatory mission for the project was organized, and a team of both national and ECE experts was formed to carry out the review. The Governments of Austria, Estonia, Finland, Moldova, Poland, Portugal and Ukraine made national experts available for the task. The Rome Division of the WHO European Centre for Environment and Health contributed its expertise and resources for the preparation of the review of environmental health issues. Two experts were funded by the Commission of the European Communities. The travel expenses of other experts from countries in transition and from the ECE secretariat were covered by extra-budgetary funds, which had been provided by Finland, Italy, and Norway. The successful conclusion of the project would not have been possible without the generous support from all these sources.

The review team prepared a report on the environmental performance of Lithuania before, during and after the review mission in Vilnius in October 1997. The Lithuanian partners in discussion with the review team did not spare time or effort in responding to the queries and requests made. The report by the review team, including draft recommendations for the solution of existing problems in national environmental policy and management, was updated in a further discussion in Vilnius in May, 1998, before it was submitted for evaluation to the ECE Committee on Environmental Policy at its annual session in Geneva, on 29 September 1998. A high-level delegation from Lithuania attended this session. It was headed by the Vice Minister of the Ministry of Environment and also included representatives of the Ministry of Agriculture and the Ministry of Health Care. The evaluation by the Committee was based on the in-depth preparation by two reviewing countries, Bulgaria and Finland. At the end of its evaluation, the Committee agreed on a final set of recommendations for inclusion in this publication.

The Peer Review of the EPR report by the ECE Committee on Environmental Policy permitted to address both strengths and weaknesses of environmental management in Lithuania during the transition process. Despite the considerable socio-economic difficulties that are being experienced, the Lithuanian Ministry of Environment has patiently succeeded in becoming an important actor in decisions affecting the development of the country's environment. The time-consuming process towards forthcoming and open partnership with all governmental and non-governmental forces involved or interested in such management has started. It can be hoped that the further evolution of the skills and means required for both the adaptation of environmental management to pan-European practices and the handling of existing management problems will enable the Ministry of Environment to develop successfully its routines for problem solution.

The ECE Committee on Environmental Policy and the ECE review team wish the Lithuanian environmental managers success in implementing and following up the policy recommendations that are included in this review.

LIST OF TEAM MEMBERS

Mr. Andreas KAHNERT	(ECE secretariat)	Team Leader
Ms. Ingrid THOMASITZ	(AUSTRIA)	Chapter 1
Mr. Vilius POGOZHELSKIS	(ECE secretariat)	Chapter 2 and Project Coordinator
Ms. Catherine CHALANDON-MASSON	(ECE secretariat)	Chapter 3
Mr. Guennadi VINOGRADOV	(ECE secretariat)	Chapter 4
Mr. Victor KARAMUSHKA	(UKRAINE)	Chapter 5
Mr. Andrzej JAGUSIEWICZ	(ECE secretariat)	Chapter 6
Ms. Lea KAUPPI	(FINLAND)	Chapter 7
Mr. Rafał MIŁASZEWSKI	(POLAND)	Chapter 7
Ms. Kaja PETERSON	(ESTONIA)	Chapter 8
Mr. Branko BOSNJAKOVIC	(ECE secretariat)	Chapter 9
Ms. Francesca RACIOPPI	(WHO/ECEH)	Chapter 10
Mr. Carlos DORA	(WHO/ECEH)	Chapter 10
Mr. Jorge BORREGO	(PORTUGAL)	Chapter 11
Ms. Margareta PETRUSEVSCHI	(MOLDOVA)	Chapter 12
Mr. Albrecht WENDENBURG	(GERMANY)	Advisor EU approximation process

The preparatory mission for the project took place on 19-21 February 1997. The review mission was organized from 1 to 10 October 1997, the update mission was carried out on 18-20 May 1998, and the peer review was held on 29 September 1998 in Geneva. The ECE Committee on Environmental Policy adopted the recommendations set out in this publication.

Information cut-off date: 30 September 1998

TABLE OF CONTENTS

List of figures... vii
List of tables.. viii
Abbreviations.. x
Signs and measures.. xii
Currency... xiii

Introduction: Features of Lithuania ....**1 - 7**
          I.   Major physical and social conditions.................................... 1
          II.   Economic development and policy... 3

PART I: THE FRAMEWORK FOR ENVIRONMENTAL POLICY AND MANAGEMENT

Chapter 1   Legal instruments and institutional arrangements.....................11 - 22
          1.1   Legislation and law enforcement.................................... 11
          1.2   Policy objectives and priorities....................................... 12
          1.3   Institutions and their mandates 12
          1.4   The approximation to the European Union...................... 15
          1.5   Environmental impact assessment 17
          1.6   Environmental monitoring and information 18
          1.7   Public participation 20
          1.8   Conclusions and recommendations 20

Chapter 2   Integration of economic and environmental decisions ....23 - 36
          2.1   Economic instruments for integration............................ 23
          2.2   Regulatory instruments.. 28
          2.3   Financing environmental expenditure 30
          2.4   Conclusions and recommendations 34

Chapter 3   Introduction of cleaner, safer and more sustainable technologies in industry........37 - 50
          3.1   Technological and environmental aspects of current industrial
                 development.. 37
          3.2   Policy setting for cleaner technology.............................. 41
          3.3   Instruments for the introduction of cleaner technologies 45
          3.4   Conclusions and recommendations 47

Chapter 4   Spatial planning ....51 - 61
          4.1   The framework for territorial development 51
          4.2   System of spatial planning.. 54
          4.3   Spatial planning in the transition period 57
          4.4   Conclusions and recommendations 59

Chapter 5   International cooperation..63 - 73
          5.1   Principles for international cooperation........................... 63
          5.2   Regional cooperation in the framework of UN/ECE 63
          5.3   Other regional cooperation 64
          5.4   Bilateral cooperation.. 66
          5.5   Global cooperation... 68
          5.6   International funding... 70
          5.7   Conclusions and recommendations 72

PART II: **MANAGEMENT OF POLLUTION AND OF NATURAL RESOURCES**

Chapter 6   **Air management**...**77 - 90**
         6.1   Air emissions and quality 77
         6.2   Policy objectives, institutional arrangements,
                available instruments and their application........................85
         6.3   Conclusions and recommendations 88

Chapter 7   **Water resources management and water quality aspects** ....**91 - 104**
         7.1   Water resources and use 91
         7.2   Water quality and major quality determinants...................93
         7.3   Objectives and implementation of water policy 99
         7.4   Conclusions and recommendations 101

Chapter 8   **Nature management** ....**105 - 118**
         8.1   Present state of nature 105
         8.2   Pressures on nature 107
         8.3   Nature policy and management 110
         8.4   Conclusions and recommendations 115

Chapter 9   **Waste management**...**119 - 132**
         9.1   Current waste flows and waste management.......................119
         9.2   Policy objectives and management instruments 126
         9.3   Conclusions and recommendations 131

PART III: **ECONOMIC AND SECTORAL INTEGRATION**

Chapter 10   **Human health and the environment** ....**135 - 152**
         10.1   Health status and environmental conditions 135
         10.2   Environmental health policy and management....................143
         10.3   Integration with other sectors 146
         10.4   Monitoring and information systems....................................147
         10.5   Conclusions and recommendations 149

Chapter 11   **Environmental concerns in energy**..**153 - 165**
         11.1   Energy production and use 153
         11.2   Environmental concerns, policy and management of the energy sector.............159
         11.3   Conclusions and recommendations 162

Chapter 12   **Environmental concerns in agriculture and food processing** ....**167 - 177**
         12.1   The present situation of agriculture 167
         12.2   Production techniques and environmental consequences 170
         12.3   Policy formulation and implementation 172
         12.4   Conclusions and recommendations 175

ANNEXES

Annex I   Selected economic and environmental data...181
Annex II   Selected bilateral and multilateral agreements 183
Annex III   Chronology of selected environmental events..185

SOURCES...**187**

LIST OF FIGURES AND TABLES

Figures:

Introduction
Figure I.1   Land cover, 1 January 1997

Chapter 1
Figure 1.1   The distribution of governmental functions in environmental protection after the Government restructuring in spring 1998
Figure 1.2   Structure of the Ministry of Environment (15 June 1998)
Figure 1.3   The full EIA procedure

Chapter 2
Figure 2.1   Environmental expenditure and share of investments, 1992-1997

Chapter 4
Figure 4.1   Preliminary EIA procedure

Chapter 6
Figure 6.1   Emissions of SO_x, 1996
Figure 6.2   Emissions of NO_x, 1996
Figure 6.3   Emissions of CO_2, 1996

Chapter 7
Figure 7.1   Water resources – intensity of use 1980-1995
Figure 7.2   Water use structure, 1996
Figure 7.3   Waste-water treatment structure, 1996
Figure 7.4   Water quality classification of the Lithuanian rivers
Figure 7.5   Water samples not corresponding to microbiological standard, 1986-1996
Figure 7.6   Water samples not corresponding to nitrate standard, 1986-1996
Figure 7.7   Changes of fertilization and nitrate nitrogen concentration in Lithuania, 1981-1994
Figure 7.8   Expenditures for waste-water treatment from the Lithuanian state budget

Chapter 8
Figure 8.1   Forest area by type of ownership, 1996
Figure 8.2   Forest area by categories of forests, 1996
Figure 8.3   Composition of mammal species
Figure 8.4   Institutional structures for species conservation and protected area management

Chapter 9
Figure 9.1   Composition of non-hazardous waste, 1992-1996

Chapter 10
Figure 10.1   Lithuanian public health institutional framework

Chapter 12
Figure 12.1   Land use by categories of farms, 1993 and 1996
Figure 12.2   Agricultural production by producer groups, 1990-1996
Figure 12.3   Use of mineral fertilizers, 1988-1996
Figure 12.4   Use of pesticides, 1988-1997

Tables:

Introduction
Table I.1   Major sector share of total output, 1991-1997
Table I.2   Main commodity groups of imports and exports in 1996

Chapter 2
Table 2.1   State budget revenues from environmental taxes, 1992-1997
Table 2.2   Reserves and extraction of selected mineral resources, 1989-1996
Table 2.3   Pollution charges in the state budget and the MEPF, 1992-1997
Table 2.4   Environmental funds, 1992-1997
Table 2.5   Share of loans and grants in foreign assistance, 1992-1996 (cumulative)
Table 2.6   Environmental expenditure, 1992-1997
Table 2.7   Environmental investment expenditure, 1992-1997
Table 2.8   Environmental expenditure and funds collected from environmental pollution, 1992-1997

Chapter 3
Table 3.1   Capacity utilization and investments in the manufacturing industry, 1992-1996
Table 3.2   Structure of industry, 1993-1996
Table 3.3   Final energy consumption sources and breakdown in industry, 1996
Table 3.4   Pollution loads generated by the main industrial activities, 1996
Table 3.5   Environmental protection expenditures and pollution taxes in industry by environmental media, 1995-1996
Table 3.6   Environmental expenditures and taxes in the main industrial sectors, 1995-1996

Chapter 5
Table 5.1   Yearly donor activity in the environmental sector, 1991-1996

Chapter 6
Table 6.1   Emissions of selected pollutants, 1991-1996
Table 6.2   Annual total classic emissions by source category, 1990 and 1995
Table 6.3   The most polluting single stationary sources, 1993-1996
Table 6.4   Transboundary import/export budgets, 1986-1995
Table 6.5   Passenger and freight transport, 1992-1996
Table 6.6   Number of road vehicles by vehicle type, 1990-1996
Table 6.7   Comparison of selected Lithuanian ambient air quality standards with recommended WHO guiding values

Chapter 7
Table 7.1   Characteristics of main rivers
Table 7.2   Water abstraction, 1992-1996
Table 7.3   Water use patterns, 1992-1996
Table 7.4   Discharge of waste-water into surface waters, 1992-1997
Table 7.5   Pollutants discharged into surface water, 1992-1996
Table 7.6   Environmental action programme in water management
Table 7.7   Investment expenditures for water pollution control, 1993-1996

Chapter 8
Table 8.1   Specially protected areas, 1996
Table 8.2   Health of trees in Lithuania and some neighbouring countries, 1996
Table 8.3   Population of the main hunted species, 1934-1997
Table 8.4   Hunting of the main species, 1965-1996
Table 8.5   Fish catch, 1991-1996

ix

Chapter 9

Table 9.1   Waste generation, 1992-1996
Table 9.2   Composition of domestic waste, 1992-1996
Table 9.3   Composition of construction waste, 1992-1997
Table 9.4   Hazardous waste generation, 1992-1997
Table 9.5   Secondary raw materials from domestic waste, 1993-1996
Table 9.6   Waste management action programme

Chapter 10

Table 10.1   Mortality rates by important cause of death, 1989-1997
Table 10.2   Standardized mortality rates for the most important causes of death, 1995
Table 10.3   New cases of occupational diseases, 1995 and 1996

Chapter 11

Table 11.1   Summary energy balance, 1991-1996
Table 11.2   Electricity capacity and generation, 1991-1996
Table 11.3   Indicators describing the energy economy, 1991-1996
Table 11.4   Power plants in Lithuania, 1995
Table 11.5   Emissions targets
Table 11.6   Consumer prices and tariffs, 1990-1996
Table 11.7   Energy prices for the 1997 heating period by producing enterprise

Chapter 12

Table 12.1   Heavy metals in the humus layer of soils in various Lithuanian regions

ABBREVIATIONS AND SIGNS

Abbreviations:

BaP	Benzo(a)pyrene
BAT	Best available technology
BATNEEC	Best available technology not entailing excessive cost
BOD	Biochemical oxygen demand
CEEC	Central and Eastern European Countries
CFC	Chlorofluorocarbon
CHP	Combined heat and power plant
CIS	Commonwealth of Independent States
CNG	Compressed natural gas
CPI	Consumer price index
CSD	Lithuanian National Council for Sustainable Development
$DeNO_x$	Denitrification
DH	District heating
EAP	Environmental Action Programme
EBRD	European Bank for Reconstruction and Development
EC	Council of Europe
ECF	Energy Conservation Fund
EEC	European Economic Community
EFF	Extended fund facility
EIA	Environmental impact assessment
EIU	The Economist Intelligence Unit
EFI	Environmental Fund for Investments
EMAS	Environmental Management and Auditing System
EMEP	Cooperative Programme for Monitoring and Evaluation of the Long-range Transmission of Air Pollutants in Europe
EPR	Environmental Performance Review
EU	European Union
FAO	Food and Agriculture Organization of the United Nations
FCCC	United Nations Framework Convention on Climate Change
FEZ	Free economic zone
FDI	Foreign direct investment
FGD	Flue gas desulphurization
FSU	Former Soviet Union
GDP	Gross domestic product
GEF	Global Environment Facility
GMO	Genetically modified organism
GTAF	General Technical Assistance Facility
IAEA	International Atomic Energy Agency
IEA	International Energy Agency
IFI	International financial institution
IMF	International Monetary Fund
INNP	Ignalina nuclear power plant
IPCC	Intergovernmental Panel on Climate Change
IPPC	Integrated pollution prevention and control
ISO	International Organization for Standardization
IUCN	World Conservation Union
HELCOM	Baltic Marine Environmental Commission
HIID	Harvard Institute for International Development
HFO	Heavy fuel oils
LAC	Limits of admitted concentrations
LEP	Law on Environmental Protection
LPG	Liquefied petroleum gas

LSD	Lithuanian State Standardisation Department
LST	Lithuanian Standards Board
MLIM	Monitoring, Laboratories, Information, Management
MEPF	Municipal Environmental Protection Fund
MAC	Maximum allowable concentration
MAP	Maximum allowable pollution
MSC-W	EMEP Meteorological Synthesizing Centre-West
MoA	Ministry of Agriculture
MoH	Ministry of Health
MoT	Ministry of Transport
NEAP	National Environmental Action Plan
NEFCO	Nordic Environment Finance Corporation
NEPP	National Environmental Protection Programme
NGO	Non-governmental organization
NIB	Nordic Investment Bank
NES	Lithuanian (National) Environmental Strategy
NSI	National Strategy for Implementation of FCCC
NU	Nutrient unit
ODS	Ozone-depleting substance
OECD	Organization for Economic Cooperation and Development
PIP	Public Investment Programme
PMU	Project management unit
POP	Persistent organic pollutant
REC	Regional Environmental Centre for Central and Eastern Europe
RED	Regional Environmental Department
RMI	Research medical and industrial waste
R&D	Research and Development
SDR	Special Drawing Unit
SEE	State ecological expertise
SIE	Statement of impact on the environment
SOE	State-owned enterprise
SME	Small and medium-sized enterprise
SNPF	State Nature Protection Fund
STF	Systemic transformation facility
TAP	Temporary allowable pollution
TBE	Tick-born encephalitis
TSP	Total suspended particulates
TU	Turbidity unit
UNCED	United Nations Conference on Environment and Development
UNDP	United Nations Development Programme
UNECE	United Nations Economic Commission for Europe
UNEP	United Nations Environment Programme
UNESCO	United Nations Educational, Scientific and Cultural Organization
UNIDO	United Nations Ogranization for Industrial Development
US$	United States dollar
USAID	United States Agency for International Development
VAT	Value added tax
VOC	Volatile organic compound
WB	World Bank
WHO	World Health Organization
WMO	World Meteorological Organization
WTO	World Trade Organization

Signs and measures:

..	not available
-	nil or negligible
.	decimal point
ha	hectare
t	metric tonne
kt	kilotonne
g	gram
kg	kilogram
mg	miligram
mm	milimetre
cm^2	square centimetre
m^3	cubic metre
km	kilometre
km^2	square kilometre
toe	ton oil equivalent
l	litre
ml	millilitre
min	minute
s	second
PJ	petajoule
m	metre
°C	degree Celsius
GJ	gigajoule
kW_{el}	kilowatt (electric)
kW_{th}	kilowatt (thermal)
MW_{el}	megawatt (electric)
MW_{th}	megawatt (thermal)
MWh	megawatt-hour
TWh	terawatt-hour
Bq	becquerel
y	year
cap	capita
eq	equivalent
h	hour
kV	kilovolt
MW	megawatt
Gcal	gigacalorie
Hz	hertz
GWh	gigawatt-hour

Currency

Monetary unit: Litas (plural: Litai), 100 Centai

Exchange rates: since 1 April 1994 Litas is pegged to the US$ at the exchange rate 1US$ to 4 Litas; the Lithuanian national currency, the Litas, was introduced on 25 June 1993. US$ exchange rate to ECU (European Currency Unit)

Annual average (in ECU)

Year	1 US$
1991	1.241
1992	1.304
1993	1.723
1994	1.189
1995	1.308
1996	1.268
1997	1.134

Source: UNECE macro-economic database.

Introduction

FEATURES OF LITHUANIA

I. Major physical and social conditions

Land and climate

Lithuania is the most southern of the three Baltic States, bordering Latvia to the north (610 km long border), Belarus to the east and south (724 km), and Poland (110 km) and the Kaliningrad region of the Russian Federation (303 km) to the south-west. The Lithuanian coastline is 99 km long. With a surface area of 65 301 km², Lithuania is the largest of the three Baltic countries. The country forms part of the great North European Plain and the landscape alternates between hilly areas and flat plains. There are two elevated regions: the Aukštaičiai Highlands and the Žemaičiai Highlands, which are a maximum of 290 m above sea level; and three plains: the Pajūris Lowland, the Central Plain and the Eastern Lowland. Lithuania has 758 rivers longer than 10 km. The longest is the Neman, or Nemunas, which is a transboundary river that flows through Lithuania over 462 km. There are 2 834 lakes larger than 0.5 ha, covering a total surface of 87 643 ha, of which the largest is the Drūkšiai (4 479 ha and 33.3 m deep). Forests cover 30 per cent of the territory; pine (40 per cent), spruce (20 per cent), and birch (18 per cent) predominate. Marshland accounts for about 7 per cent of the total area.

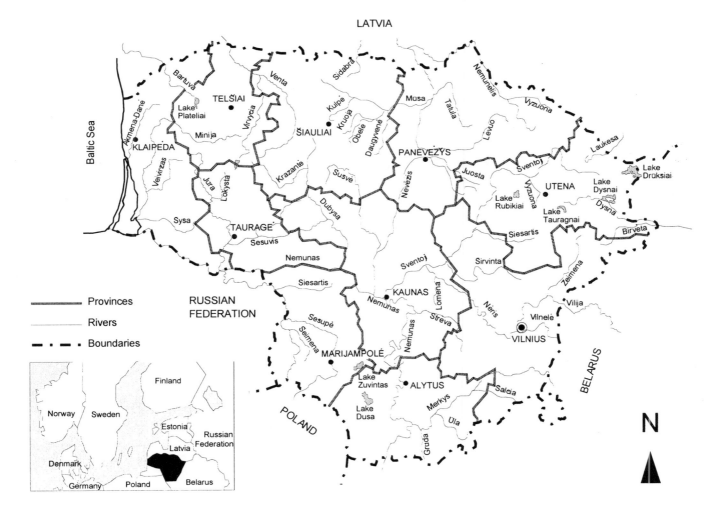

Lithuania has a maritime <u>climate</u> in its coastal zones and a continental one in the central part and in the east. Under the influence of westerly winds, the summers are moderately warm, there is 80 per cent humidity, and little snow in winter. The average temperature in January is -4.9° C and +17.2° C in July. Average annual precipitation ranges from 540 to 930 mm.

Figure I.1: Land cover, 1 January 1997

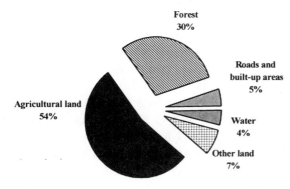

Source: Natural resources and environmental protection, Vilnius 1998.

Population and migration

The last census took place in January 1989, showing a population of 3 689 800. At the beginning of 1998, the population was estimated at 3 705 000 – some 13 000 fewer than in 1995. After an average annual growth rate of 0.83 per cent during the period 1979-1989, population growth has fallen to negative rates in recent years. From 1994 to 1996, the population decreased at an annual rate of 1.0 per 1 000. In 1996, the decline accelerated to 4.3 per 1 000 in rural areas, while in urban areas the population grew at a rate of 0.5 per 1 000. The overall decrease in the population is due mainly to the marked reduction in births, which between 1990 and 1997 declined by some 30 per cent (from 15.3 to 10.4 births per 1 000 population). The main minorities among the Lithuanian population are Russian (8.2 per cent), Polish (6.9 per cent), and Belarusian (1.5 per cent) (data for 1997). The population is to a large extent urban (68.4 per cent in 1997; 60 per cent in 1979) and the average population density is 56.8 inhabitants/km². The capital, Vilnius, had 580 100 inhabitants in January 1997.

According to the *Human Development Report*, especially the number of young rural migrants has decreased: in 1994, almost three and a half times fewer young people moved to urban areas than in the early 1980s. Job opportunities were slimmer in rural than in urban areas, but another major concern was the even wider discrepancy between educational opportunities in town and country. The impact of this trend is twofold. On the one hand, it may increase the proportion of youth in agricultural activities (a farm survey conducted in 1994 showed that only 4 per cent of farmers are under 30) and thus prevent an ageing of the rural population. On the other, due to the meagre infrastructure in rural areas, the low level of education prevalent among farmers may continue (educational levels in rural areas, according to the same survey, are below the national average and 68 per cent of all farmers do not have special agricultural qualifications).

Net emigration since the beginning of transition has been largely positive, though the rate is diminishing and in 1997 it became negative for the first time. Between 1991 and 1996, more than twice as many people emigrated from Lithuania than settled in it (77 505 vs. 28 027).

Social conditions

As in other countries in transition, worsening living standards and economic and social insecurity have an impact on health and life expectancy also in Lithuania. Life expectancy at birth peaked in 1986 (72 years). It reached its lowest level in 1994 (69 years) but increased to 70.6 years in 1996. A growing concern is the discrepancy between mortality and morbidity rates in urban and rural areas. Life expectancy nationwide is 6-8 years lower for men and 4-6 years lower for women than in western Europe. Discrepancies are also wide if broken down by gender: in 1996, Lithuanian women in cities lived 10.2 years longer than men, and in rural areas 12.9 years longer. However, life expectancy is the highest of all the three Baltic States.

The two main causes of death remain cardiovascular diseases and neoplasms. Deaths by homicide, suicide, drug and alcohol abuse increased till 1995 (11.7, 45.6 and 19.9 cases per 100 000 population respectively in 1995). In 1997, those rates improved somewhat (9.1 for homicide, 44.1 for suicides and self-inflicted injuries, 11.2 for alcohol poisoning). In general, deteriorating social and economic conditions have had a greater impact on health care provision in rural areas than in cities, leaving many rural areas with few medical services.

The annual registered unemployment rate rose from 3.8 per cent in 1994 to 7.1 per cent in 1996 and dropped to 5.9 per cent in 1997. Labour force survey unemployment rates are however twice as high. Over half of total unemployment affects women. The social dimensions of unemployment are reflected in the increase in long-term unemployment. In 1996, 32 per cent were long-term unemployed, representing a 25 per cent increase over the preceding year. The maximum duration of employment benefits is 6 months.

Legal, administrative and institutional structures

Lithuania became an independent State on 16 February 1918. In 1940, its independence was interrupted by the Soviet occupation. It was restored on 11 March 1990.

A new Constitution was adopted by referendum in October 1992, introducing a parliamentary system with a President as head of State, elected for a term of five years by universal and direct suffrage. The Seimas is a one-chamber parliament composed of 141 members elected for a four-year term. The Government is headed by a Prime Minister, who is appointed or dismissed by the President with the approval of the Seimas. The most recent parliamentary elections were held in October 1996.

The Seimas shares its right of initiative with the President of the Republic, the Government and 50 000 members of the electorate, who can propose a law which the Seimas is obliged to consider. A referendum can be held at the request of the Parliament or of 300 000 members of the electorate on the subjects of the greatest importance for the life of the State and the People (Art. 9 of the Constitution). To date, this procedure has been used seven times, but never on environmental issues.

Lithuania is subdivided into ten counties. In 1995, local government reform was introduced, consolidating 44 districts into 10, headed by governors appointed by the Government. The Governor and the county officials are responsible for implementing the regulations and policies adopted by the central Government. Local self-government is organized on the basis of the administrative territorial division of Lithuania. Local self-government takes place in 56 administrative districts and cities, represented by municipal councils elected for a period of three years by direct suffrage. The main functions of the local government are: the provision of amenities; municipal economy; municipal transport; some social security; health services and education. Local governments draft and approve their own budgets, which include notary and real estate taxes as well as some personal income tax. Local Councils have the right, within established limits and according to the procedure provided by the law, to establish local dues and to levy taxes and duties.

II.   Economic development and policy

Economic performance

Until 1991, industry was Lithuania's major economic sector. That year, it accounted for 44.4 per cent of GDP, followed by agriculture (16.4 per cent) and construction (5.4 per cent). During the first years of independence, Lithuania's industry suffered the steepest decline in the Baltic region, with production down by as much as 51.6 per cent in 1992. After a strong performance in 1995 with a growth rate of 6.2 per cent, industrial output slackened in 1996 (up a mere 2.8 per cent). The share of industry in gross domestic product has been declining (Table I.1). During the first six months of 1998, GDP increased 7.3 per cent over the same period in 1997. In June the projected annual GDP growth rate of 6.8 per cent was scaled down to 5.5 per cent, because of the Russian crisis. However, industrial production increased by 8 per cent during the first nine months of 1998.

Table I.1: Major sector share of total output, 1991-1997

% of GDP, current prices

	1991	1992	1993	1994	1995	1996	1997
Industry	44.4	37.5	34.2	27.0	26.1	25.8	24.0
Agriculture	16.4	13.8	14.2	10.7	11.7	12.2	12.7
Construction	5.4	3.9	5.1	7.2	7.1	7.1	7.3
Services	33.9	44.8	46.5	55.1	55.0	54.9	56.0

Source: UNECE Economic Survey of Europe, 1996-1997 and 1998 No.1.

Although growth in 1995-1996 was modest (3.3 per cent and 4.7 per cent, respectively on 1993 prices), the restructuring process has started to pay off. For example, labour productivity has significantly improved, with a total growth rate of 5 per cent in 1995, and even stronger growth in industry, in fact among the strongest in the countries in transition that year (14.9 per cent). The same year, 65 per cent of GDP was generated in the private sector. Investments in machinery and equipment, although modest, have increased in recent years, but have taken less than half of total investment outlays (42 per cent of total investments in 1997).

The main manufacturing sectors are food processing, light industry, machine building and metalworking, electronics and electrical appliances, chemicals, building materials, and energy industries. A major problem is that some of the main branches of industry are dependent on imports of raw materials, and production has been disrupted by the breakdown of traditional trade ties. Thus, light industry depends for around 83 per cent on imports of raw materials from the Commonwealth of Independent States (CIS) and other countries. Even though Lithuania is endowed with 1.9 million hectares of forests, and there is a long tradition of pulp and paper industry in the country, a substantial portion of the raw materials for paper and board production is imported. Bleached sulphate and sulphite pulp, non-bleached sulphite pulp, stone rosewood and waste paper are imported from the CIS. The chemical and petrochemical industries also depend heavily on the import of raw materials.

Another major problem for Lithuania's industrial production is access to new markets. The machine-building industry, for example, was a major source of exports before transition. For years, the technical and quality standards of the machine-building and metalworking industry met the former USSR and east European standards but only a negligible proportion of output was exported to western countries. Today this industrial sector is in need of restructuring to gain access to new markets. The electronics and electrical appliances industry, manufacturing audio-visual equipment, office information systems and information-related equipment, face the same problem.

The food industry is dominated by the production of meat, milk, and fish products. Lithuania's fishing industry is concentrated in Klaipėda, an ice-free trading port. In 1993, this sector was the main branch of industry by volume. However, the high prices of basic food products, the high production costs and the low purchasing power make the development of meat and milk processing difficult and have caused a decline in production. The production capacities of those enterprises are therefore not fully used. Light industry has relatively modern technology and more than half its equipment is imported from industrial countries. Its technology and qualified workforce have created the preconditions for high-quality production, giving this industrial branch a comparative advantage over other sectors for recovery.

Quarries of building materials are located in the vicinity of Vilnius, and near Kaunas. The construction industry, showing the highest level of privatization, uses local raw materials such as clay, quartz sand, gravel and dolomite. The biggest cement plant in the Baltic region is located at Akmenė in north-western Lithuania. It has an annual capacity of 3.6 million tonnes of cement. The construction sector shrank till 1993 before starting to recover. In 1997, it grew by 8.8 per cent.

The energy industry was developed during Soviet times for a Soviet-scale economy; today, Lithuania has electric power stations, developed electric and gas networks, an oil-processing industry and oil pipelines. However, the country imports approximately 93 per cent of its primary energy requirements. Mažeikiai refinery, the only refinery in the Baltic region, is Lithuania's largest industrial complex. More than 50 per cent of the refined products are exported. Lithuania is the largest electricity producer in the Baltic region, with 16.8 billion KWh generated in 1996. Lithuania's nuclear power plant produces 90 per cent of the country's electricity. Thermal power stations are mostly dedicated to meeting the heating systems' needs. Lithuania exports electricity to Belarus, Latvia, and the Kaliningrad region of the Russian Federation.

Economic policy

Economic reform was initiated as early as 1987 with the establishment of collective and personal enterprises. The transition to a market economy started after independence, when the Law on Initial Privatization of State Property was adopted in February 1991. Prices were liberalized in November of the same year.

Lithuania introduced a national currency, the Litas, in June 1993. It was pegged to the US dollar in April 1994 at an exchange rate of 4:1. Tight financial discipline and a relative stabilization have resulted in a decline in interest rates. The national budget consists of the State budget and municipal budgets. The Parliament adopts the State budget and municipal councils adopt municipal budgets one month later. Municipal budgets receive transfers from the State budget. The tax reform continues, providing an independent source of income to municipal budgets. The Central Bank cannot perform open market operations. Discussions are taking place to transfer monetary functions from the Currency Board to the Central Bank. It has been announced that the Litas will be pegged to a basket of the European euro and the US dollar.

Inflation soared in 1991-1992, with high levels continuing throughout 1993, as the economy felt the combined effects of price liberalization and wage increases aimed at compensating for inflation. The monetary policy pursued since 1994 has paid off: in 1997, inflation fell for the fourth consecutive year. Although inflation has fallen in all three Baltic States, the decline has been most marked in Lithuania, where the annual rate fell from 35.7 per cent in the second half of 1995 to 8.4 per cent in the same period of 1997. June, August and September 1998 saw deflation rates of 0.5, 0.6 and 0.4 per cent. Between September 1997 and September 1998, inflation rose 3.7 per cent.

A major priority in Lithuania's fiscal policy is to restructure the tax system, so as to minimize arrears, improve the Tax Administration System, introduce computerization and strengthen audit procedures. Budget problems exist due to corporate tax arrears, collapsing commercial banks and because of overestimated revenues. The 1994 budget earmarked 224 million Litas for subsidies. Large amounts were allotted to compensate heating

and gas enterprises for the preferential tariffs granted to households. The State-owned postal enterprise was subsidized, as was the State Railway Company for the reconstruction of railways.

The Government's economic development strategy aims at further developing market institutions, upgrading the economy's technological potential and its infrastructure by using foreign loans and foreign direct investment (FDI) efficiently. It also aims to integrate Lithuania into the EU political and economic structures, and to promote exports.

Trade

Before transition, Lithuania's trade relations were primarily with the former Soviet Union. It imported raw and exported processed materials. Since then, Lithuania has actively sought to access new markets. A free trade agreement with the EU was ratified in December 1994, and incorporated into the Association Agreement signed in June 1995. Under the terms of a 1994 memorandum with the International Monetary Fund (IMF), unified custom tariffs for all imported goods were to average 10 per cent (over a period of three years). A free trade agreement came into force on 1 January 1995. In 1996, a free trade agreement on agricultural products with the Baltic States also became effective. In spite of trade liberalization, the Russian Federation remains Lithuania's main trading partner. Mineral products represent one fifth of Lithuania's imports (Table I.2). In 1997, the merchandise trade deficit stood at 7.1 billion Litas, up from 4.8 billion Litas in 1996. During that period, exports grew 14.3 per cent, while imports surged 22.7 per cent.

Privatization

In 1990-1991, a legal framework for privatization was set up. The Law on Initial Privatization (1991) was followed by the Law on the Restitution of Property to Owners who had been expropriated in 1940. Private enterprise was regulated by a law enacted in May 1990. In December 1991 this was followed by the Law on Small Enterprises, which provided tax concessions for small and medium-sized enterprises (SMEs). According to the Law on Initial Privatization, two thirds of State property (except budget institutions, land and agricultural enterprises) was earmarked for privatization. By early 1994, over 4 000 economic units, or 69 per cent of all assets eligible for privatization, had been privatized, including 2 000 large and medium-sized enterprises. By early 1995, 77 per cent of the existing housing stock had been privatized. In 1996, 452 enterprises were listed. However, only 47 enterprises were privatized, generating 3 233 million Litas. The Privatization Programme for 1997 included 842 enterprises, with an expected sales value of 450 million Litas. In February 1997, the Government announced that the list of companies to be privatized by the year 2000 had increased, as part of the energy, communications, and transport industries would be included. The State Property Fund reported that 2.21 billion Litas worth of assets were privatized to the Fund: 17 million Litas worth of assets were privatized within local government privatization institutions during the first nine months of 1998. Also, the shares of 10 State-owned enterprises were sold at the National Securities Exchange. Moreover, by September 1998, Lithuania had managed to sell Lithuanian Telecom and negotiations have been completed to sell a third of the oil industry to a strategic investor.

Foreign investment

Between 1994 and 1996 FDI stock increased to US$ 700 million and surged to US$ 1.05 billion in 1997. FDI amounted to US$ 1.23 billion by 1 July 1998. Unlike its Baltic neighbours and many other countries in transition, Lithuania was not affected by the slump in FDI flows in 1996, probably due to the privatization and the investment policy measures described below. Sixty-two per cent of FDI capital is of EU origin. Annual FDI inflow to GDP rates were just over 4 per cent in 1996 and 4.5 per cent in 1997.

The tax legislation provides a three-year tax break if foreign capital was invested before 1 January 1992 and makes up 25 to 75 per cent of the total ownership capital. If a firm with foreign capital was established prior to 31 December 1993 and reinvested profits, the profit tax was waived. In 1996, two important bills were passed to promote foreign investment. The land reform bill enacted in July 1996 allowing foreign enterprises to buy land not only encouraged investment, but also removed a major obstacle to Lithuania's accession to the EU. The other law enacted in 1996 was the bill allowing foreign banks to operate through branch offices, which also had the twofold effect of

facilitating foreign investment operations and of being a step in the direction of harmonizing the country's banking laws with those of the EU.

In 1995, when the Central Bank imposed tighter control and compliance with the Law on Commercial Banks, enacted in January 1995, several major banks collapsed and the country faced a general banking crisis. Sweeping measures were taken to reform the banking sector and to liberalize financial services. In May 1996, of the 27 banks licensed in Lithuania, 16 were under suspension or facing bankruptcy proceedings. Only three banks met statutory requirements. In June 1996, a law introducing recapitalization securities was enacted, a condition imposed by IMF in return for a loan to overcome the effects of the banking crisis, and a plan was drawn up to restructure the banking system.

Table I.2: Main commodity groups of imports and exports in 1996

%

Imports		Exports	
		Agricultural food products and beverages	16.9
Mineral products	20.1		
Machinery and metalworking equipment	16.3	Mineral products	15.7
Transport equipment	9.9	Textiles	15.2
		Machinery and electrical	11.4
Chemicals	9.5		
Textiles	7.8	Chemicals	11.1
		Transport vehicles and equipment	7.3
Foodstuffs	5.0		

Source: EIU Country Report, 1st quarter 1998.

External financing

A major obstacle to large-scale investment had been the shortage of capital. Domestic financial markets were largely underdeveloped. Access to international financial markets was limited, and Lithuania did not have international credit standing. Since 1996, several positive developments took place, improving Lithuania's position vis-à-vis international creditors. Following its debut on the Euromarket with a

US$ 60 million Eurobond issue in December 1995 as it benefited from the favourable situation in east European markets, a 6-month syndicated loan was arranged through JP Morgan in May 1996. By the end of the summer, the country had raised US$ 158 million on international financial markets. In September of that year, Lithuania received its first sub-investment (speculative) credit rating Ba2 from Moody's. Now it has long-term investment BBB rating from Standard and Poor's (confirmed in September 1998) and a sub-investment Ba1 rating from Moody's. In 1996 alone, Lithuania issued equities worth US$ 21 million on international markets.

Lithuania is a member of IMF and the World Bank. In 1995 the former approved an Extended Fund Facility (EFF) worth SDR 135 million over a two-year period, and Lithuania received a US$ 80 million Structural Adjustment Loan from the World Bank to address structural reforms in banking, agriculture, energy and social security. Lithuania has also received grants under EU Phare programmes and from the European Bank for Reconstruction and Development (EBRD).

Lithuania's debt increased tenfold between 1993 and 1996. However, gross debt represented only 16 per cent of GDP that year. In the first three quarters of 1996, capital inflows were sufficient to finance the current account deficit and to increase foreign exchange reserves. However, because of the rapid growth in imports of goods and services, the reserve-import ratios weakened, falling short of the recommended three-month ratio. With a gross debt of US$ 1 217 million, Lithuania is the "most" indebted of the three Baltic States, Estonia and Latvia being net creditors. In 1997, the domestic debt stood at 23 per cent of GDP and foreign debt at 20 per cent of exports.

PART I: THE FRAMEWORK FOR ENVIRONMENTAL POLICY AND MANAGEMENT

Chapter 1

LEGAL INSTRUMENTS AND INSTITUTIONAL ARRANGEMENTS

1.1 Legislation and law enforcement

Like other democratic constitutions, Lithuania's lays down basic civil rights and obligations. Although it does not include a specific right to a healthy environment, it nevertheless obliges citizens to protect the environment and the State to concern itself with the protection of the natural environment. Article 53 stipulates that „the State and each individual must protect the environment from harm". Article 54 broadly outlines how the State should do this. It stipulates that: „The State shall concern itself with the protection of the natural environment, its fauna and flora, individual objects of nature and particularly valuable areas, and shall supervise the moderate utilization of natural resources as well as their restoration and growth. The exhaustion of land, water and mineral resources, water and air pollution, the creation of radioactive impact as well as the impoverishment of fauna and flora shall be prohibited by law".

The Law on Environmental Protection (LEP) of 21 January 1992 lays down the basic principles of environmental protection. Its main objective is to achieve an ecologically sound and healthy environment on which human activities have little negative impact and which can maintain Lithuania's typical landscape as well as its diversity of biological systems. The Law foresees environmental impact assessments (EIA) and prescribes the polluter-pays principle. It also encourages citizens and public organizations to participate in environmental protection.

The LEP is a framework law and forms the legal basis for the enactment of all laws and administrative acts that regulate the use of natural resources and protect the environment. It sets up the Ministry of the Environment, which initiates laws on environmental protection and, generally, sees to it that the Government also protects the environment. Legal and natural persons who violate an environmental law and cause damage to the environment can be held liable under both criminal and civil law.

```
Box 1.1 Selected environmental legislation

Laws
Law on Environmental Protection (1992),
Law on Environmental Impact Assessment (1996),
Law on Territorial Planning (1995),
Laws on Land (1994) and Land Reform (1991),
Laws on the Protection and Use of Wildlife (1991), on
Protected Areas (1993), and on Animal Protection (1997),
Laws on Plant Protection (1995) and on Wildlife (1997),
Law on Forestry (1994),
Law on Waste Management (1998),
Law on Clean Air (1981, fundamental review due in 1999),
Laws on Water (1997), and on the Protection of the Marine
Environment (1997),
Laws on Taxes on State Nature Resources (1991), and on
the Use of Oil and Gas Resources (1992),
Law on Environmental Pollution Charges (1991),
Law on Nuclear Energy (1996),
Law on Energy (1997),
Law on Environmental Monitoring (1997).
```

On 13 November 1997, Parliament passed the Law on Invalidating the Legislation Adopted Before 11 March 1990 on the Territory of the Republic of Lithuania. This Law stipulates that all former Soviet regulations will be repealed as from 31 December 1998.

There are many government resolutions, decrees and other regulatory measures aimed at protecting the environment and using natural resources rationally. Since 1991 environmental charges have been imposed on pollution and on the use of resources (see Chapter 2). The charges are meant to compensate for damage and pay for restoration. The Seimas is currently considering a new draft law on pollution charges. The envisaged system is expected to strengthen pollution prevention (precautionary principle). Lithuania is also a party to a number of international environmental conventions and treaties (see Chapter 5).

Permits are required for all significantly polluting activities. All economic activity has to comply with environmental standards. The authority responsible for permitting depends on the nature of the activity for which the permit is sought. If the activity is expected to pollute substantially, the permit has to be granted by the Ministry of the Environment. Each permit contains provisions and requirements to bring the activity in line with the applicable standards. An applicant who can meet all the requirements is legally entitled to the permit.

1.2   Policy objectives and priorities

Objectives

The first National Environmental Protection Programme (NEPP) was drawn up in 1992. It addressed the major environmental problems in priority order. However, soon economic restructuring and new environmental policy goals and priorities were required, together with more effective ways to achieve them. In 1994, the EU PHARE programme helped Lithuania to develop its National Environmental Strategy (NES). The Parliament approved the NES in September 1996. The Ministry of the Environment appointed a task force and, with the assistance of consultants from Ireland, an action programme was finalized in 1995. The Action Programme, being a constituent part of NES, was approved separately by the Government in August 1996. The working document NEPP of 1995 served as a basis for both the NES and the Action Programme and consists of three parts:

- Strategy Rationale: the assessment of the state of the environment, national economic sectors' review, environmental trends and forecasts, a description of the institutional, legal and economic systems.
- Strategy Methodology: defining the concept of the Strategy, outlining the top priorities and their justification, assessment techniques, urgency and implications of the problems.
- Action Programme: including long-, short- and medium-term action programmes, and the means to implement them.

Lithuania's NES aims to achieve sustainable development so as to be able to preserve a clean and healthy natural environment, biological and landscape diversity and ensure optimal natural resource use. Its objectives span the usual areas of protection of environmental media as well as activities giving rise to environmental risks. They include notably objectives for the protection of the Baltic Sea and for tourist areas.

Lithuania's NES includes an Environmental Master Plan with Environmental Projects for Kaunas. The city council of Kaunas had asked for help with its energy/environmental problems. Kaunas city council wanted to know whether its energy supply, primarily the heating supply, could be provided in a more effective and energy-efficient way. The Strategy also deals with questions of financing environmental protection measures. Currently a training programme is being prepared for Lithuanian officials dealing with these objectives.

Priorities

The following priorities for environmental policy and management are identified in NEPP (1995) and environmental legislation:

- Waste-water treatment and reduction of discharges
- Air pollution reduction
- Hazardous waste management
- Domestic and other non-hazardous waste management
- Protection from physical pollution
- Optimization of land use and forest structure
- Prevention of further natural landscape degradation
- Protection of ecologically sensitive and natural areas
- Rehabilitation of abandoned quarries
- Rational use of natural resources

1.3   Institutions and their mandates

The Department of Environmental Protection was created in July 1990 as an independent agency directly subordinated to the Seimas, which also appointed its Director-General. Although the Department was not formally part of the Government, its Director-General could advise the Government on environmental policy.

In 1994, the Ministry of Environmental Protection (MEP) was founded to integrate environmental protection more efficiently into the general decision-making process, and to underline the importance of pollution prevention. The Ministries of Agriculture and Forestry (protection of forest resources), of Health (effect of air pollution on human health, drinking water, hospital and medical waste treatment), of the Economy (management of

Figure 1.1: Structure of the Ministry of the Environment Please move the illustration to have it symetrically on the page

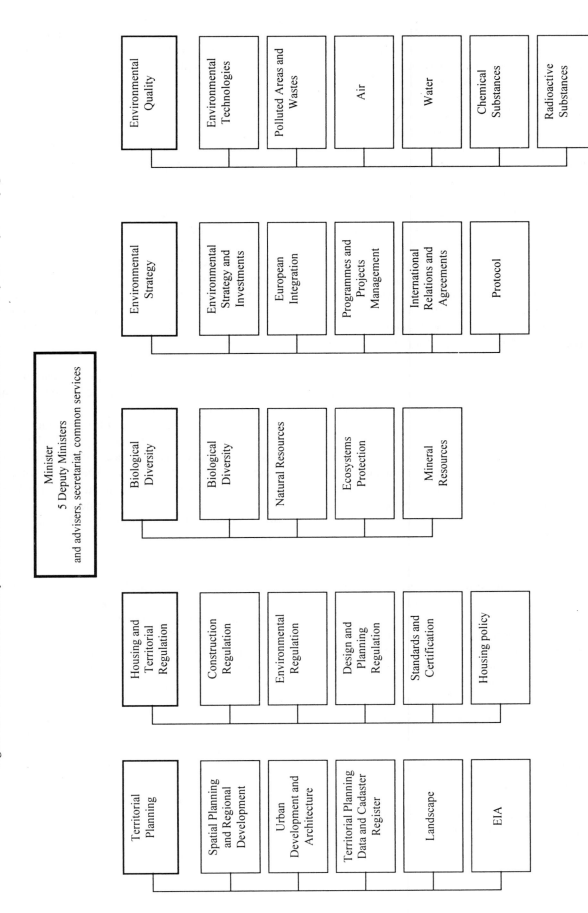

Source: UN/ECE secretariat, from more detailed material provided by the Lithuanian Ministry of the Environment

hazardous waste), and of Construction and Urban Development (territorial planning) also dealt with environmental protection issues. The Minister in charge of a certain case was also responsible for coordination. The necessity to assign issues to different authorities meant that it was difficult to find solutions quickly. An example of an issue with many ramifications was the preservation of biological resources. It fell under the responsibility of the MEP. At the same time, the former Ministries of Agriculture and Forestry and of Construction and Urban Development were also involved in related management tasks, as they regulated the economic use of resources affecting biodiversity. The National Council for Sustainable Development will be created in 1998.

In spring 1998, the Government was restructured. The number of ministries was cut from 17 to 14. The territorial planning part of the former Ministry of Construction and Urban Development and the forestry part of the former Ministry of Agriculture and Forestry were merged together with the former Ministry of Environmental Protection into the Ministry of the Environment. This new Ministry has been strengthened.

The Ministry implements all regulations on the use of natural resources and manages environmental protection. Accordingly, it prepares the main parts of the proposals on these matters. Depending on the character of the legal acts, they are issued by order of the Minister, adopted by governmental decision, or approved by Parliament. The Ministry's structure is set out in Figure 1.1. It concentrates on environmental policy and the design of management instruments (emission standards, permitting system, EIA, economic instruments). Implementation of these instruments is left to the regional and local levels. The Ministry maintains administrations in eight environmental regions. Each environmental region has its own Environmental Protection Department, consisting of 5 to 10 agencies staffed with inspectors. In all, there are 56 such agencies. Currently, it is being discussed whether or not the Environmental Protection Departments should be merged with the county administrations.

The Law on Environmental Protection and the Law on Local Government (1995) determine the responsibility of State institutions and local authorities in environmental protection. According to the Law on Environmental Protection, local governments shall:

- organize the implementation of laws and governmental decisions on environmental protection;
- prepare, approve and implement the programmes, plans and projects concerning environmental protection and use of natural resources within their jurisdictions;
- permit the use of natural resources, within established limits.

The implementation of environmental regulations is entrusted to the local authorities. Local governments may, in agreement with the Government, set stricter norms in their own jurisdictions and may establish protected areas and monuments of local significance.

The regional departments' main responsibilities concern the permitting system, environmental impact assessment, laboratory control and enforcement of environmental regulations. To carry out those functions, regional departments have centrally-based core staff and district Environmental Protection Agencies. Inspectors have access to plants and installations. Operators have to keep inspectors informed. Inspectors can order laboratories to monitor pollution, and they can impose penalties if regulations or permit conditions are violated.

Enforcing environmental legislation, regulations and standards is the responsibility of inspectors from the regional departments and agencies operating under the Ministry as well as of the Municipal Environmental Departments. The enforcement process is largely based on a system of permits and self-monitoring, with environmental inspectors periodically checking emission levels to verify the accuracy of operators' reports. All pollution is 'taxed', even if it is within the permissible limits. Failure to report (or fraudulently reporting) environmental information and releasing pollutants without a permit are considered violations subject to penal action (see Chapter 2).

There are no explicit provisions for public participation in enforcement, although broad citizens' rights to information and public consultation apply to enforcement as well.

1.4 The approximation to the European Union (EU)

General context

Lithuania applied for EU membership on 8 December 1995. As a result, its environmental policy became subject to considerable influence from the EU. The PHARE programme is used to assist the applicants in harmonizing their legislation and to provide know-how, including policy advice and training. Between 1990 and 1997, Lithuania received ECU 19.3 million from it. Between 1996 and 1999, support to Lithuania will amount to ECU 152 million. For the environment only ECU 4 million are foreseen (2.63 per cent). The General Technical Assistance Facility (GTAF) is worth ECU 29.8 million (for standards, training and institutional capacity building). Also, the European Commission published the 'White Paper - preparation of the associated CEECs for integration into the internal market of the Union' (1995). It points out key measures (Stage I measures) for different sectors of the economy. Lithuania, on its part, has developed the Approximation Strategy (1998) and is implementing it. All White-Paper laws should be transposed by the year 2000.

On 1 February 1998, the Europe Agreement with Lithuania entered into force, replacing the Free Trade Agreement of 1995. The aim is to further approximate legislation (to achieve legal security and transparency for economic agents). To achieve this and to make assessment data comparable, technical assistance will be provided. The European Commission aims at "putting in place a modern and environmentally acceptable infrastructure connected to wider European networks". The Association Committee, comprised of senior officials from the European Commission and Lithuania, has been established to this end. A Parliamentary Committee has been put in place to foster cooperation between members of the European and Lithuanian Parliaments. The Association Committee prepares decisions for the Association Council, which is the supreme institution supervising the Association Agreement. It convenes once a year to adopt decisions related to the Agreement's implementation.

White Paper (1995) and Lithuania's approximation efforts

The amendment (1996) to Article 140 of the Constitution requires each new legal act to conform to EU requirements and directives. By 30 June 1997, Lithuania had adopted national legislation referring to 316 of the 899 directives and regulations mentioned in the White Paper. The Law on Environmental Protection establishes principles for environmental protection which fully correspond to Article 130 r2 of the Treaty of Rome (namely the precautionary, the polluter-pays, and 'solving problems at the source' principles). It goes even further by establishing the principle of sustainable development, which corresponds to Article 2 of the Treaty of Rome (the principles of liability, of open access to information and of cooperation). The Law on Environmental Protection establishes an EIA procedure in which the public and NGOs can participate.

The White Paper's Stage I measures that relate to environmental policy and management can be assessed as follows:

(i) Radioactive contamination of foodstuffs: EEC and EURATOM legislation aims for an inspection and control system at the external frontiers. According to the EEC, the legal framework is not divisible and should be adopted as a Stage I measure. Lithuania's Constitution forbids "radiation impact on the environment" (Art.54). It obliges the legislator to follow "these regulations and the other acts and legal directions regulating the environment". Yet, there is no comparable legal framework in place. There is no inspection system at the external frontiers. Lithuania's Air Quality Monitoring Programme deals with toxic materials as well as with radiological air pollution monitoring and research. Analytical methods are different from those used in the EU. The Government is committed to adjusting standards of analysis to those of the EU. The draft governmental resolution on the import, export and transit of radioactive substances incorporates regulations 1493/93/EURATOM on shipments of radioactive sources between Member States.

(ii) Radiation protection: being Stage I measures, EURATOM regulations lay down basic safety standards; define a system of reporting and procedures to authorize any activity that produces ionizing radiation; and determine the supervision of radioactive waste shipments. Lithuania's National Energy Strategy (1994), which is in line with EU principles, addresses the key issues of the energy sector (security of energy supplies, rehabilitation of the energy infrastructure and increased cooperation with the other Baltic countries and EU). Although the Framework Act on Nuclear Safety has entered into force, supplementary legislation on radiation protection and radioactive waste management is necessary. Lithuania is not yet a party to all international regimes (the Nuclear Suppliers Group and the IAEA scheme for extended reporting on certain nuclear material transfers). However, Lithuania has a full-fledged safeguard agreement with the International Atomic Energy Agency (IAEA).

(iii)   Chemical   substances: the   Dangerous Substances Directive 67/548/EEC aims at harmonizing the classification, labelling, packaging and data sheets for dangerous substances, as well as notifying new substances (marketed after 1981). Lithuania   has   established   an   integrated 'Environment and Health Information System', interpreting the requirements of the Directive. For plant protection (chemical disinfection, detergents and cleansers), a list in accordance with EU norms already exists. The potential problem area is coordinating the implementation. The Ministry of the Environment has competence over chemicals needed to protect the environment (draft law on chemicals), whereas the Ministry of Health has competence with respect to the protection of human health (draft law on control of toxic substances). The White Paper also refers to the key Directive 92/32/EEC on the notification of new substances. It requires a competent authority in the member States to notify new substances. These authorities have to have the same knowledge and skills as their EU counterparts. To this end, EU is organizing exchange visits, training and technical assistance. The   draft   law   on   chemical   substances   and preparations (1998) complies with all relevant EU directives and regulations.

(iv)   Control of risk of existing substances: the White Paper requires a programme of risk evaluation. The two Stage I measures, Council Regulation 793/93/EC on the evaluation and control of the risks to man and the environment of existing substances (placed on the market before 1981) and Regulation 1488/94/EC on principles of risk   assessment,   are   widely   introduced   into Lithuania's legislation. The EIA procedure foresees a risk assessment that is compatible with that of the EC.

(v) Export/import of dangerous chemicals: Council Regulation 2455/92/EC on the export and import of certain dangerous chemicals is considered a Stage I measure.   Lithuania   has   adopted   the   EU classification, packaging and labelling system, and therefore fulfils the export requirements. It has not yet established a control system, which is also a condition of the Directive.

(vi) Environmental consequences of the deliberate release of genetically modified organisms (GMOs): the EU intention is to ensure adequate protection and to develop an international market (Directive 90/220/EEC). Lithuania's legislation has the same approach and Ministry of the Environment Resolution 6 (1993) regulates the production and use of GMOs. The Resolution only partly transposes EU requirements. The Ministry of the Environment plans to complete the transposition of EU requirements with respect to GMOs via a law that will be drafted in 1998, with the assistance of an   interministerial   working   group.   Another resolution setting standards for the containment of genetically modified micro-organisms will also be needed.   Lithuania   needs   to   set   in   place administrative systems to handle notifications of GMO research and to assess applications for permission to carry out experimental and deliberate releases.

(vii) Waste management policy: the entire waste management legislation should be adopted as a Stage I measure. It aims at setting clear definitions of waste and hazardous waste, and at establishing the administrative infrastructure to control and supervise waste management. The Approximation Strategy sets four waste management priorities. The framework requirements are the first priority (regulated by Directives 75/439/EEC, 91/156/EEC, 91/689/EEC, 94/904/EC). The Law on Waste Management (1998) contains the basic principles of the EU framework directives. The second priority concerns the Disposal of Waste Oils Directive (75/439/EEC), the Packaging and Packaging Waste Directive (94/62/EC), and the Waste Shipment Regulation (259/93/EEC). The   third   waste management priority relates to the Batteries and Accumulators   Directive   (91/157/EEC),   the Hazardous   Waste   Incineration   Directive (94/67/EEC), the Municipal Waste Incineration Directive (89/369/EEC), and the Sewage Sludge Directive (86/278/EEC). The fourth priority deals with Directives 96/59/EC and 78/176/EEC. Action plans have been prepared but need to be implemented   now   that   the   Law   on   Waste Management has been approved.

(viii) <u>Noise emissions from constructing plant and equipment</u>: while EU legislation covers only a few types of machines (like lawnmowers), Lithuania has adopted more general legislation. Allowable levels of acoustic noise, ultrasound and infrasound are regulated by Lithuania's hygiene standard HN 33-1993, which corresponds to EU directives.

(ix) <u>Air pollution - lead content of petrol and sulphur content of certain liquid fuels</u>: Directive 93/12/EEC sets limits on the sulphur content of diesel fuel (used in motor vehicles) and other gas oils (light fuel oil) used for self-propelling vehicles, heating, industrial and marine purposes. It is due to be replaced by a proposed directive on the quality of petrol and diesel fuel (COM96/0164). Directive 85/210/EEC requires the Member States to ensure the availability and balanced distribution within their territory of unleaded petrol with a content of <0.013 g Pb/l. The benzene content of both leaded and unleaded petrol must not exceed 5%. This Directive is also to be replaced by the year 2000 by the same proposed directive (COM96/0164). Lithuanian fuel standards for sulphur are currently in line with those set for the EU. In 1993, Lithuania established a concentration standard (HN 35-1993) which fully complies with that of the EU. It has established fuel quality standards (Ministry of the Economy Resolution 303, 1997) that are in line with EU requirements. In addition, the Law on Environmental Pollution Charges (under revision) includes air pollution charges on mobile sources. However, fuel quality control is poor. The roles of parties involved in controlling fuel quality have to be clarified and the system has to be improved.

(x) <u>Air pollution - volatile organic compounds</u>: to control and reduce the evaporation from petrol, the EU Member States have, according to Directive 94/63/EC, to establish control measures. The Directive applies to operations, installations, road vehicles, trains and inland waterway vessels used for the storage and transport of petrol from one terminal to another or from a terminal to a service station. Lithuania does have standards on VOC emissions, but these are not in line with EU requirements. Lithuania will have to introduce requirements for new plants and implementing the Directive will have significant cost implications.

(xi) <u>Ozone-depleting substances (ODS)</u>: EU has decided to phase out ODS (Regulation 94/3093/EEC) even before the worldwide ban comes into force in 2030 according to the Vienna Convention for the Protection of the Ozone Layer and the Montreal Protocol, as amended. Lithuania has prepared a national programme to phase out ODS. The programme was reviewed in 1997 in full accordance with the Montreal Protocol and its Copenhagen and London amendments.

1.5 Environmental impact assessment (EIA)

The Law on Environmental Impact Assessment (EIA) of 1996 determines the EIA procedure. A distinction is made between initial EIA, full EIA and State Expertise on EIA. Initial EIA is to be prepared routinely by a proponent for territorial planning documents or project proposals. The full EIA is also carried out by the proponent, but only after the Ministry of the Environment has determined that it is necessary. A full EIA is either mandatory, if the activity concerned is included in a list of activities and projects approved by the Government in May 1997 (Resolution 456), or needed, because the Ministry of the Environment deems it necessary possibly following a request from the public or public administrations – in view of the significant environmental effects of the proposed activity. The State Expertise is to be undertaken if the proposed activity is included in another special list of projects approved by the Government (Resolution 233). The State Expertise is to be financed by the proponent, but is to be undertaken by licensed experts, selected on the basis of public tender.

The list of activities and projects that are subject to a full EIA contains five groups. The energy group includes nuclear, heating and hydro power stations, boilers, and geothermal energy production. The manufacturing group contains mining and quarrying, metal processing, food and beverages industries, textile, chemical industry, construction materials, wood processing, and electronics as subgroups. The agricultural group includes poultry, cattle breeding, fish farms, melioration systems, and agricultural service enterprises. The transport and communications group includes ports, highways, railways, oil and gas pipelines, water roads, racetracks, enterprises for rail and car services and assembling. The final group is composed of 17 different activities like water treatment plants, printing shops, radioactive and hazardous waste storage and use, military fields, and use of underground resources. Conditions are laid down regarding their manufacturing capacities, water use, daily waste-water discharges, annual air pollution, and annual waste generation.

Governmental Resolution 233 (1997) determines the activities and projects that require State

Expertise. It is obligatory for 18 activities and projects. These include nuclear stations, heating power stations (capacity above 300 MW), hydro-power stations, oil exploitation and processing, oil product and chemical storage facilities and terminals, sappropel exploitation, new mineral exploitation and processing, ports (annual freight turnover above 10 million tonnes), highways and railroads, oil and gas pipelines, airports, waterways, water treatment plants (capacity above 3 000 m^3 per day), water storage facilities (capacity of at least 15 000 m^3 per day), radioactive and hazardous waste storage and use, and use of mineral resources. Governmental Resolution 88 (1998) prescribes the EIA expert licensing procedure. The Ministry of the Environment organizes the examination, processes applications and issues licences valid for 3 years.

The participants in the EIA process are called the "relevant parties" on the one hand and the public on the other. Apart from the proponent, the relevant parties include the Ministries of the Environment and of Health, the fire department of the Ministry of Internal Affairs, as well as regional and municipal administrations. The relevant parties are decisive partners in the EIA process, as they are involved in approving and concluding stages (see Figure 1.2). The role of the public is consultative. The proponent summarizes or analyses the public's comments and has to take them into account.

The Ministry of the Environment is the most important "relevant party", as it takes the essential decisions in the process, including the final decision on the proposed project. The EIA conclusions become part of the proponent's technical project. With the finalized technical project, the developer applies for a construction permit. The Law on EIA has recently been revised as part of the approximation process. The new Law replaces the initial EIA by a strategic EIA, and abolishes the State Expertise. The Law is in line with Council Directive 85/337/EEC (with amendments 97/11/EC). Lithuania is in the process of ratifying the Espoo Convention.

1.6   Environmental monitoring and information

Provisions for environmental information

The Constitution states that citizens have the right to obtain any available information that concerns them from the State in the manner established by law. Members of Parliament have the right to submit questions to and demand information from the Government, pursuant to Article 61 of the Constitution. The Law on Environmental Protection grants, *inter alia*, the right to receive accurate and up-to-date ecological information. The Government publishes environmental yearbooks, quarterly state of the environment reports, environmental monitoring and annual environmental media reports. Information on legal developments is to a large extent available in English and provided on the Internet or on CD-ROM.

Operators of facilities that pollute have to guarantee that they will make information concerning the pollution available to the public. Moreover, they are required to inform the public in the event of an emergency, which is defined as a hazardous environmental state resulting from a natural phenomenon, an accident, or another event that breaches environmental quality standards. In environmental emergencies, facility operators must remove both the causes and the consequences of the emergency and inform the public, the Ministry of Health, and the Ministry of the Environment of the hazards.

The Ministry of the Environment collects environmental data from its own observation networks and coordinates the environmental monitoring activities of these networks, but also of other institutions that are responsible for specific sectors or natural resources.

Monitoring activities

In 1989, the concept of complex environmental monitoring and the "Ekologija" information system were developed. A new ecological monitoring programme was created in 1992, because there was a need to have regional estimates. This programme prescribes monitoring at the three traditional levels: local, regional and national. It foresees a three-tier system for authority and competence: State, municipal and industrial monitoring. State monitoring covers all three levels, while municipal monitoring includes local and, partly, regional aspects. Industrial monitoring is everything else, such as self-monitoring by factories. At present, institutions and mechanisms for environmental monitoring are about to be reformed so as to modify and expand the existing infrastructure.

Figure 1.2: The EIA procedure

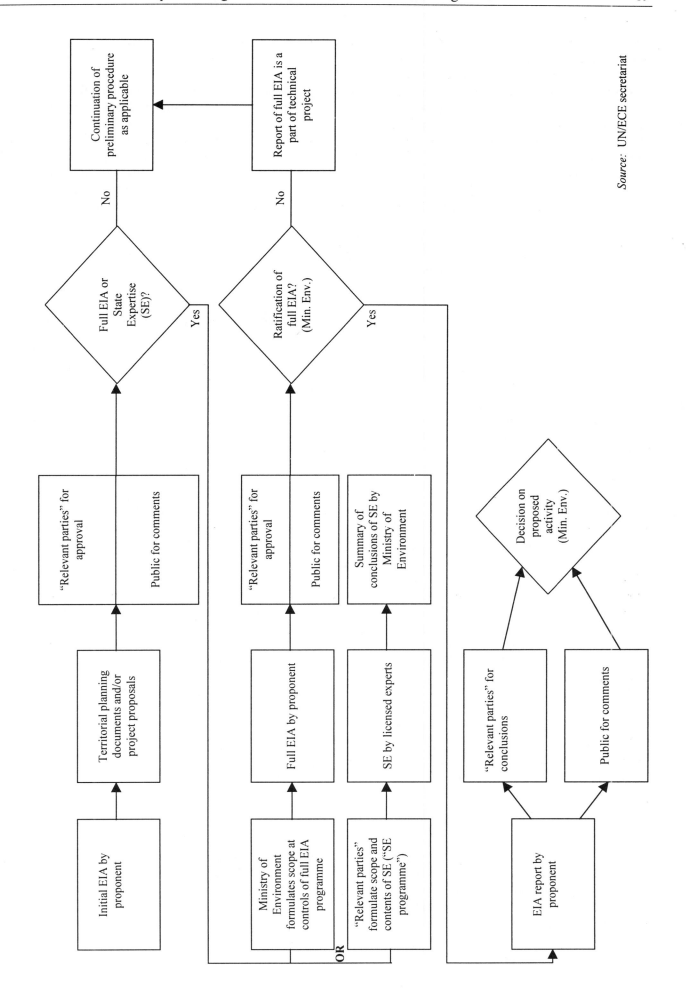

Source: UN/ECE secretariat

The State Monitoring System consists of the following interrelated subsystems: air monitoring, water monitoring, flora and fauna monitoring, and integrated landscape monitoring. Registers and cadastres of natural resources are another important source of information. The Joint Research Centre of the Ministry of the Environment and its regional departments are responsible for carrying out the monitoring programme. This is done according to a State programme, confirmed methods, and other normative documents. Data about air, water, and soil status are submitted to international data centres following international agreements. Quality assurance and quality control meet international requirements. The process to accredit the chemical laboratory of the Environmental Research Centre started in November 1997.

Integrated monitoring started in 1993. Before 1993, there was only one station, in Preila, designed for background monitoring. With the financial help of the Nordic Council, three integrated monitoring stations were established in Aukštaitija, Dzūkija and Žemaitija national parks. (For further details on monitoring, see Chapters 6 to 10.)

1.7   Public participation

Legal provisions

The main legal source of citizens' rights to public participation is the LEP. Its chapter 2 lists the duties of the State authorities to guarantee citizens' rights by establishing sound environmental standards, announcing to the public plans for any economic activity which may have an adverse environmental effect, and encouraging the participation of citizens and public organizations in environmental protection". Such rights and duties include, under Article 7, the right of the public to:

- receive accurate and up-to-date ecological information;
- take part in the discussion and implementation of programmes and projects of economic activities;
- demand that economic activities that are hazardous to the environment be terminated;
- request State ecological examinations;
- carry out public ecological examinations;
- organize public inspections of facilities for environmental protection;
- demand that State authorities and institutions organize ecological education and instruction, and

- freely advocate concepts of environmental protection.

Article 33 of the LEP specifies the organizations that can take out injunctions to restrict harm to the environment, namely legal and natural persons whose health, property or interests are affected, as well as the Ministry of the Environment and other officials if the interests of the State are at stake. Organizations, natural and legal persons can challenge decisions by environmental protection officials in court, if administrative law is violated.

Non-governmental organizations

The participation of non-governmental organizations in environmental problems is foreseen in the LEP and confirmed by the Law on Territorial Planning (1995), and also the Law on Environmental Impact Assessment (1996, which was revised in 1997). The Law on Public Organizations was approved in February 1995. This Law sets out the necessary requirements and procedures for the establishment, registration, and running of various NGOs (including environmental NGOs), as well as possible sources of finance for NGOs.

Among the public organizations dedicated to ecological issues are the Green Movement, the Lithuanian Fund for Nature and the Lithuanian Environmental Protection Society (which was recently divided into several Environmental Protection Societies in the largest cities). Their main fields of interest and activity correspond to the legal provisions listed above. Public participation is sufficiently provided for in different regulations. However, access to information appears to be a crucial requirement for NGOs.

The Regional Environmental Center for Central and Eastern Europe (REC) began its activities in the Baltic countries, including Lithuania, in 1995. The main goal for 1995 was to establish local REC offices and to set up a Local Grants Programme in Lithuania. Initially the process was slow to get off the ground because of changes in Lithuania's legislation. Later on, the registration process was renewed in the light of the new conditions.

1.8   Conclusions and recommendations

The development of a national legal system in general, and a legal system for environmental protection in particular, has made considerable progress in Lithuania. The scope of activities for environmental protection is well defined, and the legal provisions appear to be sufficient. A major obstacle to the successful development of environmental protection is the country's economic situation. A further obstacle might be the insufficient power to apply the regulations. Clear responsibility for enforcement should lie with the Minister for the Environment in order to ensure effective application.

Also, the framework programme for environmental protection has been well established. The protection strategy and the related policy programmes and priorities are transparent and convincing. The situation does not seem to be equally clear with regard to policy implementation. There are difficulties in decentralizing decision-making and problems in the integration of environmental concerns into sectoral policies and related coordination. The creation of the National Council for Sustainable Development is a convenient starting point for improving the incorporation of environmental objectives into sectoral policies. At the same time, the Council could be instrumental in questions of coordination, provided its procedures and status are strengthened.

Recommendation 1.1:
The National Council for Sustainable Development should assume the role of coordinator and bring together sectoral and environmental interests in government policy. At the same time, the Council should advise on the optimal level of decentralization of environmental decision-making with a view to maximum environmental law and policy enforcement. Finally, the Council should also see to it that an adequate general level of cooperation between government institutions is achieved with a view to promoting consistency between sectoral programmes and actions in the approximation process.

The scarcity of expertise in environmental management is an impediment to its success. The efforts made to train environmental inspectors are therefore an important step in the right direction. However, available expertise at all levels - including within NGOs - should be used more systematically, and environmental training should be extended to experts in all the ministries concerned, as well as in all the regional and local administrations involved in environmental management.

Recommendation 1.2:
The practical impediments to the full implementation of the Law on Public Organizations of 1995 should be removed. Lithuania should consider participating in EU exchange programmes like "Leonardo" or "Sokrates". A comprehensive training programme for environmental experts at all levels should be developed as a matter of urgency.

International assistance was obtained for both programme formulation and implementation. As this activity increased considerably, an organizational structure appeared to be necessary, and a special body – the Project Management Unit – was established within the Ministry of the Environment with PHARE support. Now that it has been set up, this Unit should be strengthened so that it can cope with managing more international projects.

Recommendation 1.3:
The resources of the Project Management Unit and of other units dealing with project management should be strengthened.

Public participation in environmental matters is the key to the successful implementation of the Environmental Strategy. Public awareness of environmental problems and interest in solving these problems are, therefore, necessary. Active public participation in environmental policies has to be encouraged; non-governmental environmental organizations have to be supported; environmental information and its dissemination via the mass media have to be improved.

Since the restoration of independence in 1991, and in the transition to a market economy, public participation has played an important role and has been provided for in most recent legal documents adopted by the Government. There is, however, a lack of cooperation and sharing of information within the NGO community and between NGOs and the general public. Another problem is the lack of legal assistance in courts, since lawyers are not sufficiently qualified in environmental and planning issues and thus not prepared to assist the public and NGOs in legal cases.

Recommendation 1.4:
A programme should be developed and implemented by all interested parties to promote

the legal provisions for public participation in environmental decision-making, territorial planning and development. The programme should, in particular, refer to (a) guidelines for the implementation of legal provisions for public participation at the local level, (b) improved communication and cooperation with NGOs, and (c) training of lawyers regarding administrative decisions on spatial planning and territorial development.

The new Law on Environmental Monitoring of November 1997 will most probably give new impetus to the development of monitoring information. Environmental monitoring data must be put to better use when setting guidelines for the country's economic development. Timely assessments of the environmental impact of proposed economic development are vital, particularly at a time of fundamental economic reform and priority setting.

Although air emission data are collected from 2 000 sources, systematic air emission monitoring is limited and poorly coordinated. Emission sampling at industrial plants is at best erratic. There are no protocols for uniform monitoring methods or for analytical methods, and emission data are not extrapolated to establish area-wide pollution patterns. Emission sampling should follow a special schedule and be documented. A step in the right direction would be to use the experiences with urban air quality monitoring in Vilnius to design monitoring systems for all cities.

Recommendation 1.5:
Monitoring data should be developed in regard of both their need in environmental decision-making and their comparability with data in other countries. An integrated environmental information system should be developed. Its priority should be to address the information needs for (a) the formulation of environmentally sound policies and their implementation at all levels of society, (b) the supervision of the use of natural resources, (c) investigations into causes of environmental degradation, (d) setting environmental standards, and (e) increasing public awareness of the state of the environment.

Chapter 2

INTEGRATION OF ECONOMIC AND ENVIRONMENTAL DECISIONS

2.1   Economic instruments for integration

The following economic instruments are used for the integration of economic and environmental decisions:

- Taxes on natural resources;
- Charges on the discharge of pollutants into water and air;
- Penalties for exceeding established discharge limits, for damaging the environment, for cutting trees without authorization, etc.;
- Excise duty/customs duty on fuels and cars;
- Municipal user charges for tap water, sewerage and sewage treatment, and municipal waste;
- Refundable, voluntary deposits on glass and plastic bottles;
- Grants to undertake feasibility studies and research, or to start projects;
- Subsidies to collect municipal waste.

The authorities are also considering applying the following economic instruments in the short term:

- Product charges on batteries, product packaging, and tyres;
- Pollution charges on commercial vehicles without catalytic converters.

In the long term, they are considering introducing:

- Tradable waste-water pollution permits (in Panevėžys to start with);
- A tax on harvests by State Forest Enterprises, as an extension of the taxes on natural resources.

Taxes on natural resources

The Law on Taxes on State Nature Resources (1991) obliges resource users to pay taxes to the State. The Governmental Resolution of 10 October 1995 (amended in 1997) sets the tax rates and prescribes the methodology for calculating the taxes. It links the tax directly to the resource quantity extracted. The formula reduces the tax if exploration has been carried out with little or no State funding. The tax includes royalties too. If the landowner uses mineral resources and water exclusively for his own needs, he is exempted from the tax. The same Resolution lays down the methodology for taxing the commercial use of fish resources. It applies only to the State's bodies of water that do not fall under lease agreements for commercial fishing. The tax is based on the fishing equipment used and the period for which the required fishing permit is issued. For equipment other than a conventional net, the tax formula uses a coefficient composed of the equipment's efficiency and cost ratios. The fisheries have to replenish and maintain the fish resource.

The taxes on fish resources, water, and mineral resources are paid into the State budget. Extracting more mineral resources than allowed or catching fish without replenishing leads to fines. These are paid into the State Nature Protection Fund (SNPF). The tax rate on peat is determined by Governmental Resolution (1995, amended in 1996). It favours the export of peat products over that of raw peat by reducing the rate for the former to one fifth.

The Law on Taxes on the Use of Oil and Gas Resources (1992) specifies a 20 per cent tax on the market prices of oil and gas. If the market price falls below the indicative price determined by the Government, the indicative price is used for tax purposes. An additional 9 per cent is payable, fully or partly, if the prospecting work was carried out, fully or partly, by the State. The Ministry of the Environment indexes the tax rates to the quarterly consumer price index (CPI). The tax revenues and

Table 2.1: State budget revenues from environmental taxes, 1992-1997

Million litas at current prices and percentages

	1992 a/	1993	1994	1995	1996	1997
Total revenue	**859.69**	**1 907.84**	**3 002.80**	**3 927.86**	**5 555.97**	**7 920.26**
- Other revenues	858.17	1 895.73	2 978.64	3 899.68	5 509.64	7 854.33
- Total environmental taxes	1.51	12.11	24.17	28.18	46.33	65.93
of which:						
Taxes on natural resources	1.24	9.36	18.20	18.87	28.94	44.52
As % of total environmental taxes	*81.89*	*77.32*	*75.31*	*66.98*	*62.45*	*67.52*
As % of total revenues	*0.14*	*0.49*	*0.61*	*0.48*	*0.53*	*0.57*
Taxes on pollution	0.27	2.75	5.97	9.31	17.40	21.41
As % of total environmental taxes	*18.11*	*22.68*	*24.69*	*33.02*	*37.55*	*32.48*
As % of total revenues	*0.03*	*0.14*	*0.20*	*0.24*	*0.32*	*0.27*

Sources: Ministry of Finance;
Ministry of the Environment;
Economic Reviews: Lithuania, IMF.

a/ End of year exchange rate (80 Roubles = 1 Litas) is applied for 1992.

penalties for failure to comply with tax deadlines go to the State budget. The fines for resource use over established limits are paid to the State Nature Protection Fund.

In recent years (see Table 2.1), the revenues from taxes on natural resources have accounted for 0.5 per cent of the State budget's total revenues. However, those taxes are 60-75 per cent of all environmental taxes accruing to the State budget.

Since 1990, the extraction of mineral resources has decreased (see Table 2.2) by some 85 per cent. Peat exploitation remains low despite the 1994 surge, but seventeen times more oil is being pumped.

Pollution charges

The Law on Environmental Pollution Charges (1991) sets rates for 51 water-polluting chemicals, 91 air-polluting chemicals and 9 air-polluting dust components. The rates are indexed to the CPI in the same manner as the taxes on the use of natural resources. In fact, the Ministry of the Environment issues one order indexing pollution charges, taxes two source-specific benchmarks: maximum allowable pollution (MAP) and temporary allowable pollution (TAP). The applicant for an environmental pollution permit presents the benchmarks calculations made by licensed environmental consultants. The inspectors verify

the calculations. The pollution charge is calculated per tonne of pollutant. The charge is levied at the basic, reduced or increased rate according to the degree of deviation from the benchmark set in the permit.

The basic rate is for pollution not exceeding the benchmark. The reduced rate applies when the level of emissions is below the benchmark. If the emissions do not exceed 50 per cent of the MAP level, the polluter does not pay the pollution tax. The State tax authorities collect the pollution charges. 70 per cent of the charges are paid into the municipal environmental protection funds (MEPFs), and 30 per cent into the State budget (Table 2.3). The increased charges are treated like fines and transferred to the State Nature Protection Fund.

The methodology for defining MAP and TAP is prescribed by an environmental regulation. For atmospheric pollution, the MAP is the amount of pollutants discharged into the air by a stationary source per time unit that is compatible with the established maximum allowable concentrations (MAC). The MAC in the atmosphere refers to the concentration of the substance or compound concerned that does not affect respiratory reflexes (in rural locations and within 20-30 minutes). The emissions do not conflict with the UN/ECE Convention on Long-range Transboundary Air Pollution. The MAP for water pollution is meant

Table 2.2: Reserves and extraction of selected mineral resources, 1989-1997

Selected resources	Estimated reserves	Recoverable reserves	Annual extraction of selected mineral resources									% change	Exploitation assessment	
													Years	Annually
	End of 1997	End of 1997	(Million of units)									%	Number	%
			1989	1990	1991	1992	1993	1994	1995	1996	1997	(1990-1997)	Based on 1997	
Oil (tonnes)	4.8	4.3	a/	0.012	0.033	0.064	0.072	0.079	0.115	0.161	0.212	1,707	20	4.9
Peat (tonnes)	119.2	64.1	1.745	0.763	0.650	0.342	0.190	0.438	0.249	0.267	0.284	-63	230	0.4
Limestone (tonnes)	316.1	151.7	6.800	6.850	6.370	3.554	1.317	1.395	1.376	0.963	1.109	-84	140	0.7
Dolomite (m³)	104.0	59.5	1.390	1.200	0.990	0.712	0.309	0.450	0.247	0.245	0.475	-60	130	0.8
Clay (m³)	91.2	28.7	2.388	2.665	2.148	1.057	0.493	0.458	0.296	0.193	0.239	-91	120	0.8
Sand and gravel (m³)	671.9	287.3	21.794	19.000	17.948	12.196	5.568	4.686	3.670	2.628	3.520	-81	80	1.2

Sources: Environment in Lithuania, 1996 annual report, Ministry of Environmental Protection, 1997;
Environment in Lithuania, 1994 annual report, Ministry of Environmental Protection, 1995;
Natural resources and environmental protection in 1996, Department of Statistics, 1998;
Natural resources and environmental protection in 1995, Department of Statistics, 1996.

a/ Not exploited.

Table 2.3: Pollution charges in the State budget and the MEPFs, 1992-1997

Million litas at current prices

	1992 a/	1993	1994	1995	1996	1997
Total charges for pollution	3.33	7.67	19.69	32.41	53.40	65.29
Taxes on pollution	0.27	2.75	5.97	9.31	17.40	21.41
Charges (to municipal funds)	3.06	4.93	13.72	23.10	36.00	43.88

Sources: EIU country profile, 1995-1996. IMF Economic Reviews: Lithuania.
Environment in Lithuania, Ministry of Environmental Protection, 1997;
Department of Statistics; Ministry of Economy; Ministry of Finance.

a/ End of year exchange rate is applied (80 Roubles = 1 Litas) for 1992.

to meet the water contamination standards (BOD_5 at 5-15 mg/l, nitrogen at 8-12 mg/l, and phosphorus at 1.5 mg/l) approved under the Helsinki Convention for the Baltic Sea Area.

The TAP is used only if an enterprise does not have the technical capacity to reach the MAP limit, but commits to environmental improvement. It has to put forward realistic measures to reach the MAP limits (frequently change of processes) and timetables (of financing operations). A study on the efficiency of pollution charges shows that, in 1994-1995, TAP permits were used more frequently for air than for water pollution (24 per cent of all water pollution permits use MAP, and 37 per cent of all air pollution permits use TAP).

Those air polluters that take measures to reduce emissions by more than 25 per cent can apply for an exemption from the payment of pollution charges for up to three years. Parliament is currently revising the Law. In January 1998, its Environmental Committee came up with a proposal to coordinate the revised law with the Waste Management Financing Concept (including the Law on Waste Management, which calls for product charges to be introduced). The forthcoming law on pollution charges will apply to mobile air polluters as well (private vehicles excluded). There will be a basic and an increasedrate. Exceeding the emission level specified in the permit for the activity concerned leads to the application of the increased rate. The increased rate is the basic rate multiplied by a penalty coefficient. Major pollutants are specified for stationary sources of water and air pollution.

SO_2, NO_x and suspended particles are in the list of major air pollutants. BOD_7, N-total, P-total, and suspended particles are among the major water quality parameters. All other pollutants are divided into four groups according to their degree of hazard. The rate schedule is valid for five years. During the period 1998-2003, only the basic rates for major pollutants will increase. A new schedule has to be put forward for discussion in 2001. The allocation of the revenues from the charge system is under debate. The Environmental Fund for Investments (EFI) might get 20 per cent of the pollution charges, the State budget 10 per cent (new) and the remaining 70 per cent might go to MEPFs. It could be that EFI funds will first be paid into the State budget and then appropriated for environmental investments. At present, pollution charges contribute about a quarter of a per cent to the State budget (see Table 2.1). This is more than 30 per cent of all environmental taxes paid to the State budget.

Penalties, compensation for damage, and fines

The penalty for illegal (unlicensed) extraction of oil and gas, fish catches and peat mining is ten times the regular tax on the resource use. Fines are paid into the State Nature Protection Fund. The Law on Taxes on the Use of Oil and Gas Resources (1992) lays down a fine calculated per day for the late payment of the tax, to the State budget. The sanctions for the illegal use of forest resources, damage to forests and the fines levied by State Regional Forest Inspectors are paid into the Forest Fund, which was established in 1995.

Excess pollution can be fined in two situations. If an environmental inspectorate finds evidence of unreported pollution, the polluter is liable for a fine worth ten times the pollution charge. If an enterprise pollutes more than the permit allows, it pays the increased rate. According to current practice, the penalty is four times the calculated charge. The new law proposes to apply in this case the increased rate as defined above.

Compensations for damage to the landscape are channelled to the State Nature Protection Fund. The methodology for assessing the damage to different landscape 'objects' is prescribed by the Ministry of the Environment Resolution 198 (1995). The basic rate is the essence of the compensation. The assessment formula for damage to the natural hydrological network, landscape configuration, and flora is different. The calculation is differentiated according to the damaged territory. If the violation has taken place in a State park or strict reserve, the compensation rises 10-fold. If it has taken place in a State protected area, the compensation is multiplied by 5. Finally, the compensation is increased threefold if the violation has occurred in a regional park, a reserve, a protected landscape or a protected water area. The compensations are indexed to the quarterly CPI.

The Administrative Code (articles 51-90) determines fines for individuals and officials violating environmental laws. The fines for officials are higher and vary from 25 to 10 000 Litas, depending on the violation. The fines are for unlicensed construction and issuing licences without consulting the licensing authorities. Polluting the environment with municipal, hazardous, radioactive or industrial wastes is fined. Tampering with State natural resource accounting or cadastral records, and publishing misleading environmental information or hiding correct information are fined. Infringing laws related to land, soil, mineral deposits, water resources, marine and coastal resources, water ponds, lakes, the hydrological network, forest resources, flora, fauna, the landscape, recreational areas, hunting, nature monuments, protected areas, air pollution from mobile and stationary sources, fishing and other activities is subject to a fine. Trying to interfere in the work of environmental, geological or forest inspectors can also be fined.

Excise and customs duty

The Law on Excise Duty (1994, amended in 1995) stipulates that all types of fuels and lubricants as well as luxury cars are subject to the duty, which has largely had a revenue-raising function since 1990. In the 1998 State budget, 18.3 per cent of revenues will come from excise duties. Half of it (850 million Litas) will come from duties on oil products. The Mažeikiai oil refinery (the only one in the Baltic States) processed 37 per cent (5.671 million tonnes) more raw oil in 1997 than in 1996. Stamp duty is imposed on importers of oil products. The petrol price in Lithuania remains lower than in western Europe, but is higher than in its eastern neighbours. Lithuania again raised the excise duty on petrol and oil products (by 31%) in April 1998. A new import duty of 5 per cent on fuels is planned.

Today, there is a 1 050 Litas per tonne excise duty on petrol, a 400 Litas per tonne excise duty on diesel oil and a 240 Litas per tonne excise duty on lubricants. The excise duty on those products is increasing. For example, the tax on petrol was 33 per cent (but not less than 400 Litas per tonne) in July 1995. In June 1996, it was increased to 70 per cent (but not less than 560 Litas per tonne). In April 1997, the excise duty was raised to 100 per cent (but not less than 800 Litas per tonne).

Lithuania does not manufacture cars, so all registered cars are imported. Cars manufactured before 1990 are subject to customs duty. The rate depends on the age of the imported vehicle. If it is more than 10 years old, the duty is 10 per cent of the value (but not less than 0.80 Litas per cm^3 of the engine's cylinder capacity). If it is more than 7 but less than 10 years old, the rate is 5 per cent but not less than 0.20 Litas per cm^3 of the engine's cylinder capacity. Cars manufactured after 1990 are exempted from customs duty, except luxury cars manufactured 5 years ago or less. If such cars exceed a value of 60 000 Litas, a 15 per cent excise is due.

User charges

Municipal enterprises handle waste, and treat and supply water. In 1997, the heating sector was also transferred to municipal ownership. Municipalities control the prices of water and municipal waste treatment, while the Government regulates heating and hot water prices. The intention is to liberalize these prices once social constraints are removed.

Grants

Foreign grants to undertake feasibility studies and research, or to start projects continue to be available (see Chapter 5 for details about projects). MEPFs give grants to enterprises to upgrade environmental equipment. When those funds are insufficient, SNPF might appropriate some funds (see below, financing environmental expenditure). During the past few years there have been more loans than grants (see Table 2.5).

2.2   Regulatory instruments

Licensing

The following business activities related to the environment are licensed in Lithuania: prospecting for natural resources; exploitation of natural resources; construction and operation of radiating installations; projecting and construction of State roads; production, import, transport, trade, use, storage and disposal of chemical materials that can harm the environment; import, export, wholesale and retail sale of oil and gas; inventory of forest and preparation of forestry projects; export of timber. Some activities are licensed but reserved exclusively for State and special enterprises (like the transport and use of radioactive material and its waste and related activities). For pipelines, power lines, heat networks of State importance and their technical maintenance, non-State ownership is allowed (but limited to 50 per cent). However, licences are obligatory.

Many of those activities need the approval from the Ministry of the Environment to receive a licence. For hazardous waste for instance, the licences are issued and a list of hazardous substances is validated also by the Ministry. The Ministry of the Environment established (1991) the waste grouping that includes hazardous substances. Around 2 000 industrial enterprises report according to this classification and all of them apply for an environmental permit (see below on part IV of unified permit). The Ministry issues licences for the import, export, and transit through the territory

of substances of the second to ninth classes of danger.

Permits and limits to exploit resources and pollute the environment

There is a unified system for issuing permits. It is based on Ministry of the Environment regulations and HELCOM recommendations. The system implies that the same permit determines the limits on the use of natural resources, on emissions to water and air, and on waste disposal. The Regional Environmental Departments (RED) issue these permits.

A permit comprises five parts. Water abstraction, use and transport are covered in part I. Part II deals with sewage. Part III specifies air emissions from stationary sources. Waste generation and management are addressed in part IV. Part V covers the use of natural resources. The pollution limits (MAP or TAP) are specified in the permit. Validity differs for different standards. The waste management part of the permit is valid for five years unless the waste toxicity changes.

All the conditions relating to the use of natural resources, accounting, monitoring, sanitation zone management, etc. are specified in the permit. Today, the natural resource use limits are established by the Ministry. For example, the Ministry of the Environment annually issues a resolution on the maximum permitted fish catch. Bigger catches are fined. The fines are paid to SNPF. The forest is harvested according to principles laid down in the Forest Sector Development Programme (1993). The actual volume and methods of cutting are specified in the licences granted to timber producers (Governmental Resolution 965, 1995). Violating the regulations, concerning the methods and volume of harvests (harvesting more or deviating from the rules on harvesting, cleaning the site, pest suppression), leads to fines, paid to the Forest Fund. The actual extraction of peat lags far behind its limit of 1 200 000 tonnes, and 400 000 tonnes of high-quality peat (see Table 2.2). Extraction of peat above the limits would lead to fines payable to SNPF.

Regulation 128 defines the criteria for applying for a permit. Any operating businesses (including individuals) are required to monitor the impact of their activities on the environment, and make data readily available to the respective ministries (Ministry of the Environment included) and municipal authorities. The permit conditions are monitored and enforced by inspectors. However, not all enterprises operate under a permit. A study has concluded that, in Vilnius, 200 enterprises work with permits, but another 18 000 work without.

Environmental standards and management system (EMS)

The Lithuanian Standards Board (LST) is part of the State Standardization Department (LSD). The Department is responsible for introducing the national system of standards. Relevant national legislation has changed considerably since 1990. Introducing standards is time-consuming, so, initially, the former GOST standards remained in force. They were declared inapplicable in 1998.

LST became a correspondent member of ISO in 1992. Its Technical Committee 36 (TC 36) on environmental protection was established in 1995. In 1996, the first Lithuanian environmental standard LST 1461 'Environmental Management System (Terms and Definitions)' was adopted according to BS 7 750. In 1997, TC 36 translated and adopted ISO 14001, 14004, 14010, 14011, 14012, 14021, 14024 and 14040. Currently, TC 36 is working on ISO, 14020 and 14023. The establishment of an environmental auditing and research centre is under consideration. While Lithuanian industry is working towards the ISO 9000 series, it is only preparing for the introduction of the ISO 14000 series, which is considered to be a barrier to foreign trade and access to markets.

A system of normative acts, called LAND, has been introduced by the Ministry of the Environment and reflects its approximation process to the European Union. DHV Consultants (1994) from the Netherlands carried out comparative studies on the then existing Lithuanian environmental standards and the EU ones. They found that the standards for discharges into surface water in terms of BOD_5 and total suspended solids were stricter in Lithuania than recommended by the WHO guidelines or EC directives. Air emission standards were generally stricter than those in western Europe.

Since 1994, the following normative acts on environmental standards have been developed: LAND-10, LAND-14, LAND-15, and LAND-20. LAND-10 on Norms for Sewage was based on Directives 76/464/EEC, 84/156/EEC, 91/676/EEC, 91/271/EEC and HELCOM recommendations 5/1, 7/3, 9/2, 11/2, 13/2, 16/9. LAND-14 and LAND-15 on CO, CH and Smoke Concentrations of Exhaust Fumes followed Directive 92/55/EEC and international standards ISO 3929-76, ISO 3930-93, ISO 3173-74, ISO 7644-88, ISO/TR 9310-87. LAND-20 on Standards for Sewage Sludge took into account Directive 86/278/EEC and Lithuanian Hygiene Norms (HN 44-1993, HN 60-1996).

Generally, according to the Law on Mineral Deposits (1995), water quality of all surface water reservoirs must comply with the water quality norms for fisheries. Normally, fresh groundwater is used for drinking purposes. Drinking water must meet the requirements and standards set by the Ministry of Health (see Chapter 10). The expectation is that norms may be relaxed in line with the corresponding EU ones.

Eco-labelling

The voluntary eco-labelling scheme was established and is regulated by Ministry of the Environment Resolution 81 (1995), amended by Resolution 106 (1996). The Resolution is based on EU Regulation 92/880/EEC and Directives 85/339/EEC, 75/442/EEC, 91/156/EEC, 67/548/EEC, 88/379/EEC, as well as EU Regulations 93/517, 94/10, 259/93. The Resolution applies to all products manufactured in or imported into Lithuania, except food, drinks and pharmaceuticals (as in the European scheme). The eco-label cannot be awarded to products that fall under EU Directives 67/548 and 88/379 (hazardous materials and pharmaceuticals) or to products whose production processes can harm the environment. Imported and domestic products must meet the same requirements. Building materials, ceramics, technological machinery, electronics, paper, textile, leather, fertilizers and chemical materials may qualify for the Lithuanian eco-labelling scheme.

So far, regulations have been established for the 'decorative fabric' textile product group, for toilet paper, for electric refrigerators and freezers and for leather. By comparison, EU eco-label criteria have been published for 10 product groups. The Lithuanian scheme attempts to encourage the design, production, marketing, and use of environmentally friendly products. The application fee for an environmental label is US$ 1 250. In addition, there is an annual fee of 0.2 per cent of annual sales of the certified products. These contributions are used to develop the environmental labelling system.

2.3   Financing environmental expenditure

Sources of finance

The main sources of finance for environmental expenditure are public budgetary and extrabudgetary funds, company funds, and foreign sources.

Budgetary sources

Environmental investments from the State budget are channelled through municipal budgets. The State's national and sectoral investment priorities are spelled out in the Public Investment Programme (PIP). The priority sectors are energy, transport and environment. The latest PIP covers the three-year period 1998-2000. The Government annually approves PIPs. PIP includes investment projects, which are mostly financed with a mix of grants, loans, and budget allocations. For example, the Klaipėda waste-water treatment plant receives allocations from the State and municipal budgets, grants from Sweden, Finland and the EU PHARE programme. These funds are supplemented with a loan from the World Bank.

The priority sectors will receive 48 per cent of all 1997-1999 PIP investments (25.2 per cent of total PIP expenditure is allocated to energy, 16.3 to transport, and 6.7 to the environment). By allocating funds to the environment, the PIP follows the investment priorities of the National Environmental Strategy. The construction of waste-water treatment facilities remains the highest priority. The obligations deriving from the Helsinki Convention require the building or improvement of water treatment facilities in Vilnius, Klaipėda, Šiauliai, Palanga and Kaunas (see Chapter 7). Waste management projects have been included in the PIP since 1996. The PIP for 1997-1999 earmarks 24 million Litas (or 4.2 per

cent of the PIP environmental investments) for this purpose. The National Environmental Finance Strategy (1997) indicates that bilateral donors and international financial institutions (IFIs) are willing to invest in waste management.

Extrabudgetary funds

The system of environmental funds consists of: (i) the Lithuanian State Nature Protection Fund (SNPF); (ii) 55 municipal environmental protection funds (MEPFs); and (iii) the Lithuanian Environmental Fund for Investments (EFI). The revenues and expenditures of the environmental funds are illustrated in Table 2.4. Since 1995, SNPF revenues (environmental penalties and sanctions) have stabilized at US$ 1 million a year and, therefore, the expenditure is quite limited. MEPFs are growing as the economy picks up (70 per cent of pollution charges are collected by MEPFs. See also Table 2.3).

The Ministry of the Environment manages the SNPF, while the municipalities manage MEPFs. Institutions report quarterly on the use of funds. The EFI has a completely different set-up, the difference stemming from the prevailing use of loans in EFI activity. Loans can be granted only by credit institutions according to national banking regulations. In addition, EFI will comply with banking requirements (such as capital adequacy ratios) and will have transparent rules on granting loans (the United States Agency for International Development (USAID) is helping to prepare its manual). EFI is building up its capacity and will start functioning by the end of 1998.

The Road Fund, the Forest Fund, and the Energy Efficiency Fund also have to be mentioned. The Forest Fund spent about 1 per cent of its US$ 85 million on managing protected areas in 1996. The Road Fund allocated around US$ 0.5 million for environmental purposes in 1996. The Energy Efficiency Fund started its operations in 1997. The Fund will provide loans and grants for projects that save energy and reduce dependence on standard fuels. The Road and Energy Efficiency Funds fall under the supervision of other ministries, and the Ministry of the Environment has little impact on their use. However, because of the current change in ministerial structure, the Forest Fund is with the Ministry of the Environment. There is an opportunity to coordinate the Ministry's funds.

Table 2.4: Environmental funds, 1992-1997

1 000 US$, at current prices (US$ rate at the end of the year)

	1992	1993	1994	1995	1996	1997
Total Revenues to Eco-Funds	1 098	1 530	4 205	6 923	10 352	10 951
Charges (to municipal funds)	765	1 238	3 430	5 827	9 431	9 625
Fines (to state fund)	333	292	776	1 096	921	1 326
Total Expenditure from Eco-Funds (Grants)	96	292	3 706	5 503	8 762	10 427
Investment	2	2	1 814	2 118	4 055	4 686
Current expenditure	95	291	1 892	3 385	4 708	5 741
Total Expenditure from State Eco-Fund (Grants)	96	292	610	1 087	1 079	775
Investment	2	2	203	312	430	325
Current expenditure	95	291	407	775	649	450
Total Expenditure from Municipal Eco-Funds	0	0	3 097	4 416	7 683	9 652
Investment	0	0	1 612	1 806	3 625	4 361
Current expenditure	0	0	1 485	2 611	4 058	5 291

Source: Department of Statistics; Ministry of the Economy and Ministry of Finance.

The Law on Forestry (1994) and the Governmental Resolution (1995) on the Forest Fund establish the fund that collects the revenues generated by the use of forests and their resources. There is no tax on forests as such; however, all State forest enterprises contribute to the Fund and use it to finance reforestation and afforestation and to pay forest guards. The Fund also collects the forest-related taxes such as payments for the use of forest resources other than timber. The money paid for damage to forest resources also goes to the Forest Fund.

Foreign assistance

Foreign sources cover 57 per cent of the 1997-1999 environmental investment programme. To coordinate and focus donors' efforts, the Ministry of the Environment has created a project management unit (see Chapters 1 and 5). Before 1996, foreign assistance primarily took the form of project-related grants. Later, when commercial interest rates became more affordable, loans prevailed. Table 2.5 shows that 80 per cent of those funds were committed to investments and 20 per cent to technical assistance. While technical assistance was financed by grants, the investment share was financed by both loans (52 per cent) and grants (29 per cent). Figures on pledged funds from multilateral organizations suggest a further increase in the share of loans.

Enterprise funds

The Department of Statistics has collected enterprise data on expenditure for environmental protection since 1991 (Table 2.6). However, the risk of double counting (the difficulty of matching investment expenditures with sources of finance) was reduced only from 1995. Unfortunately, the data for 1997 will be available only at the end of 1998, as the survey is conducted in July. Two specialized surveys were conducted to indicate sources of finance within enterprises in 1995 and 1997. At that time, waste-water treatment projects were financed by environmental funds and municipal grants, but the biggest share of finance was borne by enterprises. This is particularly true for projects to improve technological processes.

Table 2.5: Share of loans and grants in foreign assistance, 1991-1996 (cumulative)

Million US$ and %

	Investment	Technical Assistance	Total
Total	96.46	23.55	120.01
as % of total	80.4	19.6	100.0
Grants	34.68	23.55	58.23
as % of total	28.9	19.6	48.5
Loans	61.78	0.00	61.78
as % of total	51.5	0.0	51.5

Source: Donor and IFI Activities, Ministry of the Environment, 1997.

Table 2.6: Environmental expenditure, 1992-1997

	1992	1993	1994	1995	1996	1997
Thousand current US$ (US$ rate at the end of the year)						
Budget						
State Budget	5 499	10 756	26 565	28 541	21 609	27 432
Municipal Budgets	0	0	0	175	500	1 975
Environmental Funds						
State Environmental Fund	96	292	610	1 087	1 079	775
Municipal Environmental Funds	0	0	3 097	4 416	7 683	9 652
Enterprises a/	20 490	41 673	73 068	76 210	75 378	74 545
Funds from IFI and donors	2 454	3 152	4 304	13 313	14 982	45 090
Total Expenditure	28 539	55 873	107 643	123 741	121 231	159 470
GDP *(Million current US$)*	847	2 912	4 226	6 026	7 892	9 550
Environmental expenditure to GDP *(%)*	3. 4	1. 9	2. 5	2. 1	1. 5	1. 7
Percentages						
Budget	19	19	25	23	18	18
State Budget	19	19	25	23	18	17
Municipal Budgets	0	0	0	0	0	1
Environmental Funds	0	1	3	4	7	7
State Environmental Fund	0	1	1	1	1	0
Municipal Environmental Funds	0	0	3	4	6	6
Enterprises' expenditure a/	72	75	68	62	62	47
Funds from IFI and donors	9	6	4	11	12	28
Total expenditure	100	100	100	100	100	100

Sources: Department of Statistics; Ministry of the Economy and Ministry of Finance;
Environmental Expenditure in Central and Eastern Europe - Lithuania, Case Study, Danish EPA,
EAP Task Force/OECD, 1997;
National Environmental Finance Strategy, Ministry of the Environment-OECD-HIID, 1997;
Donor and IFI Activities, Ministry of the Environment, 1997.

a/ The methodology to account enterprises' environmental expenditure changed in 1995 and therefore data
have to be interpreted with care.

Figure 2.1: Environmental expenditure and share of investments, 1992-1997

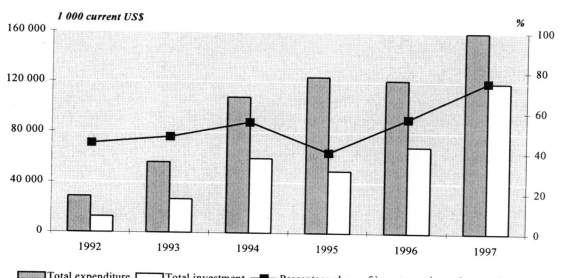

Sources: Department of Statistics; Ministry of the Economy and Ministry of Finance;
Environmental Expenditure in Central and Eastern Europe - Lithuania, Case Study, Danish EPA,
EAP Task Force/OECD, 1997.

Environmental expenditure

Table 2.6 illustrates Lithuania's total nominal environmental expenditure. Several factors need to be taken into account in the interpretation of these results. The national currency was introduced in June 1993. In 1992, an interim currency was in circulation. There has been a budget deficit since 1995. Only in 1997 did the State budget transfer the funds to the municipal budgets on time.

The diminishing share of enterprise contributions to expenditure might be a reflection of the high cost of credit. However, since 1997 the situation has improved, as inflation fell to around 6 per cent and Treasury bonds were traded at 6.5-10.5 per cent. The figures demonstrate the very small contribution of SNPF and municipal budgets to total expenditure. The State budget's contribution is falling back to 17 per cent. Extrabudgetary funds are taking up the slack as the contribution from enterprise funds dwindles. However, when commercial loans will become affordable, the enterprises' share might recover. Overall, the share of environmental protection expenditure in GDP appears to have decreased (see Table 2.6) in recent years, but is currently above 1.5 per cent.

Figure 2.1 illustrates the share of investments in environmental expenditure. In 1996, environmental investments in total environmental expenditure stood at some US$ 69 million (Table 2.7). In 1997, they surged by US$ 40 million as a result of the increase in funds from multilateral and bilateral foreign sources.

Table 2.7: Environmental investment expenditure, 1992-1997

	1992	1993	1994	1995	1996	1997
Thousand current US$ (US$ rate at the end of the year)						
Budget						
State Budget	5 182.5	9 148.0	23 800.3	24 625.0	14 275.0	18 940.5
Municipal Budgets	-	-	-	175.0	500.3	1 975.3
Environmental Funds						
State Environmental Fund	1.7	1.8	202.8	312.0	429.8	325.0
Municipal Environmental Funds	-	-	1 611.5	1 805.5	3 625.0	4 360.8
Enterprises	7 485.3	17 480.4	33 561.8	21 992.4	35 411.0	48 829.6
Funds from IFI and donors	-	-	-	480.0	14 450.0	45 090.0
Total	12 669.5	26 630.2	59 176.3	49 389.9	68 691.0	119 521.2
Gross fixed capital formation *(Million current US$)*	246.9	676.7	872.6	1 274.0	1 566.9	2 097.8
Environmental investment to gross capital formation (%	5.1	3.9	6.8	3.9	4.4	5.7
Percentages						
Budget	40.9	34.4	40.2	50.2	21.5	17.5
State Budget	40.9	34.4	40.2	49.9	20.8	15.8
Municipal Budgets	0.0	0.0	0.0	0.4	0.7	1.7
Environmental Funds	0.0	0.0	3.1	4.3	5.9	3.9
State Environmental Fund	0.0	0.0	0.3	0.6	0.6	0.3
Municipal Environmental Funds	0.0	0.0	2.7	3.7	5.3	3.6
Enterprises' investment	59.1	65.6	56.7	44.5	51.6	40.9
Funds from IFI and donors	0.0	0.0	0.0	1.0	21.0	37.7
Adjusted total investment	100.0	100.0	100.0	100.0	100.0	100.0

Sources: Department of Statistics; Ministry of the Economy and Ministry of Finance;
Environmental Expenditure in Central and Eastern Europe - Lithuania, Case Study, Danish EPA,
EAP Task Force/OECD, 1997;
National Environmental Finance Strategy, Ministry of the Environment-OECD-HIID, 1997;
Donor and IFI Activities, Ministry of the Environment, 1997;
Natural Resources and Environmental Protection in 1996 (1998).

**Table 2.8: Environmental expenditure and funds collected from
environmental pollution, 1992-1997**

Million litas, current prices

	1992	1993	1994	1995	1996	1997
Total revenues	5.9	18.2	41.0	55.9	87.7	109.7
Total taxes to Budget	1.5	12.1	24.2	28.2	46.3	65.9
Total revenues to Eco-Funds	4.4	6.1	16.8	27.7	41.4	43.8
Total expenditures for environment	114.2	223.5	430.6	495.0	484.9	637.9
Balance (expenditure over revenues)	108.3	205.3	389.6	439.1	397.2	528.1
Accumulating balance	108.3	313.6	703.1	1 142.2	1 539.4	2 067.6
Expenditure over revenues	19.3	12.3	10.5	8.9	5.5	5.8

Sources: Ministry of Finance; Ministry of the Environment.

The composition of environmental protection investments keeps changing (Table 2.7). From 1992 to 1995, the funds came from the State budget and enterprise resources. Almost no funds were available from IFI and donors till 1996. Since then, the share from the State budget has shrunk, suggesting that the Government is applying a new financing strategy for environmental investment (based on foreign loans).

Environmental investment to total gross fixed capital formation is in the upper range of 3.9 to 6.8 per cent. Gross fixed capital formation in turn represented about 22 per cent of GDP in 1997 (2-point growth over 1996). Table 2.7 suggests that the share from enterprises in the funding of environmental investments amounted to around half the total in 1996 and 1997. Loans from multilateral institutions accounted for 21 per cent and the State budget contributed almost 22 per cent in 1996. Preliminary data on funds from IFI and donors suggest that their shares were 18 and 38 per cent in 1997.

2.4   Conclusions and recommendations

Integrating environmentally related economic instruments into economic decision-making is a new concept in Lithuania. Environmental protection measures have to be backed up with economic instruments. As business standards are raised, there are new opportunities for new instruments, like product charges and tradable permits. The non-discriminatory treatment of trading partners has to be safeguarded at all times

and the need to make domestic businesses more competitive has to be acknowledged.

The Ministry of the Environment has adapted swiftly to new requirements for legislation. Incremental changes have been successful. The Ministry has also responded to foreign donors' requests for a project management unit to coordinate and streamline the many investment projects. Based on the National Environmental Strategy and according to the priorities of the Action Plan, the list of environmental protection facilities under construction shrank from 86 to 16. The financial resources available today limit the ability of the Ministry of the Environment to extend its communications network. Accordingly, the staff spends relatively more time on information gathering, processing and reporting, and less time on analysing the information available.

One could assess the economic instruments' efficiency by looking at the expenditure-to-revenue ratio. How much money do the economic instruments generate for the public coffers and how much does society spend on environmental projects? Do polluters really pay for the damage that they do to the environment or does society subsidize their activities? Table 2.8 attempts to answer some of these questions. The growing accumulating balance suggests that society continues to subsidize the polluters, although to a lesser degree. So polluters are not fully incorporating environmental externalities in their costing procedures. Yet, in the long run, they will have to internalize these costs. They should gradually prepare for this.

Recommendation 2.1
Pollution charges ought to increase in order to induce polluters to internalize external costs. The polluter-pays principle should be applied and the precautionary principle promoted.

More attention and analysis efforts need to be devoted to studying the efficiency of economic instruments. A study on the efficiency of air pollution charges suggests that they are too low. However, this inference depends on the objective of the charges. The new law on pollution charges aims at curbing pollution, but does not mention the need to accumulate funds to cope with it. The legislation related to environmental funds, by contrast, does spell out this objective.

Recommendation 2.2
The efficiency of existing economic instruments has to be analysed. Such an analysis should, in particular, shed light on the pace at which taxes, charges, and excise duties can be raised without threatening business activity as such. The analysis should also be used to design feedback mechanisms for business reactions to the applied economic instruments.

Lithuania's environmental laws are concise and to the point. Since 1990 many laws have been put in place. The current work on a new law on pollution charges relates to the Law on Waste Management, which proposes product charges and calls for an additional legislative act. There is also a Law on Environmental Funds. Such an array of laws could obscure the objective: making polluters pay for environmental damage, as called for in the National Environmental Strategy. On the other hand, in terms of law-making, the sequence of laws and their hierarchy seem quite logical.

Recommendation 2.3
A cost-benefit analysis of environmental legislation should be carried out to avoid repeating procedures and gain experience and clout and to optimize proposed instruments.

Currently, the forthcoming law on pollution charges, together with a number of resolutions on environmental standards and different penalties

and sanctions, risk overemphasizing the punitive potential of the environmental authorities. However, to encourage businesses to take low-cost measures to minimize waste or emissions during the production process, an incentive is needed rather than punishment. In this sense, the new law on pollution charges quite rightly sets lower charges with yearly increments. However, the law fails to spell out that this is an incentive for those businesses that want to take the opportunity to adapt and become competitive on the European market. In addition, studies indicate that such improvements are frequently energy- and resource-efficient.

Recommendation 2.4
In the short run, incentives should be created for businesses to make their production facilities more environmentally friendly.

Several recommendations could be made for specific instruments. The multitude of extrabudgetary funds (SNPF, MEPFs, EFI, Forest Fund, Road Fund, Energy Efficiency Fund, Health Fund and others) is creating budgetary difficulties and implies that there are inefficiencies. For instance, neither MEPFs nor the SNPF appear to have the means to finance big environmental investment projects on their own. Lithuanian experts confirm the importance of the State budget for funding environmental investments. In addition, those responsible for funds may be tempted to look for new sources of revenue and the funds are criticized by businesses. One such criticism is that environmental inspectors receive bonuses from the funds. Indeed, the Ministry should increase their salaries rather than rely on the funds to supplement their income, thus signalling its commitment to using the funds only for environmental purposes. In general, essential as they are under current circumstances, the environmental funds should be temporary and last only as long as the economic transition. EFI could grow into a credit institution or investment fund in the future with professional financial management. The other funds should in the long run be merged with the State budget.

Recommendation 2.5
The legislation should recognize that the Environmental Fund for Investments will be the main and lasting source of special funds for

environmental improvements in the private sector, while the other funds for that purpose are only temporary.

It is becoming increasingly difficult to calibrate taxes and charges. In Scandinavia, 'Green Commissions' were created for this purpose. They develop compromise solutions, frequently raising environmental taxes and charges and lowering the tax on labour. The EU approximation process (or harmonization) calls for cooperation between different governmental institutions. This cooperation is needed on tax, environment, competitiveness, and trade policies in order to achieve sustainable development. The recently created Council should coordinate the process.

Recommendation 2.6
The National Council for Sustainable Development should oversee the integration of Lithuania's environmental policy decisions into its economic development strategy.

Chapter 3

INTRODUCTION OF CLEANER, SAFER AND MORE SUSTAINABLE TECHNOLOGIES IN INDUSTRY

3.1 Technological and environmental aspects of current industrial development

Lithuanian industry today

The economic decline has levelled off since 1995. It has particularly affected the industrial sector. In 1991 industry's contribution to GDP was 44.4 per cent; in 1997 it was down to 24 per cent (Table I.1) as overall industrial output plummeted. Consequently, in 1996 manufacturing industry operated at only 48 per cent of its capacity (Table 3.1). In 1996, some sectors of activity seemed to take off, such as chemicals (including the oil industry, +14.3 per cent over the previous year), building materials and wood products (+8.5 per cent), and the textile and leather industry (+4.5 per cent), while others continued to decline (metal industry, engineering and food processing). The result was only 0.7 per cent growth in overall industrial output.

Table 3.1: Capacity utilization and investments in the manufacturing industry, 1992-1996

%

	1992	1993	1994	1995	1996
Capacity of utilization in manufacturing industry *(% of nominal capacity)*	..	50	50	44	48
Machinery and equipment share in total investment *(% of total investment)*	23	37	33	41	..

Source: UNECE Economic Survey, 1996-1997.

While privatization has resulted in many industrial assets being transferred out of State ownership (by mid-1995, 81.1 per cent of enterprises had been privatized), enterprise restructuring and productivity improvements have remained modest. Rigid vertical management structures are common in industry. Investment in machinery and equipment (Table 3.1), which is crucial for the

Table 3.2: Structure of industry, 1993-1996

	% of industrial output*			
	1993	1994	1995	1996
Food industry	32.0	31.6	33.3	33.3
Light industry (textile, leather)	12.6	13.0	13.5	13.6
Wood industries (incl. pulp and paper)	3.7	5.3	6.1	4.6
Machine building and metal working	6.5	6.5	6.4	4.9
Chemicals (incl. oil refining)	28.0	24.4	22.1	23.7
Non-metallic mineral products	3.8	4.5	4.2	3.5
Others (incl. electricity, gas and water supply)	13.4	14.7	14.4	16.4

Source: Statistical Yearbook of Lithuania, 1997.

Note:

* Total industrial output includes mining,quarrying and manufacturing.
  As of 1995, sectors are in accordance with ISIC.

Table 3.3: Final energy consumption sources and breakdown in industry, 1996

	Overall consumption	Industry consumption	Share in industry
	1 000 t coal equivalent		*%*
Total	**6 051.0**	**1 493.1**	**100.0**
Coal	260.4	13.6	0.9
Other solid fuels	26.1	11.0	0.7
Petroleum	9.9	3.5	0.2
Natural gas	529.9	200.1	13.4
Petroleum products	2 376.2	227.0	15.2
Electricity	801.4	335.1	22.4
Heat consumption	2 047.1	702.8	47.2

Source: Ministry of the Environment.

important industrial activities have been privatized, including fertilizer production, though some are still controlled by the State (e.g. oil refining). In the course of the privatization process, the new owners have not been made liable for past environmental damage.

Lithuania's major industrial sectors are listed in Table 3.2. Before independence, its industry was based mainly on food processing, the textile and leather industry and machine building. Now it has clearly shifted to chemicals (including pharmaceuticals) and energy and fuel, with food processing remaining a traditional pillar of Lithuania's industrial activities. The machine-building and metalworking industries (agricultural machinery, food-processing equipment, shipbuilding and maintenance equipment, car parts) and the electrical appliance and electronic industries used to be entirely dependent on the USSR market, as they produced military equipment. Since independence, they have shrunk dramatically, and the problem is cascading to subcontracting industries. For instance, 130 galvanizing workshops which used to work for big electronic plants that have now collapsed are struggling to survive.

Due to its very small domestic market, Lithuania's industrial sector has traditionally been strongly export-oriented. Since independence, there has been a shift westwards in Lithuania's trade pattern. In 1993, 19.9 per cent of Lithuania's exports went to EU; in 1997, the share increased to 32.5 per cent, and by mid-1998, it had risen to 33.8 per cent. Food products, fertilizers, wood products and furniture are the most successful exports. The free

trade agreement concluded in early 1995 with EU includes quality requirements. But product quality is causing problems. There is over-capacity and technology is largely outdated, because of the economic decline. In 1995, none of the slaughterhouses met EU standards and it was impossible to export meat to EU. A similar situation existed in other sectors where the quality and packing did not meet EU market requirements.

Industrial development trends and forecasts

In its Public Investment Programme (PIP), the Government put energy and environmental protection among its top priorities. The Government has also set priorities in its economic development programme, in particular for industry and agricultural processing. Accordingly, the former Ministry of Industry and Trade launched five specific development programmes in 1995:

- A development programme for forestry and the wood-processing industry;
- A modernization programme for the leather and fur industry;
- A programme to develop and expand the flax industry (growing and scutching);
- An expansion programme for the pharmaceutical industry;
- A programme to provide technology to the agricultural sector (machinery).

In addition, a programme to develop the fishing industry was prepared at the Ministry of Agriculture. All those programmes, except the last, are now coordinated by the Ministry of the Economy (which covers the activities of the former

Ministries of Industry and Trade, and of Energy). During the transition period the State was committed to helping private companies finance their projects if they fell into the priority areas, and if they were managed following strict guidelines and criteria set by it. The programmes were developed with the help of donor countries and EU, and all contained general provisions for reducing the pollution generated by industrial activities. Cleaner production were not preferred to end-of-pipe solutions. A decrease in water pollution through the construction of water purification systems, the introduction of new standards satisfying EU requirements, and a reduction in atmospheric pollution were mentioned as environmental priorities. Unfortunately, those programmes are not yet implemented.

Resource intensity of industries

In 1996 industry accounted for 24.6 per cent of the country's total energy consumption. Coal represented a negligible part of the sources, while petroleum products, electricity and heat took the lion's share. Natural gas represented 13.4 per cent (Table 3.3). Industry accounted for 45.2 per cent of final electricity consumption in 1996. Total consumption halved between 1990 and 1995. Water consumption fell 68 per cent between 1992 and 1996 (see Table 7.3). It seems that these drastic reductions are due not only to the recession; industry has also made an effort to save energy and recycle water in order to ease the burden of water user charges and energy costs (since 1992 energy prices for industrial consumers have risen sharply, see Chapter 11). It should also be pointed out that industry uses mostly "clean" sources of energy (heat, electricity and gas together amounted to 83 per cent in 1996), the share of solid fuels being very limited (Table 3.3). Nevertheless, studies show that a total energy saving of 20 to 44 per cent is still possible with a payback period of two years if best practices are applied. However, most enterprises do not have the funds for the substantial investments required.

Pollution discharges from industry

The data on pollution loads from industry presented in Table 3.4 should be interpreted with care. The enterprises which have transmitted information are those that have a permit and are therefore bound to report to the regional inspectorate. Data on air pollution are global, the breakdown of specific elements can be found in Chapter 6. The data on water seem more detailed as they are differentiated according to various polluting elements. The water data cover only those enterprises that independently discharge their waste water into surface waters., They do not send their waste water to a municipal waste-water treatment unit (MWWTU). It should be pointed out that formerly MWWTU treated municipal and industrial waste water from SMEs and larger industrial units together. SMEs potentially could do without any kind of (detoxifying) effluent pre-treatment. This could cause bio-treatment facilities to malfunction.

From the data in Table 3.4 and other elements, it can be deduced that:

- In 1996, Lithuanian enterprises generated 3 million tonnes of waste, of which about 88 tonnes was hazardous. 70 per cent of hazardous waste is accumulated on-site. Data on the waste generated by the various industrial activities are difficult to interpret and may be unreliable. Roughly, glass, paper and bone materials are reused. Building material and food wastes have grown drastically in recent years and are not recycled. The decrease in waste production is not the result of deliberate efforts, but rather of the economic crisis. The small amounts of environmental investment spent on waste would tend to confirm this assumption (Table 3.5).

- The food industry is in general a big air and water polluter, and a large solid waste producer. Its pollution is organic, mostly non-toxic, but eutrophying.

- The chemical industry, too, is a big polluter in terms of quantity. Nitrogen and phosphate discharges come from the fertilizer-producing enterprises. It is difficult to gauge the toxicity of the pollution as, even for water, there is no overall measurement of toxicity. Nevertheless, the 50.3 tonnes of hazardous waste and the presence of heavy metals in waste should be mentioned: 36 kg/year of zinc, 13 kg/year of nickel and 48 kg/year of copper (data from the Ministry of the Environment do not show their chemical oxidation degree, so it is not possible to deduce their toxicity).

Table 3.4: Pollution loads generated by the main industrial activities, 1996

	Solid waste			Air emissions				Water	Wastewater a/			
	Plants	Total Waste	of which: Hazardous	Plants	Total Emissions	of which		total discharge	Suspended solids	BOD7	N tot	P tot
						Solid	Gases and liquids					
	Number	1000 t/y		Number	1000 t/y			Million m³/y	t/y			
Total mining and manufacturing	**529**	**3,043**	**87.6**	**435**	**70.8**	**5.7**	**65.1**	**79.7**	**277.0**	**170.0**	**64.0**	**14.5**
Food industry	149	950	7.3	129	8.7	0.6	8.1	38.1	11.0	16.3	6.0	2.0
Light industry (textile, leather)	55	33	9.9	48	2.1	0.4	1.8	0.7	15.0	2.0	2.0	0.7
Machine building and metal working	123	63	18.2	88	3.2	0.4	2.8	4.2	19.0	24.0	3.0	0.1
Wood industries	42	60	1.0	48	2.4	0.5	1.9	3.5	62.0	30.0	11.0	1.9
Building materials	58	997	0.3	57	11.4	3.1	8.3	10.4	195.0	87.0	374.0 b/	46.1 b/
Chemical (incl. oil refining)	14	889 c/	50.3	13	40.2	0.3	39.9	14.8	998.0	73.0	103.0	23.4
Energy (including Ignalina NPP)	**75**	**28**	**0.9**	**153**	**60.8**	**1.3**	**59.6**	**5,285.0 d/**				

Source: Ministry of the Environment.

a/ Quantities of suspended solids, BOD₇, N and P totals include also enterprises directly discharging waste-water into surface waters.

b/ Of which 52 t/y of N and 25 t/y of P from fertilizer production facilities.

c/ Only fertilizer manufacturing.

d/ Including electricity production.

- The main heavy metal polluter is the machine-building and metalworking sector: waste emissions of 24 kg of Zn, 3 kg of Cr, 0.1 kg of Cd, 6 kg of Ni, 7 kg of Cu and 4.6 kg of Pb a year;

- The fuel industry, too, is responsible for much pollution, in particular oil emissions. Its total nitrogen and total phosphorus emissions are high.

In the absence of detailed data on the quantity and quality of industrial pollution, pollution tax revenue is a good guide to the most polluting industrial activities. Table 3.6 shows that, of Lithuania's main industrial sectors, food processing pays by far the highest pollution taxes (38.2% of total pollution charges from manufacturing industry). The chemical industry and petroleum product refining (15.6%) is followed by manufacturing of non-metallic mineral products (13.2%). Machine building and metalworking (10.3%) and the textile and leather industry (9.7%) come next. A more detailed analysis shows that taxes stem equally from air and water pollution.

It should be pointed out that about half the total tax revenue comes from the food-processing industry. The textile and leather industry and the chemical industry pay far less despite the fact that, as mentioned before, they generate toxic releases (heavy metals and toxic organics) and eutrophying agents (nitrogen and phosphate).
The chemical industry's taxes shown include the taxes paid by the oil-refining industry (contributing 29 per cent of the taxes from the chemical sector), which is responsible for much pollution, in particular oil emissions.

Pollution cost and environmental protection expenditures in industry

Since 1996, the Department of Statistics has processed data on industry's environmental expenditures (Tables 3.5 and 3.6) based on the Enterprise Register created in 1990. The share of manufacturing industry's environmental expenditures stood at 20.9 per cent of total environmental expenditures in 1995, and at 28.7 per cent in 1996.

While in 1995, current environmental expenditures exceeded investment expenditures by far, in 1996, environmental investments increased considerably, almost equalling current expenditures. Table 3.5

shows that, in 1995, 71 per cent of current environmental expenditures were spent on water, 23 per cent on air and almost nothing on waste collection and treatment, a trend which continued in 1996 (respectively 66, 22.5 and 9 per cent).

From 1995 to 1996, the manufacturing industry's environmental investments rose sharply, though the bulk is spent on end-of-pipe (78 per cent) rather than on integrated technology (22 per cent). In 1996, about 70 per cent of the investments were spent on protecting the air, 29.5% on protecting water. Till 1995, nothing was invested in waste management; in 1996 some investment started. Investments in the various industrial sectors, with the exception of the machine-building and metalworking industry, are mainly in end-of-pipe processes. 1996 investments in integrated technology were comparable to those of 1995. Most investments in integrated technology by the wood-processing,   machine-building   and metalworking sectors were spent on protecting the air. The chemicals and food-processing industries concentrated their efforts on water protection with end-of-pipe technology (Table 3.6).

3.2   Policy setting for cleaner technology

Legal framework

Clean technology is not an explicit legal requirement. There are, for instance, no best available technology (not entailing excessive cost) requirements (BATNEEC). The permitting system, which is compulsory for both new and existing industrial plants, is based on a single administrative file, bringing together water, air, waste and natural resource use issues. Yet, the authorization and emission limits for the different kinds of pollution (air, water and waste - soil is not covered) are negotiated separately; they are not considered as parts of a package. The permit is based on emission limit values expressed as pollutant concentrations in the discharged flow, and not on pollution quantities from the production process (i.e. pollution emitted per unit of product output). It does not include any requirements regarding the process technology, nor any limit values for specific substances based on BAT(NEEC). The limit values are in line with the air, water and waste acts, but these acts do not lay down technological requirements. They are based

**Table 3.5: Environmental protection expenditures and pollution taxes in industry
by environmental medium, 1995-1996**

1 000 litas

	Environmental investments				Current expenditures		Taxes on env. pollution	
	end-of-pipe		integrated technology					
	1995	1996	1995	1996	1995	1996	1995	1996
Manufacturing industry* - Total	**11 414.5**	**55 502.6**	**14 950.6**	**15 515.4**	**77 518.6**	**67 963.3**	**11 012.2**	**18 216.0**
of which on:								
Air protection	1 961.5	35 293.7	13 441.0	14 333.5	17 988.4	15 286.6	5 724.6	9 161.2
Water and soil protection	9 447.0	19 979.2	1 429.6	1 023.9	54 976.0	45 003.5	5 287.6	9 054.8
Waste collection and treatment	..	207.7	80.0	147.0	4 479.7	6 371.8	0.0	0.0

Source: Department of Statistics, Report on natural resources and environmental protection, 1995, 1996.

Note:
* ISIC 15-37.

Table 3.6: Environmental expenditures and taxes in the main industrial sectors, 1995-1996

1 000 litas

	Environmental investments				Current expenditures		Taxes on env. pollution	
	end-of-pipe		integrated technology					
	1995	1996	1995	1996	1995	1996	1995	1996
Manufacturing industry* - Total	**11 414.5**	**55 502.6**	**14 950.6**	**15 515.4**	**77 518.6**	**67 963.3**	**11 012.2**	**18 216.0**
of which in:								
Food processing	4 985.6	8 664.2	1 043.1	186.4	16 536.9	18 755.6	5 261.5	6 972.6
Light industry	64.7	2 833.7	-	-	8 064.8	13 335.5	818.6	1 765.2
Wood processing	634.4	247.4	6 570.0	-	1 154.6	2 705.9	84.5	776.0
Pulp and paper industry	763.8	258.5	25.0	-	4 191.1	4 625.0	431.6	408.0
Chemical industry (incl. oil refining)	3 775.3	6 720.6	1 130.0	1.3	30 332.7	8 769.1	1 853.5	2 839.5
Non-metallic mineral product (incl. glass)	349.3	34 738.0	44.0	11.0	2 607.1	1 470.5	1 685.1	2 396.8
Machine building and metalworking	118.8	24.0	5 948.5	10 279.7	3 661.9	5 582.2	361.8	1 874.0
Electrical and electronical industry	40.0	47.2	-	-	7 930.8	7 570.1	184.3	305.9

Source: Department of Statistics, Report on natural resources and environmental protection, 1995, 1996.

Note:
* ISIC 15-37.

For all these reasons, the integrated pollution prevention and control (IPPC) concept, which is spelled out in the IPPC Directive (96/61/EC) of EU, is hard to apply in Lithuania at the moment. Another important requirement of the IPPC Directive concerns the safety of industrial facilities, i.e. compliance with Directive 82/501/EEC (Seveso I) regarding major accident hazards of certain industrial activities (to be superseded in early 1999 by Seveso II). Lithuania has not established a list of affected facilities (about 200), and is not able to fulfil the requirements regarding monitoring and disclosure of information. However, Lithuania has recently begun to focus on new issues. In particular, since 1996 there have been more possibilities for public information and participation and for appeals against administrative decisions. There is also an effective EIA programme to prevent new pollution sources (precautionary principle). The EIA Law is a major tool to prevent the development of new pollution sources and introduce cleaner technology in the sectors of industry where investments are going to be made. It is also important to introduce economic incentives to encourage industry to improve its environmental performance and to increase its liability for the emission of pollutants. However, many SMEs slip through the permitting net, as it applies only from a certain quantity of water withdrawn or pollution discharged.

Other laws encourage cleaner production technologies, limit the use of resources and encourage their conservation, tax environmental pollution, regulate the discharge of dangerous substances, prosecute economic actors who contravene environmental regulations, empower local governments to permit or stop an activity, and lay down new standards in some sectors of activity.

Policy objectives

Lithuania's policy objectives regarding the introduction of cleaner and safer technologies are:

1. To introduce and apply the precautionary principle to protect the environment in all major sectors of activity: food-processing industry; construction and construction materials industry; chemical industry; energy; transport; textile and leather industry; and biotechnology.
2. To encourage the introduction and implementation of EMAS (eco-management and audit schemes) and the ISO 14000 series.
3. To prevent environmental pollution by introducing cleaner technologies.
4. To encourage the production of new ecologically sound products by setting environmental requirements and criteria.
5. To make both producers and consumers more aware of the environmental implications of their actions and of their increased responsibility in a market economy.

In the National Environmental Strategy and Action Programme (NES), different action items introduce, directly or indirectly, cleaner production as an important policy objective. While adherence to NES statements on cleaner technology does not appear to be very strict in practice, Lithuania, in its EU approximation strategy, is harmonizing its legislation with the EU's. The Law on Environmental Protection will be accompanied by new subsidiary legislation. Standards, in particular, should soon be in line with EU standards (end of 1998). Environmental quality standards and pollution norms based on best environmental practices and best available

technologies will be introduced for air, water and waste. Some toxic elements will be phased out. For instance, a country programme was developed and adopted in 1995 for the elimination of ozone-depleting substances (ODS). The management of chemicals can now be based on the forthcoming law on chemical substances and preparations, which was drafted early in 1998 and is expected to be enacted in the same year. It is fully in line with EU practices. More attention will in future be paid to enforcement mechanisms, to voluntary principles such as eco-labelling and environmental management of companies.

On the international scene, Lithuania is involved in some agreements that help to introduce cleaner technology. As a party to the Helsinki Convention for the Baltic Sea Area, Lithuania is committed to HELCOM recommendations. These expressly call for the introduction of cleaner technology in industry in general and for a decrease in the emissions of toxic components, organic substances and nutrients. Specific recommendations are also made to various sectors of activity such as the pulp and paper, chemical, leather, textile, oil-refining, food-processing, and metal-finishing industries. The recommendations set targets for authorized emission loads of specific elements, include a short list of preventive BAT(NEEC) technologies relevant to the particular sector and specify a deadline for reporting (in most cases late 1997). New plants were requested to comply with these recommendations by 1996-97 and existing ones by 2000. However, the recommendations are not binding.

Institutional arrangements

The *Standard and Technology Unit* of the Ministry of the Environment (four people) was created in August 1997 to start the preparations for the implementation of the IPPC Directive, which is included in the package of directives for the EU approximation process, and the introduction of cleaner technology. Adjusting to the IPPC Directive necessarily entails the preliminary adoption of emission standards, and the introduction of BAT(NEEC) into industrial production processes. The new unit will have to do both, on the basis of clear objectives and after appropriate training.

Implementation of and compliance with the BAT(NEEC) and IPPC principles at the local level will soon be the task of *the regional offices (REDs) of the Ministry of the Environment.* It seems that few offices are able to work with local enterprises to set environmental goals, develop control strategies, agree on time frames for abatement, monitor progress and, within their legal framework, impose fines and possibly close down plants or processes. Moreover, regarding the introduction of cleaner technology (BATNEEC), they do not appear to have the necessary technological support from specialists to be able to advise on technological options. They have mostly a control function and can impose fines, but have no authority to close down industrial facilities. There are examples of industrial facilities continuing to operate despite frequent violations of standards.

The Ministry of the Environment has full and exclusive responsibility for collecting information on the environmental performance of industry and for processing and dispatching this information, which is not yet done properly (see above section on pollution discharges from industry, and below section on monitoring). This explains why the Ministry of Agriculture, which oversees food processing, and the Ministry of the Economy, which oversees the other sectors of industry are unable to describe the pressures that the various sectors of industry and important industrial sites are exerting on the environment. Both ministries rely entirely on the Ministry of the Environment to describe and handle industrial pollution, and then deal with industry to solve these issues. According to both the Ministries of Agriculture and of the Economy:

- There are no priorities for industrial development yet, and development programmes (1995-1997) are not implemented;
- The development of the private sector is unfettered, as no development policies or objectives are driven by the ministries responsible;
- Small enterprises are mushrooming, and often escape the environmental permit procedures. Formerly big enterprises, which used to be subject to the permitting system because of their size, are split into small enterprises that individually no longer require a permit;
- Hazardous waste management is left entirely in the hands of the Ministry of the Economy.

The Pollution Prevention Centre (PPC) was created in April 1994 in Kaunas based on a cooperation agreement with the World Environment Centre (United States) and financially supported by USAID. PPC is a non-profit organization which promotes sustainable development, cleaner production, pollution prevention, and waste minimization. Its mission is twofold: (i) to provide industrial sectors with relevant research, technical consulting assistance and training on various environmental issues (e.g. environmental management system) and critical management skills (including problem solving and fund raising); (ii) to educate technicians and managers in industry, and also governmental organizations, NGOs and academics. It enjoys good scientific surroundings, as it is located within the Kaunas Institute of Environmental Engineering (APINI). Financed fully with foreign funds in its early stage, it will be funded 20 per cent by the State for its educational role and 80 per cent by projects from 1999.

Since 1993, specific international programmes on cleaner production have been carried out under the auspices of PPC, for example:

- Audits of Waste Minimization Opportunities to Introduce Cleaner Technologies in Lithuanian Industry (1993-1995) in partnership with Rendan AS (Denmark) and Lund University (Sweden)
- Cleaner Production Approach and its Implementation (1993-1995). Research and course for MSc and PhD students, in partnership with the International Institute for Industrial Environmental Economics, Lund University
- The Norwegian Cleaner Production Training Programme (1995-1996), with the World Cleaner Production Society (Norway)
- Implementation of Cleaner Production in Lithuanian Tanneries (1996-1997), with Chemcontrol AS (Denmark) and UAB "Ecobalt" (Lithuania)
- Implementation of Cleaner Production Project in the Lithuanian Textile Industry (1996-1997),

with IVAM, University of Amsterdam (the Netherlands)

- Second Norwegian-Lithuanian Cleaner Production Programme (1997-1998), with Det Norske Veritas (DNV, Norway)

In the course of these project identification seminars, PPC has identified many low-cost good housekeeping measures and low-cost, short-payback investments. Through the implementation of these programmes, many people have been trained and industry's awareness about cleaner production raised. As many as 80 advisers and trainers, more than 20 experts and over 120 other people have been trained and different sectors of industry have been involved (electroplating, electronic, food, paper, rubber, tannery, textile industry). Demonstration projects were launched, in particular in the textile, food-processing and plating industries: the first benefits from support by EU LIFE, while the other two, facing a bleak environmental and economic situation, are having difficulties with their practical implementation. A Danish EPA project on environmental efficiency in the Lithuanian food-processing industry includes environmental auditing in seven companies from different food sectors in the country. In general, most of the results concern improving housekeeping, saving resources (in particular water), and minimizing waste. Only the textile industry is likely to benefit in the near future from a real improvement in technology.

The Pollution Prevention Centre has capable and well-trained staff (about ten people). It is aware of the potential of cleaner production techniques. It has established a very good network of information and relationships with other specialized teams abroad - including international specialized teams (UNIDO, UNEP/IEO in Paris and UNEP/ITC in Japan) - and databases, and is developing contacts with banks (in particular NEFCO) to help industry finance its projects. The Centre is developing mobile monitoring and analytical equipment to take concrete steps and reinforce its assessment capacity. But it has no chemical engineering pilot capacity yet.

The Lithuanian Confederation of Industrialists, which plays the role of a chamber of commerce and industry, includes the Engineering Ecology Association, which is a link between industry, the Ministry of the Environment and the Government. It defends the position of industry on environmental issues, including legislation and environmental economic instruments. The Association has a project to set up a national centre for ecological auditing and management systems which will be private, but internationally accredited.

3.3 Instruments for the introduction of cleaner technologies

Environmental standards

In 1997, Lithuania was still using the air and water standards of the former Soviet Union. Air standards apply to over 1500 pollutants, water standards to almost 4 000. Some of these standards are stricter than those of the EU, but they used to serve as reference points and not to enforce compliance. Different sections of the Ministry of the Environment are currently preparing standards on air, water and waste in line with the EU's; air standards are expected to be ready in 1998.

The approach to emission standards is based on ambient quality criteria and not on the BAT (NEEC) principle. For instance, air emission limits are estimated for each polluting source (for individual components), depending on the background pollution level. Applicable air quality standards have to be met. So the inspectorate sets a maximum allowable emission which does not endanger the air quality standards in the area (see Chapter 6). There is no limit on the emissions per unit of product or process -- an approach which would push for cleaner technology. The situation is similar for water: environmental quality standards (EQS) are applied but not environmental limit values (MAP, see Chapter 7). There is no legal incentive to generate less waste, nor is there a tax on waste generated. As indulgent temporary pollution permits (TAP) are often granted, and enforcement is lax, there is no effective regulatory incentive for cleaner technology. The only exceptions are the new standards based on the BATNEEC principle that Lithuania established in 1996 for combustion installations for heat and power generation, which are comparable with the EU standards.

Monitoring

In industry, monitoring environmental pollution is a legal obligation. The modalities are discussed with the regional environmental protection departments (REDs). Many industrial enterprises have now been entrusted with self-monitoring. However, systematic emission monitoring is rare. On-line monitoring of air and water emissions is virtually non-existent because of a lack of equipment. Manual sampling is the rule, with a low sampling frequency (every three months for air pollution) and no standardized protocol for monitoring methods, or for analytical methods. All industrial pollution sources are required to report source emission data to REDs on an annual basis. However, the data are mostly calculated using emission factors which attempt to approximate actual emission levels. REDs compile the data, make a critical assessment and transmit them to the Ministry (Joint Research Centre). There, the data ought to be merged to describe the environmental situation nationwide and point out the major trends, before the results are transmitted to the Department of Statistics for publication and disclosure. But, to date, environmental data from industry have not been compiled/analysed according to activity, polluter, industrial sector, region or even medium. Therefore, as pointed out before, it is impossible to obtain a reliable picture of the important flows of pollution, who generates them, in what specific regions, urban centres or water basins, etc.

Economic instruments and incentives

Since 1991, there has been a system of environmental taxes which aims primarily at compensating for damage and raising funds to repair damage. The new system (expected in 1998) will focus more on preventing pollution. The battery of environmental economic instruments likely to encourage industry to cut its pollution has included user charges on natural resources (in particular energy and water) since 1992 and pollution fees and penalties since 1991 (for details see Chapter 2). Product charges have not yet been introduced in Lithuania.

Fees and fines levied on water and air can be partially or totally waived when action is taken to reduce pollution. Fees are included in the costs of production, while fines are paid from net profits.

The relation between the level of fees and fines appears correct. However, the level of fines is calculated on the basis of a mathematical formula which is not well understood by factory managers. As a consequence, the instruments do not always have the intended incentive and punitive effects, as the amounts are not easily predictable. Both environmental expenditures and those related to the introduction of new technology are tax-deductible.

Financing provisions

Apart from the above-mentioned tax breaks, the Government does not give any subsidies to industry to improve its environmental management and results. The State guarantee for projects in line with PIP is discouragingly long and difficult to obtain. A survey conducted from 1990 to 1995 shows that the vast majority of projects were financed by the firms themselves. In 1995-1997, all financing of process changes that reduced emissions was internal, while investments in water, air protection and waste management benefited from minority participation by banks, municipalities or other sources. For banks, the environment is not a priority investment area and the amounts involved are in most cases too small to be considered by commercial banks and international financing institutions. There are no soft loans for environmentallyfriendly projects.

Until now, there has been no mechanism for financing clean technology projects in industry. The Lithuanian Environmental Fund for Investment (EFI), created in late 1996, will be the first mechanism set up to finance industrial environmental projects. EFI will provide soft loans to industry for investment projects "yielding significant environmental benefits". NEFCO has provided a second important source since 1998, with the creation of the revolving facility for cleaner production investments. The facility will give priority to projects (i) aiming at preventing waste in industry, (ii) located in Lithuania and the Russian Federation, and (iii) identified by the Pollution Prevention Centre (PPC). It can finance up to 100 per cent of the total project costs, starting with investments with a short payback period, yielding both environmental and economic benefits. Seven million Danish kroner will be earmarked for projects in Lithuania in the first stage. The facility intends to cooperate with EFI.

Voluntary measures for industry

In 1996, the Ministry of the Environment adopted a regulation on eco-labelling (see Chapter 2 for a description). Eco-management and audit schemes are not yet introduced. However, their voluntary introduction will be encouraged by EU regulation EEC/1836/93, which is part of the EU approximation package. So far the focus seems to be chiefly on introducing the ISO 9000 series on quality management as it directly improves EU market penetration. The ISO 14000 series and EMAS seem to interest only big companies for the time being, as some international banks (e.g. EBRD) request an ecological audit as a precondition for providing funds. Ecological audits are currently subcontracted to accredited foreign consultants and are said to be very expensive.

Research, development and education

In the previous system each ministry had specific technological research and development centres. Today they have almost all collapsed: for instance, the technological centre of the Ministry of Agriculture, which was responsible for technological development in food processing, the textile and leather industry technological centre for leather and textile, etc. PPC has currently limited research and development ambitions and means, as it is only in its infancy and is developing a general approach applicable to the various sectors of industry.

Since 1994, apart from the educational and training role of PPC, the Kaunas University of Technology (APINI) has developed a course on "cleaner production/waste minimization approach and its implementation in Lithuanian industry" together with the Institute for Environmental Engineering and the International Institute for Industrial Environmental Economics of Lund University. About 50 students have already graduated. In the beginning the course was taught by foreign experts; gradually Lithuanian teachers took over. Moreover, the Lithuanian Agriculture University and the Vilnius Gediminas Technical University are introducing clean technology. Also, six Lithuanian Universities have since 1997 taken part in the Baltic University Programme, which teaches elements of sustainable industrial production.

3.4   Conclusions and recommendations

The Kaunas Pollution Prevention Centre, created in 1994 with the cooperation of several foreign countries, seems to have acted as a trigger in introducing the cleaner technology concept in Lithuania. Today, Lithuania has prepared the institutional framework and capacities to this end, although results have yet to be achieved. Much effort has already been devoted to introducing specialized education courses at universities, informing industry through training seminars, establishing links with western countries to improve skills and benefit from technical cooperation, attracting foreign financing organizations (NEFCO) ready to help realize concrete projects, etc. Moreover, with the emphasis in NES on cleaner technology, action has been taken to reinforce the institutional capacity in the Ministry of the Environment, creating a special technology unit there, to introduce a legal and tax system that favours the precautionary principle and BATNEEC, to introduce voluntary instruments to improve production process management and product quality, and to create a funding system (EFI) for environmental investments in industry. All this could soon bear fruit if the few remaining weaknesses could also be addressed.

Basically, no decisive actions in favour of the introduction of cleaner technology can be taken as long as the current situation regarding pollution discharged by industry is not clearly described. Industry duly reports its pollution emissions to the regional State inspectorate, which transmits the information to the Ministry. But, there, the data are not compiled or analysed. Therefore, the Ministry of the Environment is not able to describe the pollution generated by industry, and point out the major polluting sites and sectors of activity to the Ministry of Agriculture and the Ministry of the Economy. Consequently, none of them is aware of or feels concerned by the pollution generated by the industrial activities they oversee, and nobody knows in which sectors of activity and vulnerable geographical locations it is particularly important to make cleaner technology a priority.

Introducing cleaner technology will necessitate the full involvement of the Ministry of the Environment. The Ministry has the responsibility not only to shape the permitting system and economic incentives in a way which will encourage the introduction of less polluting techniques, it should also set up a strategy for introducing BAT(NEEC) in agreement with other ministries, and play an important advisory role to the industrial sector. This advisory role is particularly important for small and medium-size enterprises, which do not always have sufficient access to technology (often because of a lack of technical background, training or access to relevant information). The Ministry of the Environment should promote schemes assisting SMEs in searching for relevant information regarding technology. At the central level, the standard and technology division should implement the strategy, pinpoint the various problems and priorities throughout the country, give advice and provide information to the regional inspectors. At the regional level, inspectors should not limit their task to enforcing the laws and applying the permitting system. If the system is to evolve toward integrated pollution prevention and control and the introduction of BAT(NEEC), inspectors should fully play an advisory and negotiating role. Their ultimate goal should be to improve the environmental situation by helping industry diminish the pressure it exerts on the environment. This means that inspectors need to have engineering expertise to make judgements, and, if this is not possible, they should be assisted by engineering consultants. Such judgement is necessary both when national or State regulations are developed, and in case-by-case decisions regarding permits. Their policing and "money-raising" role should be seen only as a means to an end. Consequently, inspectors should be trained, and perhaps also assisted by technological advisers and experts of the Ministry of the Environment, PPC or from abroad.

Recommendation 3.1:
A key priority for the Ministry of the Environment is to draw an accurate picture of industrial pollution. To this end:
    (1)   Self-monitoring by industry should improve and become more reliable;
    (2)   Data which are transmitted by industry should be compiled, analysed (at local, regional and national levels, per environmental medium, per sector of activity, etc.); and compared with governmental data;
    (3)   Information should be published.

    (4)   The staff of the Ministry (i.e. the Standards and Technology Unit) and regional inspectors concerned with cleaner technology issues should be trained to become partners and/or counsellors of industry in the introduction of cleaner technologies.

Self-monitoring by industry poses a problem of information reliability. The problem can be solved by accrediting the laboratories that analyse samples. At the moment, there is no such accreditation system in place. As certification of laboratories is starting in some contexts (see Chapter 7), it appears timely to develop a comprehensive accreditation system for all environmental laboratories.

Recommendation 3.2:
An accreditation system for environmental laboratories should be developed in the near future, paying attention also to laboratories involved in industrial self-monitoring.

Special measures are required to improve the capacity of industrial enterprises to introduce environmental management, which can be seen as one very successful instrument to detect opportunities for cleaner technologies. While this is to some extent a question of resources - for example, industry appears to lack self-monitoring equipment - the wide introduction of environmental management systems would pave the way for successful developments in this regard.

Recommendation 3.3:
The Ministry of the Environment should take the initiative to promote the accelerated introduction of the ISO 14000 series into enterprise management, as a first step towards the implementation of EMAS standards.

Some sectors of activity are picking up, namely the chemical and pharmaceutical industries, the fuel and energy industry, or are stable, such as the food-processing and wood industries. Others, such as light industries and machine building, are declining. Figures demonstrate that the biggest polluters are the fuel industry, the chemical industry and the food industry, which are precisely those that are currently growing. It is therefore crucial that cleaner technology should be introduced in these polluting sectors that are making investments, i.e. installing new equipment. There, cleaner technologies should be preferred to end-of-pipe equipment. While actual investments are to be decided by the business sectors themselves, a policy favourable to the introduction of cleaner, safer and more sustainable technologies should be developed. Economic instruments are available or under development. They should be deliberately used to promote cleaner technologies. The various ministries involved should work out the detailed objectives, deadlines, or incentives together.

A decisive position on the part of the Government in favour of the introduction of cleaner technology would be a triggering factor. There is currently no programme, strategy or plan to introduce cleaner technology in Lithuania. Moreover, as on the command-and-control side, the sectoral laws on air and water protection, wastes and chemicals do not contain provisions for the introduction of cleaner technology or BAT (or BATNEEC), there are no incentives for industry to introduce more environmentally friendly technology.

Recommendation 3.4:
The Government should formulate a coordinated strategy and a national programme for introducing cleaner technology stepwise. In this process, responsibilities should be shared between the Ministries of the Environment, of Agriculture, of the Economy and industry. The pollution-prevention principle should be the cornerstone of the programme, in which priorities could be determined on the basis of cost estimates for individual measures. The programme should be backed up with laws and finance. Environmental auditing to assess the performances reached within the deadlines should be part of the programme, as should the disclosure of the related information. See also Recommendation 12.5.

The permitting system is a major factor when introducing cleaner technology. It should efficiently combine command-and-control and economic instruments. Currently the permitting regulations are not strict enough and, according to industry, too complicated and their implications not clear. According to the IPPC approach, the permit should encompass at the same time the generation of gaseous, liquid and solid pollution, and should take its toxicity and hazardousness into account. Industry is still discharging considerable

amounts of air and water pollutants, as only the concentration of pollution is considered. The current "media quality objectives" policy is based on nationwide quality targets, which do not reflect local situations and vulnerabilities. The toxicity of emissions is not sufficiently taken into account. A major element missing from the permit are pollution discharge limits (emission limit values) based on technology criteria and expressed as the quantity of pollution allowed per unit of product output.

Therefore, more consideration should be given to what release levels existing plants can attain and what can be expected with improved, retrofitted or new technologies. Developing specific indicators/reference values for cleaner production per sector of activity could help to set useful benchmarks. These could be used by the inspectors when negotiating permits and setting allowable pollution discharges. This approach is generally referred to as the "BAT(NEEC)" approach. It should be left to industry to choose the technical options that meet the limits in the most cost-effective manner. Specific technologies should not be imposed.

It appears that the economic instruments, namely the price put on natural resources to discourage their use (energy, water), are effective, as industry is making efforts to recycle. However, the few investments made in pollution abatement are spent on end-of-pipe rather than on process technology. This is the case, for instance, in the two main polluting sectors, food processing and the chemical industry. Moreover, the lax attitude of the authorities regarding compliance with the permit system discourages its strict application.

Recommendation 3.5:
The permits should be based both on media quality objectives and on emission limit values, and should cover all possible discharges to the different environmental media together. Legal and economic pressure should be exerted to minimize the generation of all waste residuals. Monitoring and enforcement of compliance are essential for success.

Without the participation and understanding of industry, no progress can be made towards cleaner production, as industrialists are the key players. Thanks to the action of, for instance, PPC, several industrial sectors have already benefited from relevant training (i.e. electroplating, electronic, food, paper, rubber, tannery, textile industries). They should be further encouraged to improve their environmental management, put into practice good housekeeping principles and invest in pollution combating equipment. This is being facilitated in 1998, as two important funding systems, namely EFI and the revolving facility for cleaner production investments of NEFCO, have become operational. Future action should put more emphasis on reducing the use and discharge of toxic elements in production processes. The introduction of environmental management systems in enterprises could significantly promote such action.

Recommendation 3.6:

A system of incentives for the introduction of cleaner technologies should be developed. The industrial sector should continue to be informed and trained to improve its management skills. The required information and education could be provided on a commercial basis, involving institutions like the Pollution Prevention Centre. Preferential conditions, such as subsidies, soft loans and tax rebates, should be granted for boosting the introduction of cleaner production processes. They could be attributed foremost to those enterprises that have already benefited from technical assistance and training programmes and that are introducing environmental management systems.

Chapter 4

SPATIAL PLANNING

4.1 The framework for territorial development

Human settlements network

Lithuania has a well-balanced network of human settlements, which was mainly formed after 1945. Before the Second World War, Lithuania had only two big cities, Vilnius (186 000 inhabitants) and Kaunas (154 000 inhabitants), and one medium-sized town, Klaipėda (51 000 inhabitants). Now Vilnius and Kaunas each have a population of over 400 000; Klaipėda, Šiauliai and Panevėžys have more than 100 000; Alytus and Marijampolė have more than 50 000; 13 towns have 20 000 to 50 000 inhabitants; and 19 towns have 10 000 to 20 000. There are also 72 small towns and urban-type settlements in rural areas with a population of less than 20 000.

In view of the large pool of skilled labour, many industrial enterprises (averaging 1 300 employees) set up in Lithuania, starting in the early sixties. These enterprises provided other services as well, such as housing, cultural clubs and health clinics. This industrial development took place within a comprehensive national plan for the creation of a polycentric system of human settlements based on traditional historical centres. Lithuania provides a good example of human settlements development that resulted from the distribution of different functions among urban centres: Vilnius, the historical and cultural centre and the administrative capital; Klaipėda, the country's main port; and Kaunas, the educational, business and trading centre. In rural areas, the system of farmsteads (120 000) that existed before the War was reorganized into collective farms, and many rural centres with social (child-care centres, education and health institutions) and engineering (roads, central heating and hot water supply) infrastructures were developed on the basis of existing villages and small towns. At the same time, urbanization, industrial and agricultural development and the former Soviet military sites had a negative impact on the environment and on land-use patterns (soil erosion, pollution with oil products and heavy metals).

After the restoration of independence in 1990, the system of human settlements started to change as a result of socio-economic factors, particularly in rural areas, where land was returned to its previous owners and private property rights were restored. By the end of 1995, approximately 124 000 new farms had been set up, 67 per cent of which with two or three employees. Many rural centres started to lose their economic and social importance. Job opportunities in rural areas are rare and some 70 per cent of all unemployed young people live in small rural centres. As a result, living conditions in rural settlements have worsened considerably and this has had an impact on the environment in these areas. The former rural centres are even seen by many economists as an obstacle to the development of private farming in Lithuania.

Its geographic situation makes Lithuania a bridge between western Europe, the Russian Federation and other Baltic States. This means that it has important transit functions. The railway network comprises around 2 500 km of track. The paved road network covers 35 800 km. Motorways account for 420 km. The national road system is comparatively good, but in rural areas few roads are metalled, making transport difficult in the autumn and early spring.

Population development and migration trends

The urban population has grown 3.5 times since 1950, while the rural population has decreased by 36 per cent. In 1993, birth and death rates were equal and in 1994 deaths outnumbered births by 3 600 for the first time. The birth rate fell particularly sharply in urban areas, and deaths exceeded births by 4 100 in 1995. The death rate increased from 7.8 per thousand in 1960 to 12.6 per thousand in 1995 (see also Chapter 10). Eventually, the death rate started to decrease in 1996-1997. In

1997, the net natural decrease was 2 400, while the death rate was 11 per thousand.

The deteriorating economic situation and the special regulations restricting settlement in almost all large cities (even in the suburbs of Vilnius) have contributed to a significant decrease in both rural-urban and urban-rural migration. Since 1990, there has, however, been an increase in rural-rural migration. Emigration from Lithuania has also increased, but less than one could have expected given the domestic economic difficulties. The educational qualifications of recent emigrants show that Lithuania is suffering from a brain drain, which could create difficulties for its economic, environmental and social future.

During the eighties, the number of households used to increase by 10 000 to 11 000 a year. In 1992-1994, the number of households declined by 1 per cent, i.e. approximately by 10 000. The proportion of single households is growing and women account for two-thirds of these households. The structure of consumer expenditure reflects inequalities in income distribution. Those with the highest income spend 40 per cent of it on food, while the poorest families spend 66 per cent on food. The difference in spending on other items is even more marked: 7.2-fold on clothes; 10-fold on transport; 13.3-fold on education and culture and 5.3-fold on housing. Families are facing a rise in prices of municipal services (in 1995, 15 per cent of households were in arrears for municipal services).

Characteristics of the housing stock

In 1996, there were 1 269 600 dwellings in Lithuania, i.e. 342 dwellings per 1 000 inhabitants and 20.4 m² of useful floor space per person. Despite a comparatively good provision of housing, which was particularly favourable in 1991-1995 given the demographic developments and migration, there is still a housing shortage and some 90 000 households are on the waiting list for municipal housing. There are striking differences in housing provision between rural and urban areas. In rural areas, with some 351 dwellings (mainly family houses) per 1 000 inhabitants, there is practically no demand for additional housing construction (except for new farms). In urban areas, there are, on average, 338 dwellings per 1 000 inhabitants, mainly in multi-family housing

estates, with much less floor space per dwelling unit. However, qualitative indicators - water supply, sewerage and district heating - are better in urban housing (in rural areas only 60 per cent of dwellings are connected to the piped water supply and 62 per cent have district heating). Besides being unhappy about the size of their dwellings, urban residents are dissatisfied with the levels of noise they have to endure and with the poor thermal insulation of their homes.

Territorial organization

According to the new Law on Local Government (1995), Lithuania has three levels of territorial organization and administration: the national level; the regional level (10 counties); and the local level (56 municipalities, including 44 administrative districts, and 12 city municipalities).

The average local government unit covers 1 166 km² and has approximately 66 000 inhabitants. Forty per cent of the population lives in the six largest municipalities (Vilnius, Kaunas, Klaipėda, Šiauliai, Panevėžys and Alytus) and only five local governments have fewer than 25 000 inhabitants. The local government is responsible for administering the land, and regulating land-use and physical planning. However, the division of responsibilities between central, regional and local authorities in important areas (ownership of real property, municipal service enterprises, etc.) is not always clear. At the same time, the establishment in 1994 of the Ministry for Public Administration Reform and Local Government is an indication that developing the local government is a political priority in Lithuania.

For territorial planning, Lithuania cooperates with its neighbours through a number of bilateral and multilateral programmes. Transborder cooperation between Poland and Lithuania has been carried out since 1995 on the basis of the Agreement between the former Lithuanian Ministry of Construction and Urban Development and the former Polish Ministry of Construction and Physical Planning. International agreements and programmes on the exchange of information, technical assistance, preparation of legal documents, and sustainable housing have been established with Finland and Denmark. A good cooperative framework has been established with the Nordic and Baltic countries, as well as with the

Russian Federation and Belarus.   Within this cooperation, a spatial development concept "Vision and Strategies around the Baltic Sea 2010" has been prepared. The purposes of this study were:

- to restore former ties between nations around the Baltic Sea, developing a strong regional identity, competing globally with other regions
- to support the development of networks for cooperation in the Baltic Sea region
- to provide a forum for the transfer of skills from market economies to the countries in transition
- to improve the exchange of information in the Baltic Sea region on current trends and problems
- to · assess important infrastructure projects eligible for international financial assistance
- to create a long-term planning perspective and to improve spatial planning in the participating countries
- to create a common reference document for national, regional, local authorities, comprehensive and special plans being in line with the neighbours intentions so facilitating international cooperation in spatial planning
- to create a basis to facilitate the investment process
- to prevent degradation of valuable natural areas, eliminate hot spots to the benefit of the Baltic Sea.

Land administration

The legal framework for land reform was established by: the Law on Land Reform (1991, under revision), the Law on the Procedure and Conditions for the Restoration of the Rights of Ownership to the Existing Real Property (1991), the Law on the Leasing of Land (1993), the Law on Land (1994, under revision), and the Law on Real Estate Registry (1997).   The restitution of ownership rights (or compensation) is at the centre of Lithuania's land reform. Some of these laws were subsequently amended and supplemented to meet the concern for social justice, for economic considerations and to simplify land administration procedures. Land privatization and land reform require a huge amount of work. Some 2.5 to 3 million parcels have to be surveyed, privatized or leased.   The three major types of land being privatized are: (a) agricultural and forest land in

rural areas (more than 690 000 people have applied to have their ownership rights in agricultural land restored); (b) allotments of members of gardeners' associations (there are 218 500 such members, they cultivate a total area of 21 100 ha); and (c) parcels with housing units and other buildings, mainly in urban areas.

On agricultural land, parcels are marked on the ground by temporary boundary marks, which are recorded on land cadastre maps.   To mark allotments, more precise geodetic surveying is used, but there is a lack of State and private surveying organizations. This slows down land registration and there is a tendency to do without accurate geodetic surveying. The formalities for land claims take time as it is difficult to establish proper ownership titles, and settle the legal disputes and conflicts between the former owners and those who worked and lived on this land during the Soviet period. By 1 January 1997, 231 600 applications for privatization of State land and restoration of ownership rights (or compensation) had been processed. The acceleration of the pace of land privatization, the assessment of the existing damage to the environment and effective environmental monitoring depend on the developments in the cadastre and land registration systems.

The Government's land policy has the following objectives: (a) accomplish the restitution of land and implement land reform; (b) stimulate the development of a land market by developing a land registration system and a mortgage system; (c) levy a real property tax based on market values; (d) create a land information system which will serve both the State administration and the general public for the purposes of land use, physical planning and environmental monitoring; (e) revise the current institutional set-up of land administration.   The institutional reorganization started in 1997.   In rural areas measures have been taken to reduce the number of administrative staff in favour of project design organizations and private surveyors.   At the regional level, land-use departments are being established in all 10 counties to design land reform projects. At the central level, the former National Land Survey, established in 1995, was split into two separate organizations: the Government Office for Geodesy and Cartography and the Land Management Department in the Ministry of

Agriculture (responsible for land reform policy). The State Land Cadastre and Register falls under the Ministry of Agriculture (land resources) and the former Ministry of Construction and Urban Development (registration of real estate now at the Ministry of the Environment). The fiscal cadastre is organized in the Ministry of Justice. The creation of a comprehensive, integrated State information system is envisaged. It is currently in a relatively early stage of development. The whole process can be expected to be time-consuming, because different registers use different database structures and data models.

4.2   System of spatial planning

Legislation

Spatial planning is regulated by the following three major laws: the Law on Territorial Planning (1995), the Law on Construction (1996) and the Law on Environmental Impact Assessment (1996).

The Law on Territorial Planning regulates territorial planning and the relation between the individuals, the legal entities and the public authorities involved in this process. It sets the following objectives: (a) achieving a balanced development of Lithuania's territory; (b) creating a healthy and harmonious environment to ensure better living conditions throughout the country; (c) formulating a policy for the development of residential areas and their infrastructure; (d) using natural resources rationally, protecting the natural and cultural heritage, developing recreational opportunities; (e) maintaining ecological equilibrium or restoring it; (f) harmonizing the interests of natural and legal entities or their groups with those of the population, the municipalities and the State in regard to land use and type of economic activity in a given area; (g) promoting investments in social and economic development. The Law on Territorial Planning defines four levels of territorial planning: national, regional (the county), municipal and the legal and natural entity level; and three types of territorial planning (general, special and detailed).

General planning focuses on the territory of Lithuania, the territory of a county, the territory of a municipality or its parts. For each a comprehensive planning document (master plan) has to be prepared, indicating the intended land use, related priorities, management of economic activities, use and protection of natural and cultural assets, water and other natural resources, etc. The general planning documents (master plans) are prepared by the Government, the governor of the county, or the mayor and have to be approved respectively by the Seimas, by the Government, or by the council of the municipality. The approved master plan serves as the basis for the special and detailed territorial planning documents.

Special planning focuses on (a) the land stock of the country (including forests and water resources); (b) social, cultural and economic activities; (c) infrastructure network and its parts; and (d) protected territories; natural and cultural assets. Special planning documents could be prepared in the form of land surveys; forest maps; water projects; plans for national and regional parks; projects for development of tourism and recreation facilities, infrastructure, etc. Public authorities, county governors, mayors, legal and natural entities organize the special planning.

Detailed planning focuses on (a) land plots and forest areas; (b) urban areas; and (c) territories of rural settlements. Landowners, land users, State land managers and municipal councils organize the detailed planning. They must draw up detailed plans if they envisage at least one of the following actions: (a) construction, reconstruction or demolition; (b) development of land plots, changes in their area or boundaries; (c) use of mineral resources or changes in the use of water resources; (d) changes in land use; (e) forest use, except when owners have up to 3 hectares of forest land in territories which are not reservations.

Part 3 of the Law on Territorial Planning ("Transparency of territorial planning") provides for public participation in the decision-making process on territorial planning. All territorial planning documents must be submitted for public discussion. Public discussion on these documents is arranged by the agency that organizes the planning. All natural and legal persons and public organizations concerned with planning are entitled to submit their proposals and make on regarding the planning solutions, while the property owners, tenants, other interested natural and legal persons located in the territory under planning have the right to lodge complaints. During the public hearings, the planning organizer and the planner present the changes introduced pursuant to the comments and proposals, and explain why certain proposals were found unacceptable. Detailed procedures regarding public hearings on territorial planning project documentation are specified in Government Resolution 1079 of 18 September 1996.

As a follow-up to the Law on Territorial Planning, the Government in 1996 adopted two legal acts: one on application of this Law to territorial planning documents that were already approved or in preparation when the Law entered into force, and the other on the Statutes of the Register of Territorial Planning Documents and the Statutes of the Data Bank for Territorial Planning.

The Law on Construction lays down general provisions for building research and design, construction, demolition, repair, and permits for the construction and operation of buildings and other structures. The Law specifies the relationship between all actors of the construction process, their rights and obligations, as well as areas of State regulation and supervision. A construction project should be agreed with the Ministry of the Environment (if it is subject to EIA) and with the Department of Cultural Heritage (if construction activities are undertaken in protected areas). The Law has special provisions for public information regarding construction projects.

The Law on Environmental Impact Assessment (1996) prescribes an initial EIA (see Chapter 1). As territorial planning instrument, the initial EIA is intended to determine whether a planned activity is feasible on the selected site. The developer applies to the municipality for permission to locate his business on a particular site. Before the municipality agrees to the location, the Ministry of the Environment (Regional Departments) has to issue an opinion.

The RED provides information on concepts, programmes, recommendations, methodologies, legal conditions, scientific research and other aspects that relate to the site in question. On this basis, the developer undertakes the initial EIA. Its conclusions are included in it's the report on the conceivable outcome of the project for territorial

planning. The Health Ministry, the Fire Protection Department of the Ministry of Internal Affairs, and the regional administration issue opinions. The report is submitted to the RED, which verifies, within a month, that the correct procedure has been followed. It also reviews the proposed conclusions and opinions. A public hearing also has to be convened; it can make written proposals. Such proposals from the public are also considered by the RED, when it formulates its final opinion. The RED opinion is attached to the initial EIA conclusions. If the project is not controversial, it can be approved within 10 days.

In 1997, the Law on Real Estate Registry was adopted. It regulates the legal registration of land, buildings, structures and other real property. A registry is established to register real property, titles and other interests in real property and restrictions on the right of possession, enjoyment or disposal of real property.

Institutions

Core responsibility for spatial planning lies with the Territorial Planning Department of the Ministry of the Environment (former Territorial Planning Department of the Ministry of Construction and Urban Development). In the counties the organizers and coordinators are the heads of territorial planning departments, and in the municipalities the chief architect offices. The Ministry prepares draft laws, draft governmental resolutions and other legal acts on territorial planning. It also provides substantive input for the preparation of legal acts by other ministries and governmental institutions, regional and local authorities. The Ministry prepares and approves the norms, standards and regulations in territorial planning, it supervises territorial planning at the regional (county) level. Nationwide territorial planning is supervised by the State Territorial Planning and Construction Inspectorate. The Ministry is also responsible for organizing and managing the national territorial planning data bank, which is part of the State information system under development (see above) and uses a geographical information system (GIS) comprising graphical and textual data required for territorial planning.

The Ministry of the Environment has, in its central office, an Environmental Impact Assessment

Division. It ensures ecologically sound territorial planning practice and aims to preserve the country's landscape, protected areas and ecosystems. The Department of Land Management and Biodiversity of the Ministry of the Environment defines the conditions for the preparation of territorial planning documents and coordinates the preparation of the Ministry's conclusions on these documents. The Ministry of Transport and the Ministry of Agriculture are also involved in territorial planning.

National action plan and objectives

In 1995, the former Ministry of Construction and Urban Development began to draw up a new national comprehensive plan for the period up to the year 2010. The document will define the spatial development priorities, the conditions and instruments for territorial management, as well as the actions of all actors and specific sectors responsible for implementing the plan. The full set of national policy objectives in spatial planning is also expected to be defined in the upcoming draft. However, the major policy goals and orientation of the spatial development policy had already been worked out by the Government in its national action plan for 1996-2000, which was part of the national monograph submitted to the United Nations Conference on Human Settlements (Habitat II) in 1996.

In infrastructure development and regional border area development (over half the territory of Lithuania could be classified as border region), the main strategic goal is integration into the European transport network and promotion of spatial cohesion around the Baltic Sea. Already in 1994, the Government adopted a national transport development programme which foresees: (a) the modernization of the railway system, including the construction of new railways of European gauge; (b) the development of the Via Baltica motorway (road links between Tallinn and Warsaw via Latvia and Lithuania); (c) the reconstruction of the Klaipėda Sea harbour, and (d) the modernization of the Vilnius and Kaunas airports.

In the area of regional planning, the Government's goal is to minimize the growing regional disparities. Under the centrally-planned economy, balanced regional development was sought through political decisions on the location of various economic activities and the allocation of productive and financial resources. With the profound political, economic and social changes, many rural settlements and small towns started to lose importance and development prospects, particularly in the east of the country. The Government plans to assess, together with the municipalities, the development potential of rural areas and small towns and on this basis prepare action plans to balance and regulate their development. Within the framework of the agricultural programme for rural development and employment, adopted in 1995, measures are proposed to develop rural infrastructure and increase employment, develop agro-tourism and promote small and medium-size enterprises.

Lithuania has many old towns and well-preserved architectural and historic monuments. In urban development, much attention is given to the conservation and rehabilitation of the historical and cultural heritage. Until 1990, area-based rehabilitation of old town centres was carried out with State funding. The economic difficulties as well as the processes of restitution and privatization have changed the framework for urban renewal. At present, renewal is often limited to the façades and ground floors of buildings where trading and business activities take place. The goal of the Government is to prepare programmes to mobilize financial resources for renovation and modernization. In urban areas, the Government also intends to develop programmes and measures to preserve existing green areas, retain the residential functions, and restrict traffic in old town centres. Special efforts have successfully started in Vilnius, which was put on the UNESCO list of World Heritage Sites in 1995.

In housing, the Government's goal is to develop effective programmes and instruments to make long-term housing loans available to the majority of the population. At present long-term soft loans for housing construction and renovation are provided by the State via commercial banks (for 25 years with an interest rate of 5 per cent for new constructions and for 10 years with an interest rate of 10-13 per cent for modernization). Housing loans account for 2.7 per cent of the total State credit portfolio. State support is given only to households who have less than 10m^2 per person; some 100 000 households have applied for State funding.   The Government is preparing a programme for municipal housing construction for 1997-2000. The Government's goal is to build 12 000-14 000 municipal housing units in this period, and to promote the development of engineering and social infrastructure. The Government therefore intends to set aside more money in its budget for the municipalities.

To promote the environmentally sound development of urban and rural settlements, the Government intends to promote the installation of simple, low-capacity water treatment equipment for individual homes and small settlements that are not connected to the municipal waste-water network, especially in protected areas. The Government is already carrying out the "Būstas" ("Housing") programme, which focuses on energy conservation in the building sector. This programme is implemented in cooperation with the World Bank and the technical support from the Netherlands, Denmark and Finland. In 1996, the World Bank approved a US$ 10 million loan to Lithuania for a pilot project on energy efficiency in housing and schools. The project encourages homeowners to form associations that will enable them to assume greater responsibility for the management of their homes and to take energy conservation measures. At the local level, the Government's goal is to develop a new municipal sector model based on the polluter-pays principle, on competition, and on economic incentives and business interests in environmental protection. This model should help to improve control over green areas in cities and towns; improve domestic waste collection and recycling systems; and improve the design of dumping sites, installations and their operation.

4.3   Spatial planning in the transition period

Following the collapse of the centrally-planned system of economic and territorial development, the preparation and implementation of spatial planning was initially neglected in favour of the more pressing need to cope with severe economic and social problems, as the new market-economy mechanisms were not yet in place. However, Lithuania has a deep-rooted tradition of spatial planning.. The spatial planning expertise, not only for Lithuania but also for Latvia, Estonia, and the Kaliningrad region of the Russian Federation, was concentrated in three Lithuanian institutions. They were the former Urban Development Institute (with

headquarters in Vilnius and branches throughout Lithuania), the Architecture and Construction Institute (in Kaunas), and the Industrial Planning Development Institute (also in Kaunas). In recent years the Government has made great strides in preparing the legislative basis for territorial planning, land use and environmental protection. However, the full implementation of these laws has to wait for the completion of all regulations and methodologies. In addition, the adaptation of existing laws to EU directives and norms creates new tasks, but also offers a further opportunity for improving the consistency of the entire legal system at the same time.

Regional authorities (10 counties) are a new component in the country's administrative structure and they have to develop their practices in regional development and spatial planning, including the establishment of the required coordination mechanisms with local and national authorities. The need to combine territorial and technological dimensions with a "market-oriented" approach in regional spatial development policy has produced a number of positive examples of the new approach. For example, in 1995, Parliament passed a law adopting the fundamentals of free economic zones (FEZ) in Lithuania. There are plans for three such zones: near Klaipėda port, in Šiauliai and in Kaunas. For the zone customers the Klaipėda Development Group will provide: (a) a full package of facilities and services at low cost; (b) reliable power, water and waste/sewage treatment facilities; and (c) incentives and privileges available through the FEZ law. In terms of general planning guidelines, international standards will be applied to the planning and physical development of FEZs. Seventy per cent of the total land area will be developed into industrial plots, the remaining 30 per cent will be allocated for roads, administration, green areas, commercial, residential and other non-revenue-producing purposes. The Lithuanian Development Agency was established in accordance with the Government's Resolution of 24 November 1993. The former Ministry of European Affairs founded the Agency, which is a non-profit organization. The Agency collects and disseminates information on sites and the industrial potential of different areas, investment opportunities, financial incentives and conditions for setting up; it also provides investment services and advises foreign companies.

The Canada Baltic Municipal Cooperation Programme was set up by the Canadian Urban Institute in 1994. It focuses on territorial planning as a means of enhancing democracy and strengthening local government, on using local resources in a free market economy and attracting private investment. During its first phase, the programme in Vilnius directed much of its attention to the preparation of the City Official Plan for subsequent presentation and discussion with the public. A strategic assessment of Vilnius development was made: "Vilnius Vision - 2015". This study is a good foundation for further planning activities, in particular the preparation of a comprehensive plan for the city's development.

The study has shown that (a) the spatial structure of Vilnius's landscape, as set out in the 16th century, has remained virtually unchanged; (b) segments of valuable land with a variety of landscapes and biological diversity survived even though the city expanded in the past without proper planning, the suburbs had been poorly planned, etc. The most urgent goals for the year 2015 would be: (a) integrating Vilnius's communications system into the European transport network; (b) reconstructing the airport; (c) reducing transport needs by bringing working and residential areas closer together and, for instance, creating new multi-functional integrated city centres; (d) maintaining public transport as a priority; and (e) converting collective allotments into low-rise residential areas. The ecological assessment of the environmental conditions in Vilnius indicates the high level of degradation of the city's natural surroundings: the region is polluted, the natural landscape in many areas degraded. Urbanization has devastated many valuable elements of the city's natural environment. Some stretches of the river Neris are not fit for swimming. Almost all main streets are very noisy. The plan also suggests some remedies. For example, it was proposed to regulate, in accordance with environmental protection norms, private construction of residential buildings on eroding hills and on steep Neris valley slopes.

In early 1994, the Government approved the National Transport Development Programme up to the year 2010. It defines the main aspects of the development policy for the State transport infrastructure: (a) integrate the national transport system into the west European transport network and transport service market and, at the same time, maintain the already developed transport links with the Commonwealth of Independent States (CIS); (b) harmonize the legal basis for regulating transport activities with EU laws and regulations; (c) create an open transport service market and promote private investment in the sector; and (d) ensure the stability of the transport infrastructure, its reconstruction and development, through public investment. The Government Commission for European Integration at the Ministry of Foreign Affairs was established in 1995 to coordinate the harmonization with EU legislation. The Legal and European Integration Department was established in 1995 in the Ministry of Transport. It is responsible for bringing Lithuania's transport legislation in line with EU laws.

The Via Baltica (Warsaw-Kaunas-Šiauliai-Riga-Tallinn) will be based on the existing roads through gradual renovation, the construction of city bypasses, and the construction of bridges and additional lanes. At present traffic intensity is 2 000 to 9 000 vehicles a day. It is estimated that by the year 2000, traffic flows will increase to 4 000 to 18 000 vehicles a day and by 2010 to 9 500 to 42 000 vehicles a day. The total cost of the programme is estimated at US$ 178.4 million. To modernize the railway link in the same direction, investment requirements up to the year 2005 are estimated at US$ 353 million. The road network is also developing in another direction: Klaipėda-Kaunas-Vilnius-Minsk (Belarus), i.e. the main link between Klaipėda seaport and its hinterland. The plan is to renew the road surface of certain sections, improve traffic safety and construct a bypass around Vilnius. Average traffic intensity has already reached 3 500 to 12 900 vehicles a day and it is estimated that traffic flows will increase to 5 000 to 18 000 vehicles a day by the year 2000, and up to 11 500 to 40 000 by 2010. The estimated cost is US$ 45 million.

One of the major concerns of planners is cross-border cooperation on spatial planning and territorial development. Cross-border cooperation had started first with Latvia and Belarus, now similar studies on cross-border planning are being conducted with Poland. The major problem is a lack of long-term funding. Responsibilities for cross-border cooperation are delegated to national commissions. Four commissions are composed of different vice-ministers, experts from ministries, representatives from local authorities and other organizations. Local authorities in border regions may initiate their own activities without coordination or exchange of information with the ministries.. Cross-border studies and programmes should not only be technical, but should also take economic aspects, market conditions and benefits into consideration.

The basis of economic reforms in the housing sector was established in 1991, when the Government's programme on the housing sector was approved by the Supreme Council. The programme introduced the following principles: (a) gradual transition from State housing provision to housing purchase; (b) shift away from uniform housing to individual choice, with the State remaining responsible for providing housing only to the socially and economically vulnerable population groups; (c) create favourable conditions for the provision of long-term loans for housing construction; (d) promote housing construction by different types of developers: public, private, joint-stock companies and housing associations; (e) create legal and economic conditions for the privatization of the public housing stock. These principles were enforced by the adoption of legal and normative acts.

The Law on Housing Privatization was passed in 1991, and by 1995, 77 per cent of the existing housing stock was privatized. The Law on Conditions for the Restitution of Citizens' Rights to Real Property was passed in 1991. New legal acts and regulations on the operation, maintenance and renovation of privatized residential houses and flats were approved and the Law on Homeowners' Associations was passed in 1995. However, their application caused many problems. For example, as a result of privatization there is no municipal housing and some of the housing stock has been lost because it was converted for non-residential purposes (commercial, etc.). In multi-family houses, common ownership of gardens, staircases, etc. was not initially defined and now they are taken care of either by homeowners' associations or by special municipal services. Municipal services have become more expensive. The varying financial situation of homeowners hampers the activity of their newly-established association.

Housing restitution has created tension between sitting tenants and owners. In general, the housing situation has worsened for most people. One positive result is the dynamic private housing construction sector. Lithuania's housing stock is energy-inefficient by European standards, which results in increased costs for households. Most housing units are connected to district heating networks, but heating bills do not cover costs. To cope with this problem, new housing construction regulations have recently been adopted and the Housing Renovation/Energy Conservation Fund set up. The estimated cost of improving the thermal insulation of the housing stock amounts to US$ 5.5 billion. It could save about 45 per cent of the housing sector's energy consumption, or US$ 200 million a year.

Recent legislation on territorial planning includes legal provisions for public participation in the discussions on draft territorial planning documents with time frames for the submission of comments and replies. It seems that these laws contain all the necessary elements for public participation. However, this legislation is still very new and it is difficult to gauge how it would be put in practice. NGOs, the public and even some lawyers are in many instances not aware of the legal documents, instruments and possibilities. Government/local authorities are said to be sometimes reluctant to promote public participation, not always seriously considering proposals and comments made by NGOs or the general public. It appears that the public can get only limited assistance from lawyers, since few of them are familiar with existing laws on environmental protection and spatial planning. Some NGOs have tried to promote the Law on Protected Areas, the Law on Forestry and regulations on regional parks by organizing public protest. Under public pressure, it was decided, for example, to relocate an oil terminal on the Baltic Sea coast.

4.4   Conclusions and recommendations

Over the last three years, Lithuania has made much progress in transforming its spatial planning system, particularly in the area of legislation and by strengthening local government. Thanks to local government reform, the local administration has the right to deal with the majority of local community affairs without interference from the central Government. For instance, it is responsible for urban planning, the provision of public utilities (energy and water) to residents, public transport, the educational and cultural infrastructure, maintenance of the buildings and local roads, etc. However, since it is financially dependent on the national budget and has limited administrative power, future administrative reforms to strengthen spatial planning should focus on achieving more financial and administrative independence for the local administration. As it stands, decentralization has led to a wide gap between the emerging national planning framework and local planning.

Recommendation 4.1:
The development of a clearly stated national spatial planning policy could accelerate the transition process. The policy should be based on sustainable development under conditions of a market economy. The partnership between local authorities and the private sector should be made effective.

The regional administration is a new structure in Lithuania, which started the gradual decentralization of governmental power. There is a need to give a stronger political mandate to this level as the key level for spatial planning and development, and the coordination of activities of different municipalities based on the efficient use of the region's natural, human and economic resources. The regional level is the most appropriate level for achieving a critical mass for development and, in particular, for the revitalization of backward areas. To start economic restructuring, the regional authorities have to draw up development programmes based on socio-economic studies of the region. The city of Vilnius made the country's first and very successful attempt to respond to this need for municipal development with its "Vilnius Vision - 2015". The ability to undertake such a strategic analysis depends on the highly detailed knowledge of the socio-economic and environmental conditions of the region concerned: it can be done only if there is a good, reliable regional statistical database. The former Ministry of Construction and Urban Development established a comprehensive database for all counties. While, eventually, it will most certainly be part of the evolving State information system, data requirements are already keenly felt, even before the completion of the comprehensive system. The database therefore needs to be further developed and completed

urgently. The database should also be accessible on-line to other ministries, organizations or actors in physical planning.

Recommendation 4.2:
A recently developed common database on spatial planning issues should also receive relevant data input from the databases of other ministries, bodies and organizations. All those involved in territorial planning and development should be granted easy access to this database.

In view of the complexities of the transition process, spatial planning as it is understood in the market economies does not yet exist in Lithuania, but it is emerging. Reasons for slow progress are: the economic and social transition; the early stage of administrative decentralization; the insufficient knowledge of the impact of the market on spatial development patterns; the lack of specif development priorities; the evolving status and responsibilities of ministries and the difficulties of coordination between them. The pattern of spatial development in Lithuania will, to a great extent, depend on the balance that the Government will strike between overall economic growth and regional disparities. From the point of view of environmental protection, the needs for equilibrating the development of the different regions are relatively strong.

The ongoing land reform is a precondition for the renewed planning procedures, which cannot be put into practice unless there are modern land administration instruments in place: i.e. cadastre and land registration systems. Among the reasons for conflict between environment and development are the delay in registration of land ownership and the lack of a land market and a market price, which makes it difficult to price the environmental damage and apply the polluter-pays principle.

Recommendation 4.3:
Priority should be given to making the land market more effective by speeding up the development of land valuation institutions and skills, so that land and real property values can be determined.

The political and economic transition requires considerable modifications in the transport infrastructure in view of the great changes in volumes and directions of passenger and goods transport and the adaptation to international standards. Difficult choices will have to be made between improving the national transport infrastructure and that of international transit traffic. In many instances, improving the internal transport infrastructure appears more attractive than developing international transit links. The potential environmental damage of transit road traffic and the cost of accidents, as well as a number of potential social and economic drawbacks have to be weighed against the benefits of improved communication. The corresponding analysis is complex, and requires the careful preparation of a balanced approach, if consequences are to be anticipated, and bad surprises that could give rise to substantial future remediation cost avoided. The exclusive reliance on the established EIA procedures may not be enough.

Recommendation 4.4:
Environmental impact assessment procedures should be fully applied in the decision-making on transit motorways, putting environmental issues on a par with overall economic development considerations.

The general concept of housing combines the built, natural and social environment. The key element of this concept is the provision of adequate, equitable, environmentally sound and sustainable housing for everyone, which is certainly a crucial issue for the success of the transition process. Lithuania inherited from the Soviet period inefficient, energy-intensive housing and the condition of the housing stock during the transition

has worsened as the volume of new housing construction and repairs and modernization work have dwindled. Ninety per cent of the housing stock is now in private hands, but the majority of new owners cannot afford to maintain their homes. There are not enough long-term loans available for all those who are interested in new housing construction. The lack of adequate housing is paralleled by urban-rural disparities. Environmental improvements from the reduction in economic activity during the transition were partly offset by housing-related environmental degradation. Among the local problems are: waste disposal and recycling, sewage treatment, drinking-water quality, high energy use in dwellings, as well as social problems related to the degradation of living conditions. In its Human Development Report of 1996, the United Nations Development Programme (UNDP) states that "growing human distress is shown by rising illness, suicide, social disease, and falling life expectancy". Gender problems related to the growing share of unpaid housework, unemployment and reduced child-care facilities have also worsened.

Recommendation 4.5:
Local authorities should take greater responsibility for repairing and modernizing the housing stock. This should include the preparation of simple-to-apply and practical guidelines on energy efficiency measures in spatial planning and the existing housing stock. Some of the income from local development projects and the sale of real estate should be earmarked for the maintenance of the building stock.

Chapter 5

INTERNATIONAL COOPERATION

5.1   Principles for international cooperation

Since independence, Lithuania has established close links for environmental cooperation with its neighbours as well as with other countries around the Baltic Sea and elsewhere in Europe. Lithuania has become a member of the United Nations, the Council of Europe, the International Atomic Energy Agency (IAEA) and several other international organizations. The country wants to integrate fully into Europe's economic, political and security structures. Lithuania applied for EU membership on 8 December 1995. To prepare its membership, Lithuania signed an Association Agreement as well as a Free-Trade Agreement in 1995. The latter has been replaced by the Europe Agreement, which entered into force on 1 February 1998. At present, Lithuania's major objectives for international environmental cooperation are:

1. Implement the bilateral and multilateral agreements on environmental protection and develop cooperation in accordance with international principles of environmental protection and sustainable development in an effort to implement the National Environmental Strategy and Action Plan, to develop national environmental law, to improve environmental management technologies and to attract foreign assistance for the development and implementation of environmental programmes and projects.
2. Become a member State of the European Union, harmonize national environmental legislation and regulations with EU directives and requirements and implement them so that environmental quality in Lithuania meets EU standards as well as the recommendations of the Helsinki Commission.
3. Facilitate the implementation of sustainable development policies in Lithuania, ensuring the implementation of Agenda 21 at the national and local levels.
4. Implement the provisions of the United Nations Framework Convention on Climate Change (1992), the Convention on Biological Diversity (1992), the Vienna Convention for the

Protection of the Ozone Layer (1985) and its Montreal Protocol on Substances that Deplete the Ozone Layer (1987) including the Copenhagen and London amendments at the national level.

The commitments made by the former Soviet Union (for instance, under the 1979 Convention on Long-range Transboundary Air Pollution) were not automatically continued. Instead, one of the priorities of Lithuania's international cooperation was to accede to agreements that it considered important. Lithuania has already ratified several environmental conventions and intends to become a party to more. However, it has problems meeting the conventions' obligations because of its economic difficulties and financial constraints.

5.2   Regional cooperation in the framework of UN/ECE

UN/ECE conventions

Lithuania acceded to the 1979 Convention on Long-range Transboundary Air Pollution in 1993 but has not yet ratified any of its protocols. It is still developing its legislative base for the protection against air pollution. The 1981 Law on Clean Air is still in force. It will be reviewed and amended in 1999 to adapt it to today's political, social and economic conditions.

Lithuania has signed the 1992 Convention on the Protection and Use of Transboundary Watercourses and International Lakes. It has not yet ratified it, but the procedure for the relevant governmental institutions to adopt the necessary documents for ratification has been completed. In the meantime, the development and implementation of joint projects on monitoring and assessment of the quality and management of transboundary watercourses are based on the provisions of the Convention.

The Convention on Environmental Impact Assessment in a Transboundary Context (Espoo, 1991) has been submitted to Parliament for ratification. The new environmental impact assessment procedure - introduced with new legislation in 1996 - enables public participation in the decision-making process and provides access to information. Lithuania signed the <u>Convention on the Transboundary Effects on Industrial Accidents</u> (Helsinki, 1992) in 1992. It is considering whether or not it should ratify it.

"Environment for Europe" process

The "Environment for Europe" process started in 1991. It aimed at achieving convergence between the environmental conditions in western, central and eastern Europe and consolidating efforts to apply principles of sustainable development. Since the very beginning, Lithuania has been an active participant. As the drawing-up of national environmental action programmes in central and eastern Europe was given top priority at the Lucerne (Switzerland) Ministerial Conference (1993) and again emphasized at the Sofia Ministerial Conference (1995), the Government of Lithuania has paid special attention to environmental policy development.

Lithuania's first environmental protection programme was developed in 1992. It included all major environmental problems according to their priority. New economic realities, the restructuring of economic mechanisms and the urgency to address some environmental problems led to the formulation of the Environmental Strategy and Action Programme (see Chapter 1). The PHARE programme assisted its development (project budget US$ 356 250).

The Strategy identifies public participation in environmental matters and environmental education as a key objective. Accordingly, Lithuania's governmental and non-governmental organizations actively participated in the preparation and consideration of the Convention on Public Participation, which was adopted at the Aarhus Ministerial Conference in 1998.

At the Second European Conference on Environment and Health in Helsinki (20 - 22 June 1994), the Ministers of Health and of the Environment adopted the Declaration on Action for Environment and Health in Europe, and endorsed an Environmental Health Action Plan as a basis for concerted efforts by all European States and relevant international organizations to attain the long-term environment and health policy

objectives. As a participant in this process, Lithuania started drawing up its National Environmental Health Action Plan, in close cooperation with the World Health Organization's Regional Office for Europe (WHO/EURO). Lithuania and other Baltic countries are now in the process of developing and finaliing these policy documents in coordination with the sub-regional Nordic-Baltic group dealing with these matters. This plan is to be finalied in 1998 in the run-up to the Third European Conference on Health and Environment to be held in London in 1999.

5.3   Other regional cooperation

General Baltic cooperation

In 1995, the Governments of Lithuania, Estonia and Latvia signed the Trilateral Agreement on Cooperation in the Field of Environmental Protection. It covers the most important areas, like sustainable use of natural resources, protection of the sea, environmental impact assessment and monitoring, transboundary pollution reduction and control, radiation and nuclear safety. It stipulates that the coordination and supervision of the relevant activities are the responsibility of the Baltic Council of Ministers.

The Environmental Policy Committee of the Baltic Council of Ministers discusses and prepares all environmental issues giving rise to trilateral cooperation between Latvia, Estonia and Lithuania. It also proposes activities to the Baltic Environmental Forum. The Forum is a joint project between the EU and the three Baltic States. It implements the projects suggested by the Environmental Policy Committee, and has notably developed a set of common environmental indicators for the three countries.

In 1992, Nordic and Baltic countries set up an integrated monitoring system. In Lithuania there are three transboundary pollution measuring stations that meet the EMEP standards to monitor air quality (both long-range transboundary air pollution and precipitation). During 1995-96 the project on monitoring and standards supported by Denmark (US$ 271 500) was implemented. Subsequently, the capability of the Ministry of the Environment was strengthened by a mobile air laboratory for the periodic monitoring of toxic gas emissions, combustion gases and nuclear radiation. In the framework of the project, testing and training were provided as well.

Baltic Sea protection

Lithuania has the shortest coastline of all the Baltic States: only 99 km. At the same time, the country's entire territory is within the Baltic Sea catchment area and all its pollution discharges from point or diffuse sources go to the Baltic Sea. Lithuania has participated in the Baltic Sea environmental cooperation since the end of the 1980s, when its political situation changed. A Lithuanian delegation took part in the meeting in Ronneby, Sweden (1990), where Heads of Government adopted the Baltic Sea Declaration. According to the terms of the Declaration and after two years' work, the Baltic Sea Joint Comprehensive Environmental Action Programme (JCP) was agreed upon at the Diplomatic Conference in Helsinki (1992), together with the revised Convention. JCP aims to improve the Baltic Sea ecosystem in order to support the implementation of the Convention on the Protection of the Marine Environment of the Baltic Sea Area (Helsinki Convention, 1992).

Lithuania signed the Helsinki Convention in 1992 and ratified it in 1997. The measures being taken to comply with its provisions aim at promoting the use of safer tankers and reception facilities, preventing air pollution and combating spillage from ships and generally ensuring maritime safety.

Furthermore, Lithuania has to take concrete actions to reduce marine pollution from land-based point and diffuse sources and from ships and implement a wide range of recommendations developed by the Helsinki Commission (HELCOM). The main components of the JCP are policy, laws and regulations; institutional strengthening and human resource development; investments; management of coastal lagoons and wetlands; applied research; and public awareness and environmental education. Lithuania is an active participant in the Programme Implementation Task Force, which was established in 1992 within HELCOM to initiate, facilitate and monitor the coordination of JPC implementation and periodically update it. The total cost of the Programme was estimated at ECU 1.8 billion over 20 years.

In Lithuania, the Programme is being implemented through a number of ongoing projects, above all in the water management sector. Finance is being sought from governmental and local authorities, international financial institutions and donor organizations and countries. The projects relate mostly to the improvement of the water supply and municipal and industrial waste-water treatment systems, for instance the projects to reconstruct and improve the waste-water treatment plants in Vilnius, Klaipėda, Šiauliai, Palanga, Kaunas and other cities.

To meet the obligations of international conventions and governmental decrees, a search and rescue system and a system to combat oil spills at Klaipėda port and at sea have been set up. The system involves local administrations, the rescue coordination centre, the hydro-meteorology service, the health care and nature protection services, the navy, the police, military and civil aviation, the Emergency Commission of the Government and other bodies. Lithuania participates in warning systems developed to comply with the Helsinki Commission's recommendations on the prevention of air and marine environment pollution from transport and reception facilities.

In 1992, Lithuania acceded to the Gdansk Convention on Fishing and Conservation of the Living Resources in the Baltic Sea and Belts (1973) and to the Ottawa Convention on Future Multilateral Cooperation in the North-West Atlantic Fisheries (1978). In 1996, it concluded the Agreement on Fisheries Relations with the European Community. An agreement with the Government of Denmark and the Home Government of the Faeroe Islands on the mutual fishery relations between Lithuania and the Faeroe Islands was signed in 1993 and ratified in 1997. The agreement foresees the drawing-up of a regulation to guide fishing in the Faeroe region. Negotiations are under way with the Russian Federation and Belarus on cooperation in fishing and fish-stock regulations in the Baltic Sea and transboundary watercourses and lakes.

Contamination of former military sites

Financial support from the PHARE programme and the experience of western experts were used to draw up the "Inventory of Damage and Cost Estimate of the Remediation of former Military Sites in Lithuania" (1993-1995, ECU 490 000). The survey aimed to analyse pollution patterns and environmental damage recorded at former Soviet military bases in Lithuania (totalling 421). The results of the investigation (published in 25 volumes) were considered very useful for planning and carrying out remedial activities. Since 1993, experts from Lithuania (from the Ministries of Transport, Defence, Internal Affairs, the Environment, and Health) have participated in nine pilot studies and many conferences organized by the North Atlantic Treaty Organization's Committee on Challenges of Modern Society (CCMS) and benefited from training courses on environmental issues. United States military experts promoted and accelerated the development of the Ecological Commission in the Lithuanian Defence Ministry, and the concept of environmental protection within the domain of national defence. The concept was approved by the Ministries of Defence and of Environmental Protection in 1994.

5.4   Bilateral cooperation

Countries of the Baltic Sea basin

The inter-State relations in the Baltic region are very special. Lithuania has established very close links and environmental cooperation with the northern Baltic countries. Technical assistance and financial support from these countries has led to a gradual improvement in their common environment.

Lithuania is developing bilateral cooperation on environmental protection, the sustainable use resources and nuclear safety with its neighbours and other States, mostly in the framework of joint projects and bilateral agreements. There are a number of framework agreements on environmental cooperation with these countries and, in addition, some agreements on sectoral cooperation have been concluded.

The river Lielupė is the second largest river discharging into the Gulf of Riga. Its basin covers a land area of more than 17 500 km^2, which is divided almost equally between Latvia and Lithuania. The discharge from the Lielupė basin constitutes 12 per cent of the total discharge, and 20 per cent of the nitrates carried to the Gulf of Riga. It causes many health problems: most sections of the river are unsuitable for recreational use and swimming has been banned at several beaches on the Latvian coast at Jurmala for several years.

In 1991, the River Lielupė Project was started by the Ministries of the Environment of Lithuania and Latvia. It aimed at (i) demonstrating the feasibility of cooperative river basin management in the Baltic Sea region; (ii) establishing a joint water quality database, and (iii) developing pollution abatement actions plans. In May 1993, the two Ministries signed the Agreement on Environmental Management of the Lielupė River Basin and

established the joint Lielupė River Basin Commission. The Governments of Latvia and Lithuania have expressed their intention to the World Bank to expand the scope of cooperation to include the implementation of priority action. The Project also foresees the establishment of a water quality monitoring and management system.

The Government of Sweden has helped finance the Project as a contribution to the Baltic Sea Environment Programme. The Project was finalized in 1997. Its main output was the water quality report and a GIS-based water quality monitoring and management system.

In 1996, the Environment Ministries of Estonia and Lithuania signed the Agreement on the Control of Transportation of Hazardous Wastes.

According to the Cooperation Protocol between the Environment Ministries of Finland and Lithuania (signed on 7 February 1992), Finland allocated US$ 1.5 million to the Kaunas Water and Environment Project and US$ 1.7 million to the Šiauliai waste-water treatment plant in 1996. A detailed work plan is discussed every year, and a number of projects have already been completed with Finnish assistance (pollution control and monitoring, water management, port facilities, etc.)

Since the early 1990s, cooperation with Sweden on environmental protection (Bilateral Intergovernmental Agreement on Cooperation of 1992) has aimed at technical assistance and investment projects. Attention was primarily given to pollution reduction, chemical substances and waste management control, water protection and management. According to agreements signed in 1992-1996, Sweden allocated US$ 5 million to the construction of the Klaipėda waste-water treatment plant, US$ 4.1 million to the Kaunas waste-water treatment plant, and US$ 4.65 million to the Šiauliai waste-water treatment plant. Other important projects supported by Sweden have aimed at improving the systems of environmental protection and management and nuclear safety regulation. A Memorandum between the Swedish Chemical Substances Inspectorate and the Ministry of the Environment of Lithuania was signed in 1995 according to which Sweden provides assistance to draft legislation on hazardous substance management and to regulate it.

A Cooperative Agreement with the Environment and Energy Ministry of Denmark was signed in 1991. Denmark is one of Lithuania's largest donors and its assistance represents more than 40 per cent of all donor financing for environmental programmes in Lithuania. Projects financed by Denmark (mostly in the form of grants) are related to pollution prevention and waste minimization, improvement of monitoring systems, regulation of nuclear and radiation safety, water and waste-water management. The Danish Fund for Environmental Activities in Eastern Europe supported the preparation of the National Oil Spills Contingency Plan in 1995-98. The implementation stage (delivery of oil combating equipment) of the National Plan is based on a trilateral agreement between Denmark, Finland and Lithuania.

Norway allocated US$ 1.5 million to the construction of the Šiauliai waste-water treatment plant and has helped to finance projects for the development of an efficient water quality monitoring system for the Neris River.

Assistance in the framework of the Cooperation Agreement with Germany (1993) is mainly targeted at institutional strengthening and policy development (implementation of NEAPs and environmental strategy), training and education (establishment and supporting ECAT-Lithuania) and improving INPP safety.

Lithuania signed an Inter-ministerial Agreement on Cooperation in the Field of Environmental Protection with Belarus. The Agreement sets out a wide range of cooperation areas, mainly transboundary issues. Moreover, Lithuania signed two intergovernmental agreements with Belarus: on cooperation on the use of nuclear energy and radiation safety, and on early notification of nuclear and radiation accidents and the exchange of information on nuclear facilities. Lithuania has concluded similar agreements with Poland and the Russian Federation.

On 24 January 1992, Lithuania signed a cooperative agreement with Poland (Ministry of Environmental Protection, Natural Resources and Forestry). There is cooperation on the protection of transboundary waters, control of air pollution, environmental impact assessment, protected areas and other issues. A detailed work plan is developed every two years.

A draft agreement in the field of environmental protection was prepared between Lithuania and the Russian Federation. The text is in inter-ministerial consultation in both countries, and is expected to be signed in a few months. It foresees the establishment of a joint commission and of several working groups. Cooperation will mainly cover:

- Environmental legislation
- Environmental-economic problems
- Regulations of the use of natural resources, including water and mineral resources
- Environmental monitoring and State ecological control
- Protection of environmental media from pollution
- Waste management
- Protection and management of nature
- Methodological aspects of environmental impact assessments

A general agreement is in force with the Kaliningrad region of the Russian Federation. A working group with three sub-groups on (1) water pollution, (2) environmental monitoring and joint actions during accidents, and (3) protected area management, were established at the end of 1997. Lithuania and Russia have agreed to prepare the necessary documentation for the inclusion of the Curonian Spit in the World Heritage List together.

Other countries

Active cooperation with the United States of America started in 1992, when they began assisting Lithuania's transition, mainly through activities coordinated by USAID. In 1992, the Bilateral Memorandum between Lithuania's Ministry of the Environment and the United States Environmental Protection Agency Region V on Cooperation in the Field of Environmental Protection was concluded and signed. By the end of 1997, United States assistance had exceeded US$ 45 million in technical assistance, training, equipment and investments. More than 50 projects have now been undertaken in 10 strategic areas, environment being one of the most important. The most essential projects funded by USAID are devoted to environmental policy development, improving environmental management, and strengthening the nuclear safety regulation capacity. As the main goals of the United States technical assistance have been reached, USAID is scheduled to terminate its activity in Lithuania in the near future. Joint projects will continue to be implemented in partnership with the United States Environmental Protection Agency, the Department of Energy, the Nuclear Regulation Commission and other bodies.

A number of key issues of environmental cooperation were identified in the Bilateral Memorandum between Lithuania's Ministry of the Environment and Austria's Federal Ministry for the Environment (1994).

The Agreement on Environmental Cooperation between Ukraine's Ministry for Environmental Protection and Nuclear Safety and Lithuania's Ministry of the Environment was drawn up in 1996, but it has still not been signed because of a lack of financial resources for the drawing-up and implementation of joint programmes.

Cooperation within the framework of the Agreement between the Environment Ministries of Lithuania and Slovakia (signed on 26 June 1996) is carried out in the form of expert meetings to share information and experience.

5.5   Global cooperation

Implementation of Agenda 21

Lithuania is committed to Agenda 21. It drew up its strategy for an information system on environmental protection on the basis of Agenda 21 (Chapter 40).   The leading institution is the Ministry of the Environment, obliged by national law to document the main policy trends in environmental protection, safety and natural resource use and to coordinate the generation, analysis and dissemination of environmental information.

After Parliament approved the National Environmental Strategy in 1996, a proposal was made to create the Lithuanian National Council for Sustainable Development. It consists of senior governmental officials from key ministries, other governmental bodies, scientific organizations and NGOs, and aims to integrate environmental activity and development at the country level.

In September 1996, the Ministry of the Environment issued reports on the implementation of Agenda 21 in Lithuania. They led to the report on environment and sustainable development in the Republic of Lithuania" at the end of the year. Lithuania has also participated in activities for the implementation of Agenda 21 at the regional level. In October 1997, the Ministers of the Environment of the Baltic Sea region decided at their informal meeting in Saltsjobaden to develop an Agenda 21 for the Baltic Sea region (called Baltic Agenda 21). One of the contributions to the development of

Agenda 21 is the updating and strengthening of the JCP.

Seven economic sectors were identified as being crucial for sustainable development in the region: agriculture, energy, fisheries, forestry, industry, tourism, and transport.   Lithuania has a high proportion of forested land, intensive wood production and a wealth of experience in forest management. Therefore, Lithuania became the lead country (together with Finland) in the integration of forest policy into general economic transition programmes and sustainable development.

Climate change

Lithuania signed the United Nations Framework Convention on Climate Change (FCCC) in 1992 and ratified it in 1995. The National Committee for the Implementation of the FCCC and a country team to prepare a national implementation strategy for the Convention were established in 1994. An inventory of greenhouse gases and their adsorbents was completed in 1995. The National Strategy for the Implementation (NSI) of the Convention was developed and adopted by the Government in 1996... It identifies various strategies and actions, but does not include an analysis of Lithuania's emission reduction potential. Also missing are cost estimates of the possible implementation of the various options.   Finally, a comprehensive mitigation analysis using standard methods is also missing, so there may be further options in addition to those identified.

The Ministry has started to develop the first Lithuanian national communication, which was due in December 1995.   It is based on information compiled during the preparation of NSI. However, lack of technical capacity in mitigation analysis is hampering the work.   It might have to wait for progress in the mitigation study that started in spring 1998, with GEF support requested. Lithuania's initial communication obligations in the area of vulnerability and adaptation were fulfilled with the information obtained in NSI preparation. A full vulnerability assessment using IPCC methods has not yet been undertaken.

The NSI was worked out with international technical assistance. Since 1993, there has been a special training programme for the implementation of the Convention (CC-TRAIN) under the auspices of GEF, UNDP, the international programme for the Climate Convention and other organizations. CC-TRAIN, a joint programme of the United

Nations Institute for Training and Research and the FCCC secretariat, aims to assist both developing countries and countries with economies in transition to promote the establishment of national institutions on climate change. In 1993 the programme started in three representative States of Africa (Zimbabwe), south-eastern Asia (Vietnam) and the Baltic region of Europe (Lithuania).

Since 1993, Lithuania has participated in the Swedish Programme for an Environmentally Adapted Energy System in the Baltic Region and Eastern Europe aimed at improving energy efficiency, the use of renewable energy resources, and reducing emissions hazardous to the climate and the environment. The Programme is formulated in line with FCCC and its provisions on joint implementation. Lithuania benefited from this programme, having eight projects with total investments worth more than US$ 4 million on favourable terms. All projects aim to cut CO_2 emissions by converting heating plants to the use of bio-fuels, reducing heat losses in district heating systems and other measures. Moreover, a number of projects have been carried out on energy saving and renewable energy, e.g. Klaipėda Geothermal Demonstration Project and bio-gas demonstration plants in Rokai (supported by Denmark and other donors).

Protection of the ozone layer

Lithuania has been a Party to the Vienna Convention for the Protection of the Ozone Layer (1985) since 1994, and has ratified the Montreal Protocol on Substances that Deplete the Ozone Layer (1987) as well as the Copenhagen (1992) and London (1990) Amendments to the Protocol. While Lithuania is at present not complying with the requirements of the Montreal Protocol, it is making efforts to do so. Following the provisions of the Convention, the Country Programme on the Phase-out of Ozone-Depleting Substances was developed and adopted in 1997. During the Ministerial Conference "Environment for Europe" (Sofia, 1995), the Ministers of Environment of the Baltic States signed a joint declaration on the implementation of the Montreal Protocol's requirements in the Baltic States.

The strategic action plan of the Lithuanian Government aims at phasing out CFCs and halons by the year 2000. The essential part of the action plan deals with support to Lithuania's industry for the purpose of adopting ODS-free technologies. This is done with GEF assistance, and a project

package was signed in May 1998. GEF will provide US$ 4.5 million to compensate enterprises for incremental costs of technology conversion, another part being covered by the enterprises themselves. The project targets priority ODS phase-out activities in the refrigeration and aerosol sectors. It also provides technical assistance at institutional and enterprise levels to facilitate the implementation of the Country Programme (prepared in 1996-1997, with the assistance of UNEP consultants, and based on a preliminary country programme to which both Finland and UNEP contributed) and demonstration projects for customs officials in monitoring and control of ODS, and elimination of methyl bromide.

Nature protection

In 1996 Lithuania ratified the 1979 Bern Convention on the Conservation of European Wildlife and Natural Habitats, with some reservations related to the fauna species which its Appendix II considers as strictly protected. It entered into force on 1 January 1997.

Lithuania signed the 1992 Convention on Biological Diversity in 1992 and ratified it in 1995. The Convention sets out the provisions for the conservation of the world's biological diversity. Following the provisions of the Convention and with GEF finance, Pilot National Action Plans were developed for the conservation of biological diversity in Estonia, Latvia and Lithuania. Lithuania has recently approved its National Strategy and Action Plan for Biological Diversity Conservation. The document outlines the most important issues: the current status and trends of its biodiversity, strategy elements (concept, principles, and goals), general and specific components of the action plan, and mechanisms to implement it.

In 1993 Lithuania ratified the 1971 Ramsar Convention on Wetlands of International Importance Especially as Waterfowl Habitat, as well as its Paris (1982) and Regina (1987) Amendments. Five Lithuanian wetlands have been designated for the list of Ramsar sites: Čepkeliai, Kamanos, Viešvilė, Žuvintas, Nemunas Delta (total area about 50 450 ha).

Lithuania has not yet ratified the 1973 Washington Convention on International Trade in Endangered Species of Wild Fauna and Flora, which it does not consider to be a priority. However, it is considering ratifying the 1979 Bonn Convention on the Conservation of Migratory Species of Wild Animals.

The Ministry of the Environment (and its predecessor) has been a member of the World Conservation Union (IUCN) since 1993. IUCN initiated the preparation of the environmental status report of the three Baltic countries in 1993. The Ministry is involved in the work of the IUCN European Region and the work of commissions or groups on protected areas and species conservation.

Nuclear and radiation safety

The 1996 Law on Nuclear Energy incorporates relevant provisions of the international conventions ratified by Lithuania. In 1991 the Supreme Council of the Republic of Lithuania ratified the Treaty on the Non-proliferation of Nuclear Weapons. In 1992,Lithuania ratified the Vienna Convention on Civil Liability for Nuclear Damage . In 1993, Lithuania deposited its instruments of accession to its Protocol on Enforcement of Application of the Vienna Convention on Civil Liability for Nuclear Damage (1963), and the Common Protocol Relating to the Application of the Vienna Convention and the Paris Convention (1988). The Convention on the Physical Protection of Nuclear Material (acceded to in 1993), the Convention on Early Notification of a Nuclear Accident (acceded to in 1994) and the 1994 International Convention on Nuclear Safety (ratified in 1995) have also entered into force for Lithuania during the past few years. In 1997, Lithuania signed the Joint Convention on the Safety of Spent Fuel Management and on the Safety of Radioactive Waste Management, among other agreements. It intends to become a party to other important conventions in this field, such as the Convention on Supplementary Compensation for Nuclear Damage (signed on 29 September 1997) and the Convention on Assistance in the Case of a Nuclear Accident or Radiological Emergency (1986).

Moreover, Lithuania has signed several intergovernmental and inter-sectoral agreements on cooperation on different issues of nuclear and radiation safety (such as peaceful use of nuclear energy, nuclear safety, radiation protection, early notification of nuclear and radiation accidents, exchange of information on nuclear facilities) during the past few years with foreign parties (e.g. Commissariat for Nuclear Energy of France, Gosatomnadzor of the Russian Federation, United States Nuclear Regulation Commission, as well as the Governments of Belarus, Canada, Denmark,

Norway, Poland, Ukraine and others). The Baltic Sea States Arrangements on Regular Exchange of Radiation Monitoring Data and other Information of Radiological Significance (Denmark, Estonia, Finland, Germany, Iceland, Latvia, Lithuania, Norway, Poland, Russian Federation, Sweden, and EU) were worked out in 1997.

As a member of IAEA (full membership since 18 November 1993), Lithuania participates in several IAEA programmes covering a broad range of safety-related topics. Quite a large number of multilateral and bilateral projects, mostly concerning the safety of the INPP (INPP Safety Enhancement Programme alone counts 18 projects), and financed by Sweden, Germany, United States of America, France, Japan, United Kingdom, Italy, Belgium, Canada, Finland, Switzerland, Denmark, the PHARE programme and international finance institutions (mainly EBRD), are now being carried out.

Transboundary movement of hazardous waste

Lithuania has not yet ratified the 1989 Basel Convention on the Control of Transboundary Movements of Hazardous Wastes and their Disposal. However, the Government has already approved it, and now Parliament is considering its ratification.

Marine pollution

Lithuania has been a full member of the International Maritime Organization since 1995 and has participated in its programmes since 1991. Nevertheless, Lithuania has not ratified the International Convention for the Prevention of Pollution from Ships (MARPOL, London, 1973/1978), nor has it ratified the Convention on Civil Liability for Oil Pollution Damage (Brussels, 1969).

5.6   International funding

Donors and purposes

Since independence in 1991, Lithuania's environmental sector has received substantial foreign assistance, mostly in the form of grants and soft loans. For many reasons, it is difficult to assess the exact amount. General figures and trends in 1991-1996 suggest that the environmental sector received more than US$ 120 million, in the form of grants (US$ 58 million) and loans (US$ 62 million) for both investments (US$ 96.5 million) and technical assistance (US$ 23.5 million). Various bilateral donors and international financial institutions have backed Lithuania's environmental sector. Most support has come from the Nordic countries: Denmark 41.46 per cent; Sweden 11.21 per cent; Finland 3.97 per cent; and Norway 1.45 per cent of the grand total for 1991-1996. In the same period, support from EU PHARE programme stood at 15.92 per cent, from EBRD at 12.33 per cent, from the World Bank at 11 per cent, from NEFCO at 2.5 per cent and the United States provided 0.16 per cent of total assistance (approximately).

The yearly amount of resources for investments and technical assistance to the environmental sector increased gradually from 1991 till 1995 (see Table 5.1), but decreased in 1996. Western assistance is becoming more effective and focused. The technical assistance was directed especially to institutional strengthening (26.1 per cent), waste-water treatment (27.1 per cent), nature protection projects (10.7 per cent), waste management (9.7 per cent), and pollution prevention and waste minimization (11.1 per cent), clean-up (5 per cent), protection against radiation (5.5 per cent), and monitoring and standards (4.6 per cent). The investments focused on the waste-water sector, which took 96 per cent of total environmental investments.

PHARE assistance

Since 1991 PHARE assistance to Lithuania has focused on several sectors. In environment, two are defined as priorities: water/waste water, and institutional strengthening and policy development. In the framework of PHARE assistance, the Project Management Unit has been established within the Ministry of the Environment. The Unit's main objective is to coordinate projects carried out with foreign assistance and to manage projects. The Unit benefited from a PHARE project which

provided US$ 360 000 for long-term planning and institutional support for the Ministry (project began at the end of 1994). Since the end of the project, the size of the Unit has been reduced to two staff. It provides general assistance to the Ministry in investment planning and project preparation, including supervision of bilateral and multilateral donor projects.

PHARE is also giving technical assistance (worth US$ 625 000) for the approximation of Lithuania's environmental legislation. With PHARE support, Lithuania has drawn up its Environmental Strategy and Action Programme. In the framework of a PHARE-supported project, the Comprehensive Strategy for Transport and Environment (Lithuania) has been completed (1997) to harmonize Lithuania's laws and regulations with those of EC.

World Bank and EBRD

The World Bank has supported two projects devoted to the preparation of the National Biodiversity Strategy and Action Plan and the National Report on Biodiversity Conservation in Lithuania (1991-1996).

EBRD and GEF granted US$ 18 million for the development and implementation of the Klaipėda Geothermal Demonstration Project aimed at optimizing the use of the geothermal resources in Klaipėda. The Project's technical assistance and training component is complemented by an investment component for the Klaipėda geothermal demonstration plant. As a result, the plant will reduce its annual CO_2 emissions by an estimated 56 000 tonnes and significantly reduce its SO_2, NO_x and SPM emissions.

The most significant support from the World Bank and EBRD is directed at projects to improve municipal waste-water treatment facilities in Lithuania's biggest cities. The World Bank, EBRD and other donors (EU PHARE, Denmark, Sweden,

Table 5.1: Yearly donor activity in the environmental sector, 1991-1996

1 000 US$

	1991	1992	1993	1994	1995	1996	1991-1996 period
Total	280	2 454	6 215	25 353	53 983	31 729	120 013
Investments	0	0	3 063	21 049	41 150	31 197	96 458
Technical assistance	280	2 454	3 152	4 304	12 833	532	23 555

Source: Donor and IFI Activities, Ministry of the Environment, 1997.

Finland, and Norway) have provided grants and investments for waste-water treatment plants in Vilnius, Kaunas, Klaipėda, Šiauliai and other municipalities.

One such project, the Klaipėda Environment Project, consists of two components: (i) water and waste-water improvement; and (ii) environmental management. Its main objectives are: (i) to reduce the discharge of waste water into the Baltic Sea; (ii) to restore and improve the water quality in Klaipėda and nearby beaches; (iii) to improve the water supply and sanitation in Klaipėda; (iv) to improve the operational efficiency and management systems of the Klaipėda State water and waste-water enterprise; and (v) to promote the environmentally sustainable management and development of the Kuršių Lagoon and nearby coastal areas. The project was evaluated in July 1994 and at the end of 1995 a loan agreement worth US$ 7 million was signed between the World Bank and the Lithuanian Government. Additional funds come from domestic sources and other donors (Sweden, Finland, and PHARE - in the form of grants).

5.7   Conclusions and recommendations

It can be concluded from this general picture that Lithuania has succeeded in developing international environmental cooperation in many directions with countries, international organizations and financial institutions. It has an overall concept for international cooperation and applies it. The main aims of such cooperation are the protection of joint ecosystems and the integration of national policies into common action for environmental improvement. To this end, Lithuania has established a reliable network of bilateral and multilateral partnerships by concluding framework and sectoral cooperation agreements.

Lithuania has signed and ratified a number of international conventions according to its priorities in marine environment protection, improvement of nuclear safety, conservation of landscape and biological diversity, water protection and transboundary issues. To meet the requirements of these international acts, Lithuania has adapted or introduced specific provisions in its legislation and drawn up general (Environmental Strategy and Action Plan) and specific (National Implementation Strategy for the United Nations Framework Convention on Climate Change, Biodiversity

Conservation Strategy and Action Plan, etc.) policy documents and programmes.

The responsibility for implementing the environmental conventions is mostly concentrated within the Ministry of the Environment. However, international conventions and treaties often require intersectoral cooperation. Thus, their implementation requires closer links and better coordination between the Ministry of the Environment and other relevant ministries, governmental institutions and non-governmental organizations. Some actions require consolidated efforts and goodwill to achieve results. In this respect it seems advisable to accelerate the drawing-up of the national environmental health action plan by combining the efforts of the Environment and Health Ministries.

Recommendation 5.1:
Routines for cooperation should be established between all institutions involved in the management of international projects that are intersectoral.

The Government and Parliament are still considering a number of very important international conventions. Parliament is in the process of ratifying some of them, and Lithuania can, in the near future, be expected to become a party to the Basel Convention on the Control of Transboundary Movements of Hazardous Wastes and their Disposal, the Convention on Environmental Impact Assessment in a Transboundary Context, the Joint Convention on the Safety of Spent Fuel Management and on the Safety of Radioactive Waste Management. At the same time, it seems also important that it should ratify the Convention on the Protection and Use of Transboundary Watercourses and International Lakes, the protocols to the Convention on Long-range Transboundary Air Pollution, and the Convention on the Transboundary Effects of Industrial Accidents - all of which regulate transboundary issues. The Convention on the Conservation of Migratory Species of Wild Animals, as a global convention on biodiversity, plays a very important role in the protection of migrating wild animals. Its ratification should be seen as a priority in the implementation of the national biodiversity conservation strategy.

Recommendation 5.2:
Lithuania should ratify all UN/ECE conventions and related protocols on transboundary issues. It

should also reassess its priorities concerning the ratification of the Bonn and Washington Conventions.

Lithuania's priority to become a member of the EU is clear and translated into action (Chapter 1). PHARE provides technical assistance and supports projects. It seems difficult to move toward EU legislation and requirements without European expertise. The institutional capacities for that should be strengthened.

Recommendation 5.3
Concrete plans for EU/PHARE projects, including twinning projects, should be worked out as a matter of priority, in order to prepare smoothly for the upcoming EU accession negotiations, and implement EU directives in the most expedient way.

PART II: MANAGEMENT OF POLLUTION AND OF NATURAL RESOURCES

Chapter 6

AIR MANAGEMENT

6.1 Air emissions and quality

Air emissions

Since 1991, the estimated air emissions of the main pollutants from stationary and mobile sources in Lithuania have decreased on average by a factor of 2. However, the situation differs depending on the pollutant, the sector and the city. The emissions of classic pollutants such as sulphur oxides, nitrogen oxides and carbon monoxide have fallen more than half during the period 1991-1996, while those of volatile organic compounds (VOCs) and methane have decreased by one third only (see Tables 6.1 and 6.2).

In the last few years, SO_2 emissions from the plants of Lithuania's State Power System have fallen by nearly 70 per cent compared to 1980. NO_x emissions are well below their 1987 level. CO_2 emissions were considerably lower in 1995 than in 1990 (24 and 42 e.g. million tonnes, respectively). CH_4 emissions fell from 412 000 tonnes in 1990 to 285 000 in 1996. The decrease in emissions was caused first of all by the industrial collapse, though new regulations and norms are also beginning to have an effect. However, emissions from traffic in urban areas, energy production and the chemical industry continue to be a problem. In 1993, the main sources of atmospheric pollutants were: transport (58 per cent), energy (11 per cent) and industry (31 per cent). According to the Ministry of the Environment's estimates (1997), around 70 per cent of all current air pollution stems from transport. Changes will come about only if new policy objectives and environmental quality targets are set and attained.

While the emissions from the energy sector and industry have decreased along with economic activity, those generated by the transport sector have been on the increase since 1994 at least. The present emissions of NO_x and VOCs, from all transport modes and fuels combined, are respectively 15 per cent and 100 per cent higher than in 1993 (see also Table 6.1), although the share of mobile sources in the national total classic emissions has risen only slightly, from about 60 per cent to 65 per cent, since 1991.

The emissions of heavy metals are not important in the country as a whole, but the emission of lead, mostly from leaded petrol, was relatively high (~10 tonnes) in 1995. The emission of nickel was in the same order, while that of zinc accounts for less than half of that amount. A survey conducted in 1996 showed a decrease in the consumption of ozone-depleting substances (ODS) to 648.3 tonnes compared to 859.5 tonnes in 1994. However, they have not yet been phased out, as required by the Montreal Protocol. Only 80 per cent of the target had been reached by 1996.

As far as the emissions from the main districts and cities are concerned, the most spectacular decrease has occurred in Akmenė's district, while emissions in Kaunas, Klaipėda and Vilnius have been on the rise since 1995. In the first case, this is due to the drop in production at the Akmenė's cement plant, while in the second it is due to the quickly growing share of the emissions of carbon monoxide, NO_x and VOCs from road transport (up to 75 per cent of urban pollution).

Apart from the polluting transport sector, the main stationary emission sources are in the energy, petrochemical and metal industries and in the construction and building materials industries located in the main cities and industrial centres in Vilnius, Kaunas, Klaipėda, Šiauliai, Panevėžys, Kėdainiai, Jonava, Naujoji, Akmenė and Mažeikiai. The single most polluting source is the refinery in Mažeikiai, which emitted almost 28 000 tonnes of pollutants in 1996 (Table 6.3).

Table 6.1: Emissions of selected pollutants, 1991-1996

1 000 t

		1991	1992	1993	1994	1995	1996
SO_x	**Total**	**234**	**139**	**125**	**117**	**107**	**93**
	Stationary sources	224	133	120	112	102	84
	Mobile sources	10	6	5	5	5	9
NO_x	**Total**	**166**	**98**	**78**	**77**	**67**	**65**
	Stationary sources	80	51	45	44	29	26
	Mobile sources	86	47	33	33	38	39
NMVOC*	**Total**	**122**	**76**	**62**	**62**	**82**	**87**
	Stationary sources	71	50	43	43	42	49
	Mobile sources	51	26	19	19	40	38
CO	**Total**	**599**	**351**	**292**	**303**	**244**	**312**
	Stationary sources	88	42	34	35	16	94
	Mobile sources	511	309	258	268	228	218
Total							
(SO_x, NO_x, NMVOCs, CO)		**1,121**	**664**	**557**	**559**	**500**	**557**
Stationary sources *(as % of total)*		*41.3*	*41.6*	*43.4*	*41.9*	*37.8*	*45.4*
Mobile sources *(as % of total)*		*58.7*	*58.4*	*56.6*	*58.1*	*62.2*	*54.6*
CH_4*	Total	412	391	381	379	293	285
NH_3*	Total	85	81	80	80	44	36
PM*	Stationary sources	65	39	26	21	18	8
Pb	Total	0.0488	0.0324	0.0282	0.0330	0.0172	0.0174
Ni	Total	0.0574	0.0599	0.0570	0.0578	0.0182	0.0456
Zn	Total	0.0552	0.0300	0.0132	0.0089	0.0075	0.0179
CO_2	*(Million t)*	45	29	25	25	24	19

Sources: Ministry of the Environment; EMEP emission database.

* NMVOC - Non-methane volatile organic compounds.
  CH_4 - Methane.
  NH_3 - Ammonia.
  PM - Particulate matter.

Table 6.2: Annual total classic emissions by source category, 1990 and 1996

1 000 t / year

	1990				1996			
	SO_x	NO_x	NMVOC$_s$	CO	SO_x	NO_x	NMVOC$_s$	CO
Total	**222**	**158**	**119**	**521**	**93**	**65**	**87**	**312**
Public power, cogeneration and district heating	105	47	1	5	58	19	0	9
Commercial, institutional and residential combustion plants	64	9	1	4	13	4	7	74
Industrial combustion plants and processes with combustion	38	18	29	36	13	3	1	7
Non-combustion processes	6	3	10	12	0	0	25	4
Extraction and distribution of fossil fuels	..	..	7	..	..	..	..	..
Solvent use	..	..	11	..	..	..	8	..
Road transport	6	53	45	450	2	25	37	214
Other transport	3	28	4	12	7	14	1	4
Waste treatment and disposal	..	..	..	2	..	..	..	..
Agriculture	..	..	3	..	..	..	..	..
Nature	..	..	8	..	..	..	8	..

Sources: National Environmental Finance Strategy, Ministry of the Environment,
    OECD and the Harvard Institute for International Development, 1997.

Table 6.3: The most polluting single stationary sources, 1993-1997

1 000 t

	1993	1994	1995	1996	1997
Refinery company Ma zeikiai	35.5	31.5	29.0	28.9	27.7
Thermal power plant Ma zeikiai	11.1	10.4	9.9	9.5	8.9
Lithuanian power plant Elektr enai	8.0	9.0	9.3	9.3	11.3
Power plant (VE2) Vilnius	5.3	5.9	4.8	6.1	5.1
Cement plant Akmen e	11.5	18.2	8.1	5.8	6.3
Chemical complex Achema	6.0	4.9	6.7	5.8	5.6
Chemical plant Dirbtinis Pluoštas	1.7	1.4	2.7	4.2	3.8
Power plant Kaunas	4.1	7.4	4.2	4.1	2.8

Source: Ministry of the Environment.

As the national reporting system on emissions concerns only those stationary sources which emit more than 10 tonnes of pollutants annually (1 012 such sources report at present), it is completed by emission calculations done at the Ministry of the Environment on the basis of material and fuel balances, including also mobile sources and using relevant emission factors. The calculated total emissions of Lithuania as given in Table 6.1 for example were one-third higher in 1995 for most pollutants than reported, although for CO and VOCs the situation was just the opposite.

The emissions per capita of the main classic pollutants, SO_x and NO_x, of the order of 25 kg and 17.5 kg respectively, are almost half the OECD average and much lower than in most countries in transition, particularly with respect to SO_x (see Figures 6.1 and 6.2). For NO_x, Lithuania's emission factor is equal to Hungary's. The same goes for its CO_2 emission factor, which is comparable to that of Hungary but lower than that of Austria, Italy and Slovenia (see Figure 6.3).

In a transboundary context, according to the model

Figure 6.1: Emissions of SOx, 1996

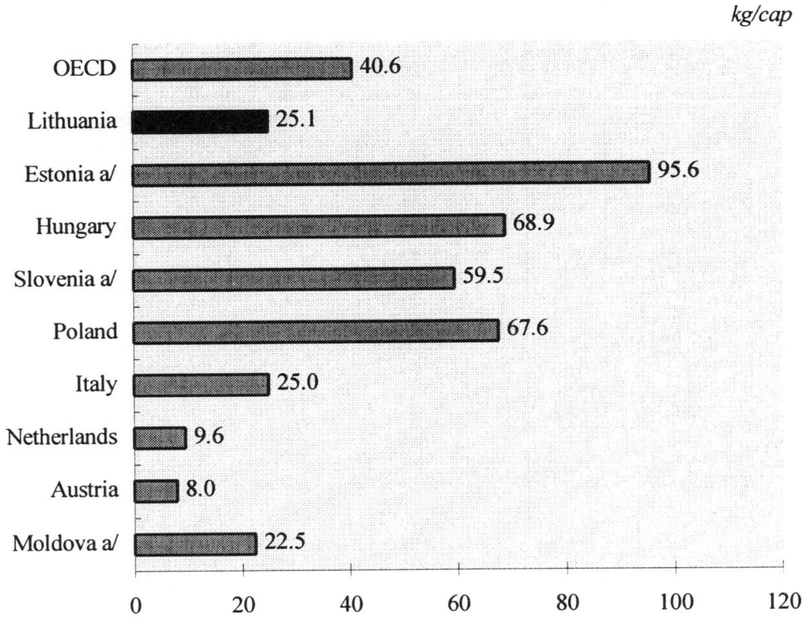

kg/cap

OECD	40.6
Lithuania	25.1
Estonia a/	95.6
Hungary	68.9
Slovenia a/	59.5
Poland	67.6
Italy	25.0
Netherlands	9.6
Austria	8.0
Moldova a/	22.5

Sources: Ministry of the Environment;
OECD, Environmental data, Compendium 1997.

a/ Data refer to 1995.

Figure 6.2: Emissions of NOx, 1996

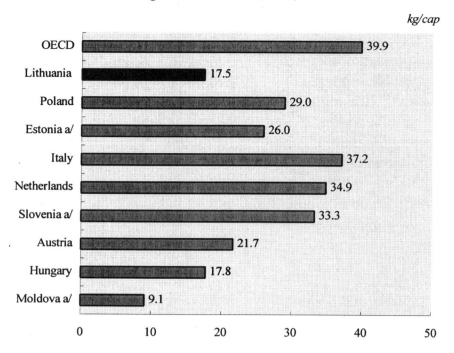

kg/cap

Sources: Ministry of the Environment;
          OECD, Environmental data, Compendium 1997.
a/ Data refer to 1995.

Figure 6.3: Emissions of CO$_2$, 1996

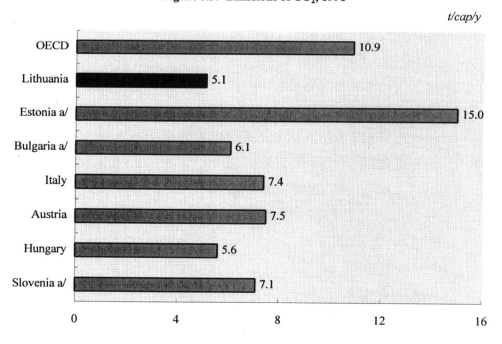

t/cap/y

Sources: Ministry of the Environment;
          OECD, Environmental data, Compendium 1997.
a/ Data refer to 1995.

calculations by the EMEP Meteorological Synthesizing Centre-West (MSC-W) for 1986 to 1995, Lithuania exported on average 20 000 tonnes of SO_x and NH_3 and over 50 000 tonnes of NO_2 more than it imported each year. Although the rate of imported oxidized nitrogen deposition exceeded 90 per cent, the percentage of exported emissions was higher still (Table 6.4).

Table 6.4: Transboundary import/export budgets, 1986-1995

1 000 tonnes

	Oxidized S	Oxidized N	Reduced N
Export mass	898	380	368
Emission *(%)*	*83*	*94*	*55*
Import mass	754	297	206
Depositions (%)	*80*	*93*	*41*
Net export	144	83	162

Source: Meteorological Synthesizing Centre-West.

Sectoral pressures and underlying factors

At present most sectoral pressures come from traffic-generated air pollution followed by combustion processes and to some extent from different industrial point sources. Since independence in 1990, the Government has recognized transport as a priority sector of the national economy. In 1993, the contribution of transport to gross domestic product (GDP) reached 8.3 per cent, in 1994, 8 per cent, and in 1996, 6.9 per cent. The transport services market has been demonopolized and privatized, leading to the rapid development of small private transport companies, particularly those involved in road transport and forwarding haulage services. Almost 98 per cent of passengers and 62 per cent of freight haulage are transported by road (Table 6.5).

The number of vehicles registered in Lithuania during the period 1990-1997 increased by 56 per cent (Table 6.6). However, the number of vehicles actually used could be lower, because Lithuania has a permanent (not annual or biennial) registration system and is home to a major car-refurbishing and re-exporting sector. Taking this into account, it is estimated that 212 passenger cars per 1 000 inhabitants (1996) are used in Lithuania. In 1995, this level was at 46 per cent of the EU level and it was expected to reach 50 per cent in 1997.

Table 6.5: Passenger and freight transport, 1992-1997

	1992		1993		1994		1995		1996		1997	
Passengers carried	*Million*	*%*	*Million*	*%*	*Million*	*%*	*Million*	*%*	*Million*	*%*	*Million*	*%*
Total	997.10	100.0	816.50	100.0	788.50	100.0	694.70	100.0	593.10	100.0	532.30	100.0
of which by:												
Road	973.00	97.6	789.90	96.7	768.10	97.4	678.20	97.6	578.20	97.5	519.40	97.6
Railway	21.90	2.2	25.10	3.1	18.30	2.3	15.20	2.2	13.20	2.2	11.20	2.1
Inland waterways	1.50	0.2	1.30	0.2	1.84	0.2	1.00	0.1	1.47	0.2	1.40	0.3
Air	0.70	0.1	0.20	0.0	0.26	0.0	0.24	0.0	0.24	0.0	0.27	0.1
Sea	..	..	0.02	0.0	0.03	0.0	0.04	0.0	0.04	0.0	0.04	0.0
Freight transport	*Million tonnes*	*%*	*Million tonnes*	*%*	*Million tonnes*	*%*	*Million tonnes*	*%*	*Million tonnes*	*%*	*Million tonnes*	*%*
Total	263.80	100.0	214.80	100.0	165.16	100.0	170.60	100.0	123.00	100.0	94.50	100.0
of which by:												
Road	201.20	76.3	170.20	79.2	130.10	78.8	138.30	81.1	88.60	72.0	58.80	62.2
Railway	56.20	21.3	38.40	17.9	29.50	17.9	26.00	15.2	29.10	23.7	30.50	32.3
Inland waterways	1.40	0.5	0.70	0.3	0.66	0.4	0.50	0.3	0.60	0.5	0.70	0.7
Air	0.003	0.0	0.003	0.0	0.005	0.0	0.003	0.0	0.002	0.0	0.003	0.0
Sea	5.10	1.9	5.50	2.6	4.90	3.0	5.80	3.4	4.70	3.8	4.50	4.8

Source: Statistical Yearbook of Lithuania, 1997.

Table 6.6: Number of road vehicles by vehicle type, 1990-1997

	1990	1991	1992	1993	1994	1995	1996	1997
Passenger transport								
Cars	492 978	530 824	565 320	597 735	652 810	718 469	785 088	882 101
of which: personal	477 911	510 562	542 516	575 980	627 105	685 552	745 742	835 462
Buses	15 157	15 627	16 284	16 339	17 103	17 052	15 482	14 888
of which: personal	414	563	930	1 699	2 967	5 824	5 552	6 208
Trolleybuses	550	563	548	535	532	532	544	547
Freight transport								
Motor vehicles, including pick-ups and vans	83 035	84 341	87 321	89 530	93 593	101 422	81 291	84 731
of which: personal	3 383	3 105	6 537	14 786	24 105	37 873	37 703	41 953
Tractors for semi-trailers	7 752	7 728	8 911	9 241	7 467	7 469	7 992	8 939
Trailers	11 836	12 311	11 469	11 813	12 810	9 136	7 077	6 840
Semi-trailers	11 474	11 969	11 794	10 952	10 696	9 119	8 730	9 359
Road transport of special purpose (incl. special cars)	30 928	26 850	24 172	23 677	22 459	15 346	15 269	15 148
Total vehicles	**653 710**	**690 213**	**725 819**	**759 822**	**817 470**	**878 545**	**921 473**	**1,022,553**
Motorcycles	192 123	196 075	192 148	180 452	172 946	171 292	a/	a/

Source: Statistical Yearbook of Lithuania, 1997.

a/ Stock not known. After new registration data are for 1996: 19 402 and for 1997: 19 128.

Although imported vehicles from western Europe and elsewhere have gradually been replacing ex-Soviet models, resulting in better fuel economy and lower emissions, the vehicle stock is old. Registration data indicate that 44 per cent of registered vehicles are more than 13 years old. A survey of private car owners conducted in 1997 indicated that 62 per cent of all cars were more than 10 years old and that 71 per cent of all private cars purchased were more than 10 years old. Only 24 000 cars were produced after 1992, of which 10 000 were produced in the Russian Federation without exhaust control system. In 1998, the new car sales have finally started to surge (by 88 per cent in the first quarter compared to last year's figure). Western cars dominate sales.

In 1995, Lithuania's only oil refinery in Mažeikiai still produced leaded petrol, which accounted for more than 40 per cent of total petrol refined. In 1996, the refinery stopped producing leaded petrol (following a ministerial order) and all petrol refined in Lithuania became lead-free. However, lead pollution has not decreased as much as one might expect. Legal imports of leaded petrol were still allowed in 1997. Illegal imports of poor-quality leaded petrol 76 OCT, mainly from Belarus and the Russian Federation, were often mixed at filling stations with better fuel. In 1997, the "smuggled" petrol officially accounted for only 5 per cent of the petrol used (down from 45 per cent in 1993). The problem was addressed in 1998, when fuel quality inspections and controls at the borders and at the pumps intensified (backed by legally binding requirements for higher fuel standards).

All this results in relatively high unit emissions and high pollution from road vehicles and the transport sector as a whole (rail transport accounts for 2.5 per cent of SO_x and NO_x emissions), which could even intensify in the coming years. Substantive improvements cannot be expected, for example in compliance with the EU regulations, without vehicle and fuel upgrading accompanied by efficient and effective controls.

Another pressure comes from industrial combustion processes, which in 1995 accounted for 85 per cent of SO_x emissions and 40 per cent of NO_x emissions from the whole territory. Due to the recession and the severed economic ties with eastern countries, final energy demand (heat, electricity and fuel) in Lithuania has halved since 1990. In the power plants using fossil fuels, electricity production has decreased eightfold. Heat production has also decreased. The Lithuanian Power Plant uses only 60 MW, slightly more than 3 per cent of its available capacity.

The decrease in energy consumption shows in all industrial sectors, but particularly in the construction and building materials industry, in agriculture and in manufacturing, where energy consumption is at only two-thirds of its 1990 level. In the transport sector, the demand for energy has fallen almost 40 per cent, while in the household sector it has decreased only by 4 per cent. The structure of energy in the most consuming sectors has changed considerably, for example the share of household demand has increased. The country remains relatively energy-intensive (for more details see Chapter 11).

The future air pollution from the power sector depends primarily on the complete closing-down of Ignalina NPP, scheduled in two stages: unit 1 in 2003 and unit 2 in 2008. To prepare for this eventuality, a number of scenarios have been developed to predict investment in the power generation sector and the related environmental impact. All scenarios predict increases in the sector's air emissions. According to the Lithuanian Energy Institute, the optimal strategy is to keep Ignalina open as long as possible, and to make the Lithuanian Power System fully operational, more efficient and environmentally friendly.

As no decision has yet been taken, it is difficult to estimate the pressure of the power generation sector in the coming years. However, it is likely that the use of conventional thermal power plants will increase, leading to basic energy sector restructuring costs, including primary and secondary gaseous emission control measures, which are almost non-existent at present.

Concerning other stationary sources, the pressures come from industrial complexes (Table 6.3) located within 3 to 5 km from cities and are the result of the so-called temporary emission limit values, which in many cases by far exceed legally established emission norms, particularly for specific pollutants.

Ambient air quality

In general, the ambient air quality is good and most pollution indices have improved since 1990. However, Lithuanian standards, i.e. maximum allowable concentrations (MAC), for long-term or average exposure to particulate matter and short, 30-minute exposure to nitrogen dioxide are exceeded, mainly in big cities, due to traffic-related emissions and those from the largest industrial stationary sources located on their outskirts.

The 1996 monitoring data for 10 cities, capitals of counties, provided by the Ministry of the Environment and its Regional Departments clearly indicate that average concentrations of total suspended particulates (TSPs), although in general on the decrease in most cities, are much higher than WHO annual guidelines. They range from 0.06 to 0.09 mg/m³ in Vilnius, Kaunas, Šiauliai, Kėdainiai, Jonava, Venta and Naujoji Akmenė. In the last two cities they also exceed Lithuania's 24-hour MAC of 0.15 mg/m³ and have been rising since 1992. Moreover, as TSPs come mostly from the cement plant, in Naujoji Akmenė the 24-hour MAC, at 0.1 mg/m³, is lower still and the excess higher.

Average NO_2 concentrations are on the increase mainly in Klaipėda and Panevėžys and rather stable in Vilnius, Naujoji Akmenė and Jonava. Nowhere did they exceed Lithuania's 24-hour MAC of 0.04 mg/m³, which is also the WHO annual guideline. In most cities they ranged between 0.02 and 0.03 mg/m³. However, the 30-minute MAC was attained at some monitoring stations located close to transport routes. For example, in Vilnius 30 per cent of samples taken at two city monitoring stations exceeded the standard. It should also be noted that maximum concentrations of NO_2 rose in 1996 compared to 1995 in five cities and in Vilnius they more than doubled.

Average SO_2 concentrations, although constantly increasing in Vilnius, Panevėžys, Venta and Jonava since 1992, were far below both Lithuania's 24-hour standard and the corresponding WHO guideline (for a comparison of both values, see (Table 6.7). Maximum SO_2 concentrations reached 40 per cent of Lithuania's 30-minute MAC in Vilnius.

**Table 6.7: Comparison of selected Lithuanian ambient air quality standards
with recommended WHO guiding values**

Substance	Lithuania MAC mg/m^3, 30 min	Lithuania MAC mg/m^3, 24h	WHO guideline value/ averaging time
Classical air pollutants			
Carbon monoxide	5.00	3.00	100 mg/m^3, 15 min
			60 mg/m^3, 30 min
			30 mg/m^3, 1h
			10 mg/m^3, 8h
Ozone	0.16	0.03	0.120 mg/m^3, 8h
Sulphur dioxide	0.50	0.05	0.5 mg/m^3, 10 min
			0.125 mg/m^3, 24h
			0.050 mg/m^3, annual
Organic pollutants			
Formaldehyde	0.035	0.003	0.0001 mg/m^3, 30 min
Styrene	0.200	..	0.26 mg/m^3, 1 week
Tetrachloroethylene	0.500	0.060	0.25 mg/m^3, 24h
Toluene	0.600	0.600	0.26 mg/m^3, 1 week
Trichloroethylene	4.000	1.000	4.3×10^{-6} mg/m^3, lifetime
Inorganic pollutants			
Arsenic	..	0.003	1.5×10^{-6} mg/m^3, lifetime
Cadmium (compounds)	..	0.0003	0.005 mg/m^3, annual (deposition)
Lead	..	0.0003	0.0005 mg/m^3, annual
Mercury	..	0.0003	0.001 mg/m^3, annual

Sources: Ministry of the Environment and WHO.

There did not seem to be any excess of heavy metals. The average concentrations of seven heavy metals (nickel, lead, cadmium, chromium, copper, manganese and vanadium) measured in three cities, Vilnius, Kaunas and Klaipėda, were much lower than Lithuania's 24-hour MACs, reaching at worst only one tenth of the MACs.

Average concentrations of benzo(a)pyrene (BaP) were close to the Lithuanian standard in Kaunas, Vilnius and Šiauliai. In the last, it is believed that the BaP emissions originate at a major jet engine repair facility located on the military airbase just outside the town.

Average concentrations of formaldehyde were on the increase compared to 1995 in Vilnius and Klaipėda, where they were close to the Lithuanian 24-hour MAC. Average concentrations of ammonia and sulphates were well below the standards in all 10 cities.

The concentrations of carbon monoxide are poorly documented, because of the lack of measuring devices. Their maximum concentrations do not exceed 1 to 2 mg/m^3 or 20 to 40 per cent of Lithuania's MAC in most cities, but they are on the increase in Klaipėda and Vilnius and could rise elsewhere as the vehicle stock is ageing and poor-quality petrol is widely used.

Systematic measurements at three background monitoring stations have confirmed the acidic nature of precipitation, as in much of Europe. The 10-year average pH ranged from 4.26 to 4.63. However, the concentrations of hydrogen (H+) and nitrates (NO_3--) have risen and those of sulphates (SO_4--) and calcium (Ca++) decreased. These results attest to the successful implementation of the first Sulphur Protocol and the growing NO_x emissions, mainly from road traffic, in the ECE region.

6.2   Policy objectives, institutional arrangements, available instruments and their application

Objectives and institutional arrangements

According to NES, to reduce air pollution from mobile sources it is necessary to solve the fuel quality issue in line with EU requirements and gradually shift to vehicles which meet EU standards and introduce regulation systems to achieve optimal transport streams. This involves in particular the Ministry of the Environment, the Ministry of Transport, the Ministry of Internal Affairs, the Ministry of the Economy and the municipalities. The deadlines range from 1996 to 1998 for most of the actions. The NES takes into account the relevant parts of the 1992 programme of transport and the environment.

To prevent air pollution from stationary sources by NO_x, SO_2, CO_2, VOCs and suspended solids from getting worse, NES recommends, following the EU standards, to speed up and finalize the development of legislation for the regulation of their emissions, to take energy-saving measures, promote the use of cleaner production programmes, including upgraded fuels, and to introduce treatment techniques based on best available technology (BAT). The main partners involved are also the Ministry of the Environment, and the Ministry of the Economy.

The main task of the Ministry of the Economy is to revise the financing scheme for environmental protection measures and to establish an environmental fund for investments (see Chapter 2 for details), thus providing more favourable conditions for the implementation of NES. The deadlines range from 1996 up to the year 2000 and some are even continuous, for instance those relating to BAT.

Available instruments and their application

Air management is based on the 1992 Law on Environmental Protection, the 1996 Law on Environmental Impact Assessment and the 1981 former Soviet Clean Air Act, which has simply been transformed into Lithuanian law (1995), without any changes. Command-and-control mechanisms are combined with economic instruments, primarily emission charges and fines.

A new draft law on atmospheric protection is under preparation and is expected to be ready in 1999. It should be based *inter alia* on integrated pollution prevention and control and impose fewer, but more realistic, ambient air quality standards. The 1993 ambient air quality standards applied to 421 pollutants. Emission limit values (MAPs) for stationary sources are set by the Regional Departments on the basis of a simplified computer dispersion model, applied also in the former Soviet Union within the ecological evaluation procedure, and compared with the 1993 air quality standards.

In practice, in addition to legally binding MAPs, so-called temporary emission limits (TAPs) are very often established reflecting the real situation of the emitting source during the time period set. Their values can be lower than MAPs, if the level of activity is lower than initially proposed, or higher than MAPs, if control measures have not yet been implemented. According to the Ministry of the Environment's survey (1996) of 348 pollutants emitted by 1 012 sources in quantities above 10 tonnes a year, TAPs were set for most of the cases reported and were very often much higher than the MAPs.

The differences between TAPs and MAPs are the most striking for hydrocarbons or VOCs (more than 30 times higher), acetone (22 times higher), ammonia (6 times higher) and dust (3 to 4 times higher). For specific chemical pollutants the differences were also of several factors. In total, TAP values were 1.5 times higher than MAPs, and much higher for gaseous pollutants (1.6) than for solid ones (1.2).

The situation differs with respect to mobile sources. Vehicle fleets of large transport companies should meet individual exhaust gas emission standards, established for CO and HC from Otto engines and for soot (opacity) from diesel engines. However, transport activities are not on the list of activities subject to a full EIA. After the abolition of GOST norms, new values for CO and smoke are already in force. The values for CO are less strict than GOST values were, while those for HC are twice as strict and will come into force on 1 January 2000 (the EU does not standardize HC for the time being).

Private cars are subject to these standards too. First, they are checked during vehicle registration at licensed stations and then periodically (every 1 to 2 years) and on the road during joint spot checks by the Road Police and the State Environmental Inspectorate. At present, 61 technical vehicle inspection stations accredited by the Ministry of Transport are applying ISO measurement methods. Most of them are equipped with CO and soot analysers, but not yet with HC analysers. However, garages have insufficient equipment and cannot help inspection stations by guaranteeing vehicle performance.

Spot checks of vehicles are generally carried out in spring and autumn. At present the Road Police and regional inspectorates are able to check about 3 000 vehicles a year. Their spot checks focus on vehicles that are more than 10 years old and concern primarily CO and opacity. More than 30 per cent of checked vehicles are found to breach the standards. Depending on the pollution level, fines can go up to 100 Litas.

In parallel, the Ministry of the Economy in 1996 introduced quality standards for leaded and unleaded petrol, limiting their lead content from 0.35 g/l to 0.15 g/l and 0.013 g/l, respectively. Regardless of the type of petrol, the sulphur content has been limited to 0.05 per cent of the mass and benzene volume to 5 per cent. As of 1 January 1998, only unleaded petrol can legally be sold in Lithuania.

There is another, stricter and broader draft norm aligning the quality of all selected fuels used in Lithuania, including "city diesel" and fuel oil, with EU directives. It has been prepared by the Board of Standards and is expected to be approved by the Ministry of the Economy and issued as a ministerial order soon.

When checking emission limits, regional laboratories take samples annually and analyse them automatically for classic pollutants, e.g. sulphur and nitrogen compounds, or manually for specific pollutants like phenol and formaldehyde. The results are compared to the norms (MAPs or TAPs) and sent to the Ministry of the Environment for its annual reports and to the State Environmental Inspectorate, which calculates charges and imposes fines for non-compliance.

The Regional Departments and district environmental agencies are not adequately equipped to ensure regular and complete control of the licensed polluting sources. Therefore, the inspectors must rely on estimates of emissions based on energy and material balance. However, they do not check even sporadically the quality of motor fuels and fuel oils, leaving it up to the transport companies and power/energy generation plants.

The situation is even worse within the licensed stationary sources. They usually have no equipment to monitor their own emissions and air-source sampling by continuous monitoring is almost non-existent. Their emission data are mostly calculated using emission factors based on energy and material inputs that cannot integrate process variations and therefore provide only an approximate indication of emission levels.

At present, the laboratories of the Regional Departments are being equipped with mobile gas chromatographs to enforce the control of exhaust gas emissions from vehicles, mainly VOCs, as the deadline for the entry into force of new standards is approaching. The regional laboratories, under the leadership of the Central Environment Research Laboratory, which organizes inter alia regular inter-calibration exercises for them and analyses centrally very specific samples, are much more involved and achieve better results in monitoring ambient air. Their ambient air monitoring forms an integrated subsystem of the State Monitoring Programme and consists of two fairly autonomous parts; systematic observations and studies, both related to chemical and radiological pollution.

The chemical observations cover 16 air pollutants and are carried out at 23 stations in cities, industrial centres and residential areas. They focus on the local level. Sulphur dioxide, nitrogen dioxide, carbon monoxide and dust are monitored in all monitoring sites. Other pollutants are monitored according to the specificity of the city's or the industrial centre's emissions and the probability that their ambient air quality standards will be exceeded.

Most measurements at the local level are done manually. Samples are taken three times a day and then analysed in regional laboratories according to the methodology of the former Soviet Union based on photometry, mass spectrometry, chromatography and atomic absorption methods. Automated air monitoring is still in its infancy and takes place in Vilnius at only three stations. Its results go directly to the Ministry of the Environment to be used in monitoring-related studies, but have not so far been integrated in the city's pollution report by the Regional Department in Vilnius.

The air monitoring network of Vilnius consists of seven stations, located primarily along the transport routes, three of which are automated. Apart from standard components, NH_3, H_2S, HCl, formaldehyde, sulphates, heavy metals and benzo(a)pyrene are monitored at the four manual stations, and SO_2, NO_2, CO and O_3 at the two automated stations.

Monitoring also takes place at the regional level. A dozen precipitation stations are evenly distributed throughout Lithuania's territory, away from industrial centres. When operational, regional monitoring should consist of 30 to 35 precipitation and air sampling stations and be operated by the Institute of Physics, which is responsible for relevant studies. In addition, four stations located in Preila, Aukštaitija, Dzūkija and Žemaitija are integrated within the international programmes of EMEP and EUROTRAC, mainly thanks to financial support from the Nordic countries. They contribute to controlling transboundary air pollution and to global scientific air and precipitation programmes and are also operated by the Institute of Physics.

Local radiological monitoring covers the area around Ignalina NPP; its regional counterpart provides information on the radioactivity of precipitation and atmospheric aerosols using the existing conventional stations.

The Regional Departments verify the quality of all monitoring results before they are transmitted to the Ministry of the Environment. There they are once again checked by the Environmental Quality Department or, if they concern air pollutants, by the Air Division. Subsequently, the Joint Research Centre consolidates them into annual reports. It also takes account of the results of different monitoring-related studies, e.g. model calculations.

The most widely applied economic instruments are emission charges and fines (for tax exemptions, waivers and penalties applicable to stationary sources see Chapter 2). In practice, transport companies are not subject to pollution taxation. They also escape the Ministry of the Environment's reporting system due to the dynamic, but scattered privatization of the sector (often consisting in the splitting-up of big State enterprises into small businesses that emit less than 10 tonnes a year). Drivers can be penalized if their vehicles fail to comply with standards during road checks. Excise duties on motor fuel and fuel prices do not have an environmental tax component.

As alternative fuels, only liquefied petroleum gas (LPG) is used and new filling stations are adapting to it. Their wider use, for instance, in public transport or production from biomass is still under investigation and subject to several project proposals for international financing.

According to the Law on Environmental Pollution Charges (1991), 70 per cent are paid to the municipal nature protection funds, which transfer 20 per cent to the municipal health funds. The taxes levied on some large-scale plants are distributed differently by law, e.g. Ignalina NPP pays 90 per cent to the State and 10 per cent to the municipality, Mažeikiai refinery and Akmenė's cement plant pay fifty-fifty (for more information see Chapter 2).

Unfortunately, since 1992, no investments (only current expenditures) have been allocated to air pollution abatement, although air protection has been declared one of the top priorities and many actions included in the NES cannot be implemented without capital investments.

As a result of the lack of investments in air emission abatement, existing control equipment has aged or none has been installed (no flue gas desulphurization (FGD) or denitrification (de-NO_x) systems). The efficiency of existing equipment has dropped, resulting in higher unit emissions from different sources (TAPs and exhaust gas emissions on the increase) and ambient air excess for some pollutants.

Any pro-environmental development depends to a large extent on the municipalities, which are responsible for enforcing the environmental laws, for decisions on their territories and for fining the legal entities that fail to comply. The Elektrėnai municipality has a strong interest in keeping air pollution below ambient air quality standards, because of the health care complex located on its territory.

Vilnius has an environmental protection unit, which has not yet been directly involved in air pollution management. However, through its Nature Protection Fund, it supports the monitoring activities within the city network. Moreover, it promotes, via territorial planning including initial EIA, better traffic management, e.g. bypassing downtown and biking paths. Unfortunately, the Vilnius municipality has not so far made the monitoring results or data concerning its other environmental achievements (in the areas of waste or waste-water management) available to its citizens (except that available on the city's Internet homepage). Nor has it strengthened public awareness via the mass media and particularly through the widely distributed newspaper *Lithuanian Future* with its section devoted exclusively to the city.

6.3   Conclusions and recommendations

Lithuania has laid down clear political guidance on the principles and goals of air management. Consequently, it has achieved quite impressive results in terms of policy documents. At the same time, the legal foundations for many aspects of management are not always fully adapted to current requirements in terms of both substance and management routines. For instance, the legal framework for air management is still based on the Law on Clean Air (1981), with its old-style air management concept. It does not integrate or further develop new principles and rules as provided for in the 1994 framework Law on Environmental Protection and the 1996 Law on EIA. Based on a critical review of the current situation, a draft law on environmental taxes has recently been drawn up. The changes that it proposes would seem to make the taxation system more efficient.

It seems that partnership and mutual understanding between the key players, including the public at large, is still to be developed, in particular with respect to policy goals, mainly environmental

standard-setting and designing cleaner production and energy-saving programmes. The decision-making process in that respect has been deficient: e.g. personalities rather than institutions have so far been involved, sometimes the Ministry of the Environment and its Regional Departments prevail. The role of municipalities in the process has not been evidenced, although they have a mandate.

Recommendation 6.1:
The revision of the Law on Clean Air of 1981 should be a priority. The new law should pay particular attention to all matters of enforcement. The implementation of the new law should clarify the rights and responsibilities of all levels of administration in air management. It should also help to develop routines for cooperation between all interested partners in air management.

Concerning the main policy objectives and actions in air management, which are clearly reflected in the NES, most of them are being achieved or are expected to be achieved in the near future. However, enforcement is not systematic, partly because the existing legal and institutional framework for air pollution management cannot guarantee NES implementation. Concerning the basic principles contained in the framework Law on Environmental Protection, most have lost their practical meaning during the transition. The improvement in air quality, which has occurred in Lithuania since its independence, has been due to economic recession rather than the result of control measures applied to either stationary or mobile sources.

As a result, it can be feared that air pollution will rapidly turn into a major problem, once the economy recovers more vigorously - unless an action plan is drawn up and implemented. Such an action plan should focus on completing the legal and regulatory framework for air pollution abatement, including more realistic but fewer ambient air quality standards, emission standards for major stationary sources based on BATNEEC and exhaust gas emission standards for vehicles. These last should initially be in line with the relevant ECE regulations and then shift gradually to the EU standards.

Recommendation 6.2:
Based on a critical review of the National Environmental Strategy (NES) and its present

implementation, an action plan should be implemented that meets the declared policy needs, including assigning precise responsibility and putting in place financing schemes. The action plan should be formulated in cooperation with the key players, i.e. various administrative bodies, line ministries, industry and the general public, as well as with different decision-making levels (local, regional and central).

The approximation to the EU is progressing, but requires Lithuania to make substantial efforts. Being a Party to the Convention on Long-range Transboundary Air Pollution, Lithuania's accession to the Convention's protocols could be seen as a mid-term target in the area of air emissions on the way to membership of the European Union.

Recommendation 6.3:
Lithuania should consider complying with the Protocols on SO_x, NO_x, VOCs, POPs and Heavy Metals to the Convention on Long-range Transboundary Air Pollution.

Although air protection in Lithuania is based on environmental impact assessment, whose procedural and methodological aspects are close to those of EU and ECE, the lack of technology-based standards and poor enforcement, particularly through economic instruments, are undermining its results. The situation is particularly critical with respect to road vehicles, where the polluter-pays principle is insufficiently enforced. To bridge these gaps, more realistic but fewer ambient air quality standards and related emission limits should be set and enforced for the main stationary and mobile source categories. In particular, the process of setting new ambient air quality standards and technology-based emission standards for stationary sources has not yet been undertaken. Also, big, publicly owned transport companies should be prompted to switch to less polluting vehicles and/or fuels by adequate means, thereby complementing the efforts made in the same direction by, for instance, environmental impact assessment of transport infrastructure.

Recommendation 6.4:
New ambient air quality standards in accordance with EU practices and technology-based emission standards should be urgently developed, approved and enforced.

According to different studies, 80 per cent of the potential reduction of air pollution could be achieved by energy savings. The marginal cost per tonne of pollution abated would thus be US$ 368. It is estimated that a nationwide average 40 per cent reduction in the main pollutant emissions (total annual cost estimates for SO_2, NO_x, CO and particulates) could be achieved at an annual cost of up to a mere 0.33 per cent of 1995 GDP. Most of this sum would be needed for abating SO_x emissions. However, there may be a cheaper option for cutting SO_x emissions, namely switching to natural gas.

The emission factors per unit of output from the main stationary sources have risen relatively since 1992. The emission structure is characterized by many small polluters and only few large ones; the latter can be effectively and efficiently controlled with a relatively low marginal cost per tonne of pollution abated. An abatement programme using the available instruments appears feasible.

The cost of implementing that part of the NES that relates to air protection has been evaluated at 1 per cent of its total. In practice, not even this trifle 1 per cent has been spent on anti-pollution measures, confirming that air protection, although declared priority number 2, has in terms of investment been completely neglected. Although revenues from pollution charges increased from 81 per cent of total revenues in 1993 to 91 per cent in 1996, revenues from fines have decreased from 19 per cent to only 9 per cent during this period. This confirms that stationary polluters are willing to pay charges, rather than invest in control measures, and are benefiting from less stringent emission limits (TAPs), thus paying relatively fewer fines. At present BAT has not been introduced in industry, for example no FGD or de-NO_x system has been installed and technologies to reduce emissions of VOCs have not been produced or applied.

Recommendation 6.5:
Increasing the use of natural gas in the national energy economy should be seriously considered. The Ministry of the Environment should prepare an abatement programme for all stationary sources with temporary emission limits and set established emission limit values as targets.

With regard to mobile sources, particularly road

motor vehicles, a relative reduction in emissions in the long term requires a number of preparatory measures. Among them is certainly the attempt to control traffic flows with the available planning instruments.   Such measures are particularly important for the larger towns.

Recommendation 6.6:
Traffic minimization through better integration of transport policy and traffic management with territorial planning and particularly land-use planning should be promoted in the main cities, especially in Vilnius.

Lithuania aims to develop national requirements for vehicles and fuel quality in line with EU directives. However, it cannot meet this challenge without retrofitting and upgrading most of its car fleet - on which 5 per cent of 1995 GDP would have to be spent, as estimated by OECD and the Harvard Institute for International Development. This is obviously unrealistic.   Moreover, the decision to set stricter vehicle standards has not been preceded by economic and technical studies and has not been made by consensus of the main two ministries concerned (the Ministry of the Environment and the Ministry of Transport).

Economic instruments to encourage cleaner motor fuels and cleaner vehicles (import duties, excise duties, annual vehicle taxes, petrol pricing, etc.) are non-existent - drivers enjoy a virtual tax holiday. The relevant taxes are currently in revision. Appropriate economic instruments will be required to manage air emissions from mobile sources. If they cannot be included into the draft law, they will have to be created in another way.

Recommendation 6.7:
The new environmental taxation system should include such market-oriented instruments as differentiated import duties (lower for safer and cleaner vehicles), and differentiated excise duties depending on the fuel's pollution potential.

The vehicle standards in place cannot be properly or efficiently enforced because of the vehicle registration system and vehicle pollution control

regarding air emissions at inspection stations. Spot checks can reach only about 3 per cent of the vehicle stock owing to a shortage of resources and equipment. Moreover, a coherent maintenance and inspection system for in-use vehicles is still to be put in place.

Recommendation 6.8:
Vehicle inspection should be based on the present standards (outcome of the Vienna Regional Conference to be taken into account) and rely on certified and adequately equipped stations and garages.   In addition, spot checks of vehicles should be strengthened and become continuous and be extended to transport companies, particularly those with public transport vehicles.

The process of aligning the quality of fuels used in Lithuania with EU requirements is much more advanced and almost complete for motor fuels. However, in practice the lack of quality checks and illegal imports of poor-quality fuels cause a high risk of misfuelling (tampering).

Recommendation 6.9:
The existing fuel quality control system should be strengthened, including strict border control of imported fuels, and controls on the transport of fuels and on filling stations.

Ambient air quality monitoring is quite well developed and sufficiently integrated into international, regional and global programmes. The air pollution monitoring network in Vilnius, although still not fully homogeneous since it is partly manual and partly automatic, can be seen as a model for other Lithuanian cities and industrial areas.   However, the measurements of emission rates are not yet integrated into the air monitoring programme.   Also, there should be automatic sampling at least at large stationary sources, which should be integrated with this programme to ensure swift reaction if ambient air quality standards are exceeded. The regional laboratories are also not adequately prepared or equipped to provide such services.   The situation could be gradually improved while awaiting the entry into force of technology-based emission standards.

Chapter 7

WATER RESOURCES MANAGEMENT AND WATER QUALITY ASPECTS

7.1 Water resources and use

Availability and ownership of water

Lithuania is located in the wet part of the world and is rich in freshwater resources. Rainfall during an average year amounts to 748 mm (from 570 mm to 902 mm). From a total average precipitation of 44.0 billion m³/year, about 13.7 billion is river outflow (mainly to the Nemunas). The remaining 30.3 billion (or almost 69 per cent) evaporate and infiltrate groundwater.

The average density of the river network, including artificial water streams, is 1km/km². In recent decades, with the excavation of numerous land-reclamation canals, the total density of the hydrographic network has almost doubled. There are over 29 900 rivers, rivulets and canals longer than 250 m; 758 rivers longer than 10 km; 18 rivers longer than 100 km and 9 rivers longer than 200 km.

The characteristics of Lithuania's main rivers are described in Table 7.1. The length of the main water artery, the River Nemunas, is 937 km, of which 475 km flow through Lithuania. It rises in Belarus. The Nemunas is a tributary of Lithuania's largest inland water source, Kuršių Lagoon. 413 km² of that Lagoon (out of 1 610 km²) are in Lithuania. The rest lies in the Kaliningrad region of the Russian Federation. It is separated from the Baltic Sea by the overgrown and picturesque Kuršių Spit. The total length of the second largest river - the Neris - is 510 km, of which 276 km flow through Belarus. The river Šventoji runs entirely through Lithuania and is 249 km long. The total annual river flow in Lithuania (including transit flow) is 26.1 billion m³. Over 75 per cent of rivers and rivulets have been regulated by land reclamation. Of the 63 700 km of natural rivers only 17 000 have remained unregulated, including the 9 largest rivers.

Table 7.1: Characteristics of the main rivers

	Flow m³/s	Length in km		Catchment area, km²		Measurement point number
		Total	In Lithuania	Total	In Lithuania	
Nemunas	665	937	475	97 928	46 692	9
Neris	178	510	234	24 942	13 850	6
Šventoji	51	246	246	6 889	6 801	4
Nevezis	36	209	209	6 140	6 140	5
Musa (Lielupe)	125	284	146	17 600	8 716	3
Dubysa	15	139	139	2 033	2 033	1
Jura	41	172	172	3 994	3 994	2
Venta	95	346	161	11 800	5 140	3
Bartuva	22	101	55	2 020	748	2
Minija	40	202	202	2 942	2 942	4
Akmena-Dane	7	63	63	580	580	4
Sesupe	33	298	209	6 105	4 899	4
Merkys	34	203	190	4 416	4 333	2
Zeimena	22	80	80	2 793	2 793	4

Source: Ministry of the Environment.

There are over 2 800 lakes in Lithuania which are over 0.5 ha and their total area accounts for 880 km², or 1.5 per cent of the country's territory. The Ignalina NPP is located near the largest lake, Drūkšiai (45 km²). With a depth of 60 metres, Tauragnai is the deepest lake. About 400 reservoirs (ponds) of not less than 5 ha have been created. There are more than 10 000 smaller ponds. The Kaunas Lagoon is the largest reservoir (63.5 km²). It was formed by damming the Nemunas River after the construction of a hydroelectric power plant.

The list of Nationally Significant Bodies of Water was approved by Government decision No. 2 on 10 January 1998. Groundwaters are the exclusive property of the State. Surface bodies of water can become private property if they are sold or returned to their previous owners. The 1997 Law on Water and other relevant legislation provide that only small surface bodies of water can be sold to private owners. Restitution to previous owners is the main process leading to privately owned bodies of water. This process is still under way, so that it is impossible to say at this time how important private ownership will be.

Water abstraction and use

Figure 7.1: Water resources - intensity of use, 1980-1995a/

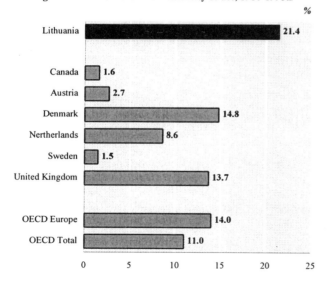

Source: OECD, Environmental data, Compendium 1997.
a/ Long-term annual average.

Annual water abstraction (including cooling water) per capita is 1 508 m³. This is still relatively high compared to other European countries, as is the intensity of use (Figure 7.1). In 1996, total water

abstraction amounted to 20.5 per cent of all water resources. This amount includes water used for cooling in power plants and to produce electricity in hydroelectric power plants. However, if the water used in the energy sector is excluded, water abstraction amounts to 1.2 per cent of all water resources. In 1996, 5.1 per cent of water was abstracted from groundwater and 94.9 per cent from surface waters. About 94 per cent of water is used for energy needs.

Water abstraction during recent years is shown in Table 7.2. The abstraction of surface water increased by some 30 per cent between 1992 and 1997. This rise was caused by an increase in water use at the Ignalina Nuclear Power Plant and the Kruonis Hydroelectric Station. Surface water is the dominant source of cooling water in electricity generation. In 1996 the Ignalina Nuclear Power Plant abstracted more than 5 billion m³ from Drūkšiai Lake for cooling. However, the abstraction of groundwater decreased by more than 51 per cent between 1992 and 1997. Groundwater is the major source for the public water supply.

Table 7.2: Water abstraction, 1992-1997

Million m³/year

	1992	1993	1994	1995	1996	1997
Total abstracti	3 984	4 388	3 997	4 582	5 696	4 786
Surface water	3 504	3 972	3 632	4 278	5 407	4 552
Groundwater	480	416	365	305	289	234

Source: Ministry of the Environment.

The withdrawal of groundwater has affected groundwater levels practically throughout the country. A brief analysis prepared by the Geological Survey of Lithuania states that groundwater extraction in most well-fields in 1993 was lower than in previous years. The data on well-field operation in 1994 show a slight increase in 26 well-fields and stabilization in 14. In 1994, the total volume of groundwater withdrawal in all the well-fields was about 707 000 m³/day, or some 18 per cent less than in 1990. The withdrawals at many well-fields amounted to about 35-40 per cent of the groundwater resources.

The reason for this decrease in groundwater withdrawal was the general decline in the Lithuanian economy and the concurrent increase in the prices of drinking water. There was a vigorous campaign to install water meters in many blocks of flats in town.   The volume of groundwater withdrawal is still decreasing in Vilnius, Panevėžys, Mažeikiai and Marijampolė.   Since 1995, groundwater withdrawal in the Kaunas, Klaipda, Alytus and Jonava well-fields has been increasing. This may indicate that the economic situation in these towns is improving.

The data presented in Table 7.3 show that due to economic reform, from 1992 to 1997 the consumption of water for industry (except energy needs), municipal and household, agricultural, fishery and other needs fell in the range from 25 per cent (other) to 75 per cent (agriculture). Figure 7.2 shows the water use structure in 1997 (excluding cooling water). More than 48 per cent of water is for municipal and household needs and less than 1 per cent for agriculture. The water data for agriculture are considered accurate. In 1989 water use in agriculture stood at some 15.9 million m³, but after Lithuania's economic restructuring it dropped to its present 2.3 million m³.   No water is used for irrigation.   Only those water users that withdraw more than 10 m³ of water per day are included in the statistics. A natural resource tax for the abstraction of surface and groundwater was introduced in 1995. The 1998 rates are the following: groundwater for domestic needs (0.037 Litas per m³), groundwater for industry (0.087 Litas per m³), surface water for energy (0.0012 Litas per m³), surface water for fisheries (0.0006 Litas per m³), surface water for agriculture (0.006 Litas per m³).   Prices for the supply of treated water to households and industrial plants are set by municipalities and take into consideration the cost

of water treatment and distribution. Prices for households range from 1.7 to 3.0 Litas per m³.

Figure 7.2: Water use structure*, 1997

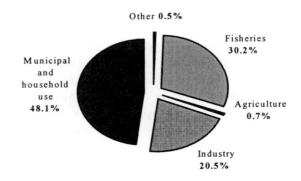

Source: Ministry of the Environment.

Note:
* Excluding cooling water.

7.2   Water quality and major quality determinants

Waste-water generation and treatment

Pollution from urbanized areas along rivers is especially severe. The discharges from the seven biggest cities, or 44 per cent of the population, make up about 67 per cent of all discharges. In terms of BOD_7, this is 74 per cent, nitrogen discharges are 64 per cent of the national total and phosphorus discharges 60 per cent.   Pollution

Table 7.3: Water use patterns, 1992-1997

Million m³/year

	1992	1993	1994	1995	1996	1997	% change 1992-1997
Cooling water	2 969.0	3 755.0	3 374.0	4 099.0	5 271.0	4 411.0	48.6
Municipal and household use	297.0	260.0	251.0	196.0	167.0	148.0	-50.2
Industry	145.0	102.0	76.0	49.0	47.0	63.0	-56.6
Agriculture	8.0	6.0	4.0	4.0	3.0	2.0	-75.0
Fisheries	157.0	107.0	124.0	116.0	102.0	93.0	-40.8
Other	2.0	2.0	2.0	1.0	1.0	1.5	-25.0
Total water consumption	**3 578.0**	**4 232.0**	**3 831.0**	**4 465.0**	**5 591.0**	**4 718.0**	**31.9**
Water consumption m³ per capita	956.3	1 134.5	1 029.6	1 202.0	1 507.2	1 271.9	33.0

Sources: Ministry of the Environment;
         Statistical Yearbook of Lithuania 1997.

caused by industry has decreased over recent years, partly as a result of reduced economic activity in certain key sectors. Trends in waste-water discharge are shown in Table 7.4. The discharge meeting quality standards without treatment (primarily cooling water from the energy sector) increased by about 69 per cent between 1992 and 1996, but shrank to 41 per cent in 1997. In 1996 and 1997, it amounted to some 95 per cent of the total waste-water discharge. This waste water from the energy sector is discharged into Drūkšiai Lake and Kaunas Reservoir and to the Nemunas River. The remaining 5 per cent of waste water discharged to surface water bodies has to be treated. The amount of waste water requiring treatment decreased by 36.5 per cent between 1992 and 1997.

Figure 7.3 shows the structure of waste water requiring treatment. In 1997, the total amount of waste water requiring treatment was 233 million m³. Of this amount 115 million m³, i.e. 49 per cent, were treated to meet Lithuania's effluent standards. A slightly smaller amount of waste water (79 million m³, i.e. 43 per cent) was discharged into surface waters without sufficient treatment (mechanical treatment only or cleaned in ineffective biological treatment facilities). Some 39 million m³, i.e. 17 per cent, were discharged into surface waters without treatment.

In 1997, there were 787 waste-water treatment plants in Lithuania. 49 are equipped with mechanical treatment technology only, and 668 with biological treatment technology. The average

capacity of village treatment plants is about 100 m³ per day.

Six towns (Kelmė, Lazdijai, Šilalė, Raseiniai, Pakruojis, Molėtai) remove both phosphorus and nitrogen in their treatment plants. The same facilities are being installed in Vilnius, where they are expected to go into operation at the end of 1998. The capacity of the plants in the six cities mentioned above amounts to 5.6 million m³ a year. Treatment efficiencies in the major cities in terms of BOD removal vary between 93 per cent and 97 per cent in biological treatment installations (Vilnius, Šiauliai, Panevėžys, Alytus, Marijampolė), and reach 42 per cent at the

Figure 7.3: Waste-water treatment structure*, 1997

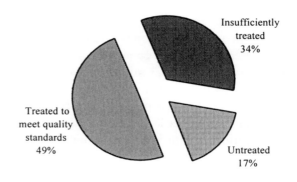

Source: Ministry of the Environment.

Note:
* Excluding water meeting quality standards without treatment.

Table 7.4: Discharge of waste water into surface waters, 1992–1997

Million m³/year

	1992	1993	1994	1995	1996	1997	% change 1992-1997
Total amount discharged standards	3 537	3 338	3 779	4 493	5 598	4 709	33.1
without treatment	3 170	2 993	3 443	4 189	5 346	4 476	41.2
Waste waters including:	367	345	336	304	252	233	-36.5
- *Untreated*	*70*	*78*	*68*	*54*	*42*	*39*	*-44.3*
- *Insufficiently treated*	*201*	*178*	*183*	*172*	*110*	*79*	*-60.7*
- *Treated to meet quality sta*	*96*	*89*	*85*	*78*	*100*	*115*	*19.8*

Source: Ministry of the Environment.

Table 7.5: Pollutants discharged into surface water, 1992-1997

t/year

	1992	1993	1994	1995	1996	1997
BOD_5	31 900	27 920	34 500	21 000	16 600 a/	15 000 a/
Suspended solids	36 900	30 430	38 500	26 000	17 900	15 000
Oil products	340	270	280	220	160	150
Phosphorus	1 438	1 535	1 502	1 184	960	879
Nitrogen	10 601	10 209	10 773	7 663	6 446	5 401
Iron (Fe)	173	101	166	72	30	10
Copper (Cu)	16	18	9	7	5	5
Zinc (Zn)	50	53	51	33	29	27
Nickel (Ni)	11	9	9	6	4	5
Chrome (Cr)	22	13	12	9	7	5
Manganese (Mn)	8	3	9	4	3	4
Lead (Pb)	2	1	3	0	0	0

Source: Ministry of the Environment.

a/ BOD_7.

Figure 7.4: Water quality classification of Lithuania's rivers, 1996

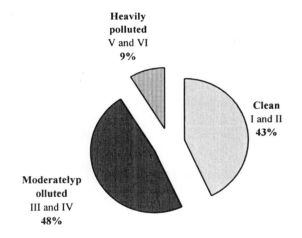

Source: Ministry of the Environment.

Klaipėda mechanical treatment plant. Between 62 per cent and 80 per cent of nitrogen and 37 per cent and 80 per cent of phosphorus are removed. Sludge management is hampered by a lack of dewatering technology, while its disposal and reuse of heavy metals. Most sludge is dried in land-intensive facilities that are not lined or monitored and are then disposed of in landfills or abandoned gravel pits. This practice presents a major risk of groundwater contamination.

Surface water quality

Surface water quality is monitored in 47 rivers and 9 lakes, at the points which most characteristically reflect the impact of municipal, industrial and agricultural activities. The set of parameters, about 70, is quite extensive. Natural background concentrations are observed in the 6 smaller rivers least affected by economic activity. Forty-three per cent of rivers are classified as being clean (Figure 7.4), 48 per cent as moderately polluted and 9 per cent as heavily polluted. In the heavily polluted rivers – Sidabra, Kulpė, Obelė, Tatula, Laukupė – concentrations of organic matters exceed standard limits 10-fold, those of nitrates 13-fold and ammonium and phosphates up to 26-fold.

The water quality of the main river Nemunas varies along the course of the river. In the uppermost reaches it is excellent or good, downstream from the main cities it is polluted. There have been no significant changes in recent years in the water quality of the Nemunas. It is estimated that one third of organic and total nitrogen loads of the river are discharged from sources in the Kaliningrad region. The poorest water quality is observed in the Šiauliai region. The main problem in Lithuania's rivers is heavy loading of organic matter. In many cases phosphorus and nitrogen concentrations as well as hygiene parameters indicate serious pollution.

The only significant trend in the water quality of Lithuania's lakes is the increase in nitrate concentration in almost all the lakes and increasing BOD in two lakes. Lithuania's lakes have a high buffer capacity and thus acidification is not a problem. Assessing the likely future development of the lakes is difficult, since no information is available on the activities affecting them.

Groundwater and drinking-water quality

Groundwater monitoring consists of three programmes:

- national groundwater monitoring
- monitoring of wells
- monitoring of groundwater in contaminated sites.

In 1996 there were 26 main and 14 subsidiary monitoring stations in the national monitoring network. Groundwater pollution has been detected in almost one third of the country. Groundwater is the main source of drinking water in Lithuania. Particularly in rural areas and on the outskirts of cities, where piped water supply is less common, drinking-water supply is facing serious problems. Today 300 000 dug wells produce drinking water from shallow wells for 1 million Lithuanians. Due to intensive land use, shallow groundwaters are heavily polluted in large areas. It has been

estimated for 1996 that 60 per cent of the dug wells did not meet hygiene standards and 37.5 per cent were polluted by nitrates (Figures 7.5 and 7.6). Chloride and sulphate levels often exceed the drinking-water standards as well. In some localities, such as the site of Jonava 'Achema' company, or at oil storage facilities as well as former Soviet military sites, groundwater is heavily polluted by nitrates and oil products. Groundwater in the Karst region in northern Lithuania contains increased amounts of nitrogen compounds and organic matter.

The main problem with the piped water supply is the high content of iron caused by natural enrichment of groundwater, and also by the widespread presence of ferrous pipes in the water supply networks, which are not protected against corrosion. In approximately 90 per cent of water abstracted from underground sources, iron concentrations are above 0.3 mg/l. Natural iron is being eliminated from abstracted groundwater in 32 treatment plants, which treat about 40 per cent of the groundwater that should be treated for iron. Manganese is found at concentrations of more than 0.1 mg/l in approximately 26 per cent of the drinking-water supply.

Another problem is fluorides, which may be locally present in drinking water. In north-western and west Lithuania high concentrations of fluorides (4-5 mg/l, sometimes up to 7 mg/l, compared to the standard for drinking water of 0.7-1.2 mg/l) are common and fluorosis has been diagnosed. On the

Figure 7.5: Water samples not meeting microbiological standards, 1986-1996

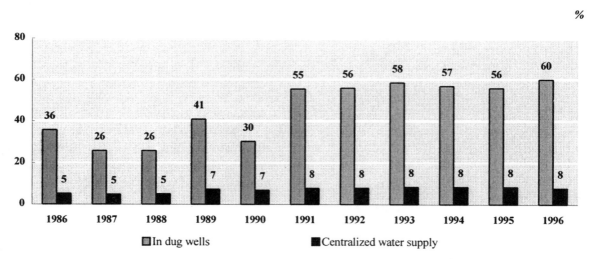

Source: Ministry of the Environment.

Figure 7.6: Water samples not meeting the nitrate standard*, 1986-1996

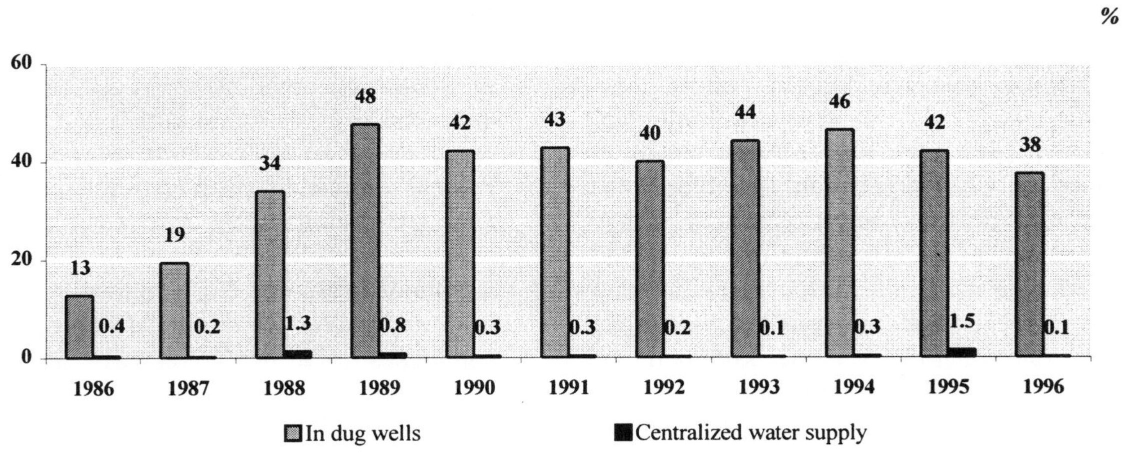

%

In dug wells   Centralized water supply

Source: Ministry of the Environment.
* Standard: 50 mg/l NO$_3$

other hand, in eastern and southern parts of the country, drinking water has low fluoride concentrations, paralleled by a high occurrence of caries among children.

Coastal and marine water quality

Currently, marine water quality is monitored at 32 monitoring stations, four of which belong to the international Baltic Sea monitoring programme. Three of the stations - Būtingė, Melnragė and Nida - cover the heavily polluted sea areas. The Kuršių Lagoon is monitored at 13 stations. The estimation of the riverine loads to the Kuršių Lagoon and to the Baltic Sea is based on daily measurements of the water level and monthly sampling of water quality. The loads are calculated using linear interpolation between sampling days.

Most of the river waters enter the Baltic Sea via the Kuršių Lagoon. It has been estimated that about 80 per cent of the Lagoon and 45 per cent of the Lithuanian coastal waters are heavily polluted with nitrogen and phosphorus. During the 1984-1996 period nitrate and phosphorus concentrations in the central parts of the Lagoon rose sharply. Phytoplankton biomasses have increased as well, and today blue-green algal blooms last from June-July to October-November. Several potentially toxic algal species are common. Comparison of historical data shows that since the 1920s the abundance of today's dominant blue-green alga has increased more than one order of magnitude and

the Lagoon can be classified as highly eutrophic. Even fish kills are common in early summer, coinciding with the maximum phytoplankton biomasses.

There was no clear trend in nitrate or phosphate concentration in the coastal waters during the 1992-1996 observation period. The Lithuanian coast is quite open and thus the water exchange between the coast and the open sea is efficient. However, during the hot summer days the beaches of Klaipėda, Giruliai and Palanga often fail to meet sanitary standards.

Non-point sources of pollution

Almost half the Lithuanian territory is used for agricultural purposes: 38 per cent is arable land and 11.5 per cent pasture. Therefore, agriculture has a strong impact on water quality in rivers, lakes and coastal waters. Lithuania has reported to HELCOM that 50 per cent of the total riverine N load and 22 per cent of the total riverine P load originate from non-point pollution sources.

The pollutants discharged from non-point pollution sources into bodies of water are difficult to calculate and treat. There are different pollution sources such as storage sites for manure, oil products, agrochemicals, toxic solutions, land affected by erosion, increased effluent from drained lands. The main reasons for water contamination are inadequate agricultural practices that do not meet ecological requirements and poor sanitary practices.

The run-off results from the application and storage of natural and chemical fertilizers, and from large-scale, intensive pig and poultry units located throughout the country. Pollution of surface and groundwater resources with fertilizers is caused by (a) poor application technology, (b) overfertilization in some areas, (c) poor tillage practices that fail to incorporate fertilizer into the soil, and (d) open storage facilities. Plants take up only 15-25 per cent of phosphorous fertilizer. The fertilization rate in 1995 was 62 kilograms of nitrogen, 32 kilograms of phosphorus, and 56 kilograms of potassium per hectare, of which an estimated 20 to 30 per cent do not penetrate the soil, but are washed away.

According to the Ministry of Agriculture, a tenfold increase in fertilizer prices and a sixfold increase in pesticide prices since 1991, have contributed to a massive decline in their use - together with the economic depression. From 1990 to 1994, agricultural production declined by almost 50 per cent and the use of fertilizers by as much as 80 per cent. This was not, however, reflected in the river water quality until 1994 (Figure 7.7). There are, of course, several reasons for this time lag. The nitrogen storage in the soil was high enough to

enable the leaching to continue after inputs had dramatically decreased. Hydrological conditions also vary strongly from year to year and affect the leaching of nitrogen. It is expected that when the agricultural process stabilizes, fertilizer and pesticide consumption will once again increase. The Ministry of Agriculture predicts that, as a result of privatization, small farmers will increase the use of natural fertilizers and will use better fertilizer techniques.

A major national environmental management problem results from the 24 large pig-breeding complexes each producing between 12 000 and 54 000 pigs per year (in 1997, 520 000 pigs were raised), and 5 large poultry farms, all of which cause severe local pollution of surface and groundwater. Meat being a major export commodity for Lithuania, these large-scale farms will in all likelihood remain viable.

Marine transport

In addition to (municipal and industrial) waste water and agricultural pollution, marine transport also creates risks for the Baltic Sea environment. Klaipėda is Lithuania's only seaport and the fifth biggest port in the Baltic Sea region in terms of cargo trans-shipment volumes. Container traffic is increasing steadily. A project for a new container

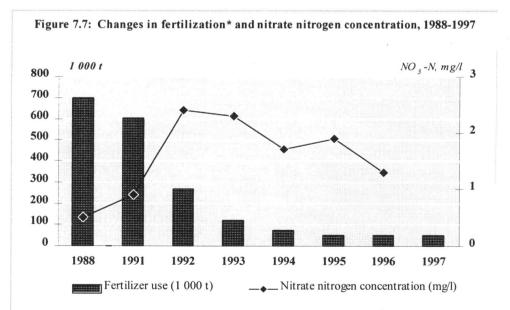

Figure 7.7: Changes in fertilization* and nitrate nitrogen concentration, 1988-1997

Fertilizer use (1 000 t)   Nitrate nitrogen concentration (mg/l)

Source: Ministry of the Environment.

Note:

* In terms of pure ingredients.

terminal is already being carried out. The new oil terminal to be constructed in Būtingė will strongly increase oil transport, since the envisaged capacity of the terminal is about 20 million tonnes of oil products.

Increasing traffic implies an increasing risk of accidents and oil spills. Accidents were already common in the past, the most serious one being the breaking apart of a British tanker outside Klaipėda in 1981. In general, the dramatic increase in activity on the Lithuanian coast calls for proper risk management plans and facilities for oil pollution prevention.

7.3 Objectives and implementation of water policy

Legislation

Water management in Lithuania is mainly based on the Law on Environmental Protection (1992), together with the Law on Water (1997), the Law on the Protection of the Marine Environment (1997) and numerous other legal instruments. Implementing regulations have also been adopted. The most important are Special Conditions for Use of Land and Forest (1992, amended in 1995), Waste-water Pollution Standards (1996), Methodology for Estimation of Environmental Water Flow (1997), and the Regulation on Obtaining Permits for the Use of Natural Resources and Discharges of Effluents into the Environment (1995). Currently, the first priority in preparing legislation is harmonizing existing laws with EU legislation, as well as preparing legal instruments to implement the Law on Water and the Law on the Protection of the Marine Environment.

Policy objectives and action programme

The Lithuanian Environmental Strategy (1996) and the corresponding action programme for implementation provide the basis for a new approach towards more efficient water resource use and water management. The governmental goals for water protection are to:

- reduce surface water pollution from municipal waste water;
- reduce pollution with industrial and agro-industrial waste water;
- reduce groundwater pollution;

- reduce non-point source pollution of bodies of water;
- reduce pollution with surface (storm water) run-off;
- reduce the pollution load flowing into the sea;
- prevent sea water pollution from oil product transport;
- reduce the polluted water inflow from other countries.

The objectives of water resources protection are to:

- protect freshwater resources from overuse while extracting water from water intake sites;
- prevent further changes in the natural hydrographic network structure.

The corresponding priorities in water management are:

- waste-water treatment and reduction in discharges;
- rational use of natural and water resources.

Domestic waste water from cities, with the exception of Panevėžys, is discharged into rivers after being only mechanically treated or after receiving insufficient biological treatment. In Kaunas, waste water is discharged totally untreated. Waste water in Vilnius, Klaipda, Šiauliai and Palanga is already biologically treated. Therefore, it is expected that when the waste-water treatment plant in Kaunas starts operating, only 1 per cent of waste water will remain untreated. The construction of waste-water treatment facilities remains a top priority for investments, particularly for funds from the State budget, and loans and subsidies received by the State. In parallel, it is necessary to implement codes of good agricultural practices to reduce non-point source pollution of soil and water and introduce the polluter/consumer-pays principle, and develop the necessary water protection laws.

The environmental Action Programme, approved by the Government on 5 August 1996, lists numerous actions for water pollution prevention. Several technical actions aim at improving waste-water treatment in municipalities and rural areas. Training the technical staff of treatment plants is also part of the Programme. The time schedule for

Table 7.6:   Environmental Action Programme in water management

Develop personnel training and certification programmes for waste water treatment facilities …	1996
Reducing Baltic Sea pollution and contaminated water influx from other countries	
Prepare a draft government decree to improve the system of combating accidents at sea and sea-	1997
Work out a sea water protection programme for the transport of orimulsion and oil products …	997-199
Conclude bilateral or multilateral inter-State agreements for the use and protection of transbound	996-200
Reducing groundwater contamination, improving drinking-water quality	
Develop drinking-water standard ………………………………………………………………	996-199
Establish water intake sites and sanitary zones (lines) in cities according to the Ministry of Healt	996-200
Build drinking-water preparation facilities in central water intake sites (Klaipeda, ☐iauliai, Joni☐	ince 1996

Source: National Environmental Strategy, Ministry of the Environment.

its implementation is very challenging. It is strongly dependent on funding, particularly the construction of waste-water treatment plants in big cities.   The part of the Action Programme concerning water management is summarized in Table 7.6.   In 1992 Lithuania acceded to the Helsinki Convention on the Protection of the Marine Environment of the Baltic Sea Area. According to the 1998 Ministerial Declaration, Lithuania should reduce pollution discharges to the Baltic Sea by 50 per cent, including organic and biogenic substances as well as heavy metals.

Institutional aspects

The Ministry of the Environment and the Ministry of Health are involved in water management in Lithuania. There are 8 Environmental Protection Departments, which issue water permits. Fifty-six regional agencies and city inspectorates within the Environmental Protection Departments are responsible for the use and protection of water resources locally. Institutions such as the Hydrometeorological Service of Lithuania (responsible for estimations of water quantity), the Joint Research Centre (responsible for monitoring water quality), the Marine Research Centre (responsible for monitoring the Kuršių Lagoon and the coastal waters), and the Hydrographic Network Service (State control of technical status of dams, reservoirs and other hydrotechnical constructions) are subordinated to the Ministry of the Environment. The State Centre for Public Health and the State Hygiene Inspectorate, which are subordinated to the Ministry of Health, are responsible for monitoring compliance with

drinking-water standards and controlling recreational bodies of water. The Lithuanian Geological Service, subordinated to the Ministry of the Environment, is responsible for groundwater resources.

Instruments and measures

Standards for basic physical and hydrochemical values, for nutrients and metal content in surface and sea water, for hazardous pollutants (metals, organic compounds and their halogenic derivatives) content in water sediments will be reviewed shortly, with a view to adapting them to the EU environmental standards. Currently, the implementation of the Helsinki Commission's recommendations regarding the technological processes of paper, chemical, leather, textile, oil-refining, food, and metal-finishing industries is being considered.

There are three important economic instruments in use in water management: natural resource taxes, pollution charges, and subsidies for the construction of waste-water plants. Taxes on the use of water resources have been in effect since 1992. Of late, the use of water resources has declined to levels below permissible limits.

The environmental fund for investments is necessary to provide incentives for waste and pollution minimization and to raise additional funds. These are aimed at paying for resource-saving or industrial pollution minimization projects. Once the project is on stream, its revenues will be used to repay loans to the environmental fund for investments, thus revolving and increasing it.

In connection with the development plans for Klaipėda port and the Būtingė oil terminal, several studies have been carried out on the environmental management of the marine transport sector. The Būtingė oil terminal project also included an EIA and plans for its proper environmental management.

The most significant management project regarding the marine transport sector was the preparation of the National Oil Spill Contingency Plan. The Plan (Phase 1) was finalized in 1995. The proposal for its implementation (Phase II) includes the description of the administrative structure and responsibilities of different authorities as well as operational activities (see also Chapter 5).

It is foreseen that biological waste-water treatment plants will be constructed in Alytus, Utena, Vilkaviškis. Biological treatment plants will be built in Ukmergė and Širvintai, and the construction of a plant in Anykščiai will be finished in 1998. The capacity of all the above-mentioned plants will be 28.5 million m^3/year. Nitrogen and phosphorus will be removed from the discharge in all plants in the above-mentioned towns (except Širvintai). In addition, it is foreseen that nitrogen and phosphorus will be removed from the discharge in new treatment plants in Klaipėda, Šiauliai and Palanga. The plan is also to modernize the biological treatment technology in Vilnius so

that it will remove nitrogen and phosphorus. Experimental plants applying natural treatment methods are going to be built in villages, several of them with foreign assistance (Denmark, Switzerland). According to data from the Statistics Department, 105 cities and towns have a centralized sewage pipe system or separate sewage networks.

Most environmental expenditures go to water protection, i.e. waste-water treatment plants. The main sources of finance are the State budget, foreign loans and grants. In 1996, 56.6 million Litas were allocated from the State budget for waste-water treatment plant investments (Table 7.7) and 29 million Litas for current expenditure (Figure 7.8). SNPF allocated 0.27 million Litas and 2.6 million Litas, respectively. The Municipal Environment Funds allocated 10.5 million Litas for investments and 16.2 million Litas for current expenditure.

In addition to national funding, foreign loans and grants provide an important source of financing. So far committed foreign grants for water protection total about US$ 31 million and loans almost US$ 62 million. Investment expenditures for water pollution control for the period from 1993 to 1996 are described in Table 7.7.

7.4 Conclusions and recommendations

Lithuania has succeeded in preparing the ground for modern water management in all respects, and has also in many ways improved the aquatic

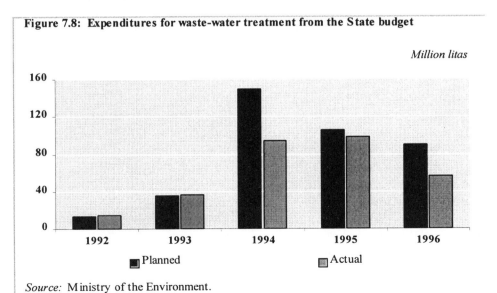

Figure 7.8: Expenditures for waste-water treatment from the State budget

Million litas

Legend: ■ Planned ▨ Actual

Source: Ministry of the Environment.

		1993	1994	1995	1996
Total		**68 186**	**189 264**	**160 796**	**143 027**
State budget		36 250	94 600	98 500	56 600
Municipal budget		-	-	700	1 979
State Nature Protection Fund		-	298	351	265
Municipal Environmental Protection Funds		-	5 905	5 024	10 500
Enterprises' own funds		31,936 a/	88,461 a/	56,221	73,683

Thousand litas

Sources: Ministry of the Environment; Department of Statistics.

a/ Data do not include expenditures for integrated technologies.

environment. It appears that the need for further improvements is well understood, and that most of the measures that are now required are well known. For example, basic environmental protection requirements for different sectors, as well as environmental protection policy enforcement measures, should be incorporated into the Law on Environmental Protection at its next revision.

The legal and regulatory framework for water resources management exists, but important laws still remain to be passed, particularly for municipal water-supply and sewerage services and for land uses that have major consequences for water resources management. It is not possible to develop and adopt all needed legal acts at the same time. The recent adoption of the new Law on Water was a big step forward. Now, implementation becomes the priority – i.e. the development, adoption and application of new legal instruments, such as new standards. These standards need and will be harmonized with applicable EU practices.

Recommendation 7.1:
The necessary legislation required after the recent adoption of the new Water Law should be a priority for future work on legal instruments. The introduction of integrated water management for individual river basins should be considered, including institutional changes in line with the new water management policy of the European Union.

As elsewhere, a mix of regulatory and economic instruments is progressively being implemented in Lithuania's water management. In the near future, the developmental focus should be on new economic instruments to encourage pollution and

waste minimization and prevention and the preservation of water resources. Such instruments would make management more flexible. The instruments should be consistent with the polluter-pays principle. They should promote the introduction of cleaner production.

Recommendation 7.2:
The tool kit of water management should be extended primarily with economic instruments. Appropriate taxation should be developed in particular for water resource management.

The main area of concern for water management is water pollution. Problems with water use continue to exist, in terms of both pollution and resource management. The Ministry of the Environment imposes a water tax to make industries and households reduce their water use. With regard to industrial water users, the wide introduction of closed circuits should be monitored, as it could give indications as to the adequacy of the tax rate level. At the municipal level, programmes aimed at saving water resources and reducing losses as well as using resources rationally and preventing their exhaustion (and contamination) should be developed and implemented. Finally, decreasing public water supply probably means that, from an economic point of view, there is no need to maintain all well-fields.

Recommendation 7.3:
The full-fledged introduction of a modern water use policy requires stronger municipal programmes and capabilities. The economics of individual well-fields should be reassessed from the point of view of expected developments in water supply and use.

Water quality has improved to some extent during recent years, mainly because of the construction of treatment plants. Now that the economy is in recession and investments in some municipal and industrial waste-water treatment are increasing, the challenge for Lithuania is to keep improving its water environment, effectively using the available diversified tools such as technical, command-and-control, and economic instruments. When determining new needs for water quality management, the economic aspects need to be analysed. The experiences with local networks should be taken into account in such analysis, which should therefore preferably be organized in a decentralized framework.

The completion or modernization of a large number of municipal waste-water treatment plants and industrial pre-treatment facilities will increase the scale of the sludge problem in the future. As proper land markets develop following restitution and privatization, land-intensive solutions will need to be replaced by modern sludge management technology.

Recommendation 7.4:
The introduction of modern sludge treatment technology should be expected to become a priority for investments in the foreseeable future. Establishing quality standards for industrial waste water might promote the introduction of pretreatment of industrial effluent waters before they enter municipal sewage systems.

Special protection zones have reduced the impact of agriculture on water pollution. However, many rivers and lakes have no such zones or have only partially established ones. The establishment of private farming will help to reduce pollution from cattle farms and arable lands. However, the problem of waste water from farmsteads will become acute. During the process of privatization and land reform, there is the possibility of constructing small waste-water treatment plants for small farms and private businesses. Lithuanian engineers, with the assistance of foreign colleagues, are working on projects to develop such treatment plants.

Baltic Sea pollution from Lithuanian agriculture has eased recently. However, this improvement does not stem from deliberate environmental measures, but from the economic recession. Therefore, it can be expected that in the near future, as agricultural production increases, agricultural impacts on watercourses will also increase. The above issues can be managed successfully only through close cooperation between the Ministries of the Environment and of Agriculture.

Recommendation 7.5:
The Ministry of the Environment and the Ministry of Agriculture should seek institutional solutions and set up adequate routines for cooperation to manage environmental issues of common concern.

Eutrophication and oil spills are the main problems of Lithuania's coastal waters. The development of a national contingency plan for oil spills is a clear achievement in this regard. It is now crucial (1) to implement the plans for the construction of biological waste-water treatment plants, first in the main cities and industrial plants and later on in smaller municipalities, (2) to implement the HELCOM recommendations regarding agricultural activities, and (3) to implement the National Oil Spill Contingency Plan.

Recommendation 7.6:
Efficient improvement in water quality along the Baltic Sea coast requires the swift implementation of the relevant HELCOM recommendations and of the existing National Oil Spill Contingency Plan.

As neither point nor non-point sources of pollution are adequately monitored, their pollution cannot be reduced. To be able to participate fully in the cooperation within HELCOM, special attention should be paid to the harmonization and quality assurance of the whole monitoring process (design, sampling, laboratory analyses, data storage, data analysis, reporting and dissemination of results). This recommendation covers the monitoring of both natural waters and waste water.

There are many data on Lithuania's water resources, their quantity as well as their quality. These data are, however, only partly used. Strong efforts should be put into developing data banks as well as into reporting and particularly into a thorough analysis of cause-effect relationships in order to be able to make full use of the data in decision-making. The publication of results in international journals should be promoted.

Recommendation 7.7:
Existing monitoring should be improved in accordance with HELCOM practices, as should the quality of monitoring data and of other environmental data. Their accessibility and their actual use in analysis should be improved by all possible means.

Chapter 8

NATURE MANAGEMENT

8.1 Present state of nature

Landscape and ecosystems diversity

Lithuania occupies Boreal and Temperate Continental biogeographic regions, where mixed forests and coniferous forests prevail. Lithuania belongs to three biogeographic provinces: the Eastern Baltic, the Central European and the Baltic Sea Marine Province.

Its ecosystems include natural/semi-natural (such as forests, wetlands, marshes, meadows, coastal, sandy, aquatic and marine systems) and anthropogenic (such as rural and urban) types.

The forest cover has increased over the past 50 years, from 21.8 per cent in 1937 to about 30 per cent in 1997. However, it is lower than in Latvia (41.7 per cent), Estonia (39.2 per cent) or Belarus (34.6 per cent). The dominant tree species are pine (37.6 per cent) and spruce (24.0 per cent). The other tree species are deciduous, predominantly birch (19.5 per cent). Mixed stands occupy 56 per cent and relatively homogeneous stands 44 per cent of forests. The annual average increment is 6.3 m^3 per hectare. Mature forests account for only 9.6 per cent of all forests.

Most of Lithuania's forest is in State hands (Figure 8.1). At present, private forests make up about 5 per cent (91 400 ha). It is estimated that, by the end of the land reform, private forests will cover one third to one half. The forests fall into four management categories (Figure 8.2).

Six to seven per cent of Lithuania's land area is covered by marshes. Most are in the west, the south and the east. Some 77 per cent of wetlands have been drained for agricultural purposes (incl. landscape management and land reclamation). By January 1993, 2.4 million ha of land had a functioning drainage system. It is estimated that over the past 30 years about 70 per cent of wetlands have been lost. According to the National Environmental Strategy, 35 000 ha of land is damaged, 20 000 ha of this are peatbogs.

Figure 8.1: Forest area by type of ownership, 1996

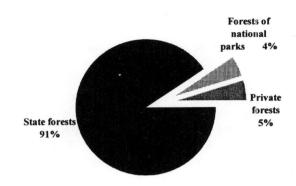

Source: Natural resources and environmental protection, 1996, Department of Statistics.

Figure 8.2: Forest area by category of forests, 1996

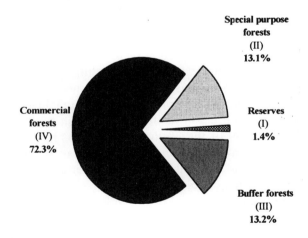

Source: Natural resources and environmental protection, 1996, Department of Statistics.

The phytocenotic diversity of meadow communities is high, yet in the past 30 years a fast decrease in the natural meadow ecosystem has been observed. For example, in 1956 meadows covered 19.6 per cent of the country's territory; in 1980 the coverage had diminished to 6.5 per cent. Due to the collapse of the large-scale collective farms of the Soviet era, pastures and meadows are currently set aside and overgrown with shrubs and coppice.

The Baltic Sea <u>coast</u> of Lithuania (98 km long) is an area for recreation, but also an important habitat for migrating water-birds, the Nemunas River Delta and the Curonian Lagoon in particular. The history of observation and ringing of migrating birds dates back to 1929, when the Ventės Ragas Ornithological Station was founded. About 167 bird species have been recorded on migration over Lithuania, 82 species on spring and 62 species on autumn migration. About 30 wintering seabird species are regularly recorded. Two wintering sites are of international importance: Palanga and Curonian spit. <u>Sand ecosystems</u> are confined to coastal and riverine areas. They are not very diverse.

Lithuania has a dense network of rivers. In all, there are more than 29 000 watercourses over 250 m long. There are 758 rivers more than 10 km long, 18 of which are longer than 100 km. There are 2833 lakes which exceed 0.5 ha. The majority of lakes are located in Aukštaičiiai Upland. All four development types of lakes (meso-, eu-, hyper- and dystrophic) are present. Meso- and eutrophic lakes, however, prevail.

According to the Biodiversity Conservation Strategy and Action Plan, <u>agrarian ecosystems</u> occupy some 53.7 per cent of Lithuania. They are the poorest from a biodiversity point of view. <u>Urban ecosystems</u> occupy nearly 5 per cent of the country's territory, and are expanding. Despite the high population density, the high concentration of industry and heavy traffic and the high levels of pollution, the urban landscape is rich in biological diversity. 39 of the 70 mammal species have been recorded in urban landscapes. The urban parks provide a suitable habitat for a number of local and alien species of trees and vascular plants. Species have been inventoried in 239 urban parks. <u>Ruderal communities</u> emerge on wasteland, dumping sites and fallow land. 200 plant species have been recorded in ruderal plant communities.

The Plant Communities Red Data Book (1992) includes 57 rare association communities grouped into five categories (from 0 to 4). Thirty rare communities (i.e. 55 per cent) occupy aquatic ecosystems (wetland or water body). Thirteen rare communities (or 24 per cent) occupy meadows. Six rare communities (i.e. 11 per cent) are forests. Rare sand and ruderal ecosystems (5) comprise about 9 per cent of listed ecosystems in the Plant Communities Red Data Book of Lithuania.

Species diversity

Due to the ecotonial character of Lithuania's biogeographic provinces, there is a rich variety of species: 1 796 species of plants, 6 050 species of fungi, 70 species of mammals (Figure 8.3), 321 species of birds, 7 species of reptiles, 13 species of amphibians, 96 species of fish and 3 species of Cyclostomata, some 15 000 species of insects, some 200 species of arachnids, some 170 species of molluscs, 300 species of Rotatoria, and 6 species of Porifera.

Figure 8.3: Composition of mammal species

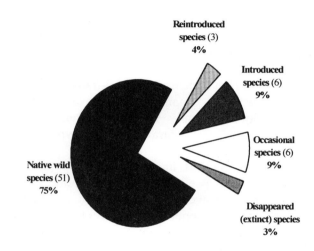

Source: Ministry of the Environment.

There are 1 450 species of higher plants (1992). Over 20 000 species of invertebrates have been recorded. There are 63 terrestrial and 5 marine mammal species. This century 50 new species have been added to the list, most of them accidental visitors. The terrestrial mammal fauna largely comprises species that live in mixed forests, a few species are typical of coniferous and broad-leaved forests. The Red Data Book of Species (1992) includes 501 species: 210 plants, 210 animals and 81 fungi species.

The largest diversity of mammal species is recorded in the forests. The second most important habitats in terms of mammal variety are the wetlands, shrubbery, natural meadows and pastures and bodies of water. Areas diverse in geo-morphological and hydrographic composition, such as afforested sandy plains and hilly moraine uplands, provide far more favourable habitats for mammals than the clay plains, which form the majority of fertile agricultural land.

During this century, 13 mammal, 1 bird and about 15 fish species have been introduced or re-introduced. Whereas the beaver, the European bison and the red deer have been successfully re-introduced and the raccoon dog and the Canadian mink have become common species, the fallow deer, the European muflon and the pheasant cannot adapt to the harsh winters.

Protected areas

Lithuania has achieved outstanding results in landscape protection: 11.2 per cent of its total territory is protected. Its five national parks, 30 regional parks, 6 strict reserves and 290 reserves of different types represent the most valuable landscapes (both natural and cultural) and natural ecosystems.

The Law on Protected Areas (1993) distinguishes four categories, which are not identical to but are compatible with IUCN (1994) categories:

1. Conservation areas (including strict nature and culture reserves, managed reserves, protected landscape objects/nature or cultural monuments);
2. Preservation areas (i.e. buffer zones for other protected areas and objects/protected bodies of water, roads);
3. Recuperation area (including natural resource restoration areas);
4. Integrated protected areas (including national and regional parks, biosphere reserves and polygons).

There is one historical national park (Trakai), which is manageg by the Ministry of Culture. The park's primary objective is to protect the cultural heritage, whereas the four other parks (under the Ministry of the Environment) aim at conserving nature and landscapes. Among the 30 regional parks, there is also one historical park (Dieveniškės). In addition to four strict nature reserves, there are two strict cultural reserves (Kernavė, Vilniaus Pilys), established in 1989 and in 1997, respectively. Other protected areas comprise reserves: geological (10), geomorphological (46), hydrographical (35), pedological (12), botanical (38), telmological (27), teriological (1), ornithological (6), herpetological (2), ichtyological (11), entomological (20), botanical-zoological (20), landscape (61), cartographical (1) and cultural (10) reserves established by the State authorities. There are also

62 reserves established by local authorities. 700 single objects of natural heritage also enjoy protection.

Table 8.1: Specially protected areas*, 1997

	Number	Area (1 000 ha)	Share of total area %
Integrated areas:			
- National parks (IUCN II)	5	138.1	2.1
- Regional parks (IUCN V)	30	380.9	5.8
Conservation areas:			
- Strict nature reserves (IUCN I)	4	23.5	0.3
- Strict culture reserves	2	0.2	0.1
- Reserves (IUCN IV)	290	176.4	2.7
- Landscape objects	688	..	..
Total of above listed data	*1,113*	*734.0*	*11.2*

Source: Statistical Yearbook of Lithuania, 1997.
Natural resources and environmental protection, 1996, Department of Statistics.

Note:
* There are 9 preservation areas that are not included in the total.

By October 1997 no natural resource restoration areas had been identified. However, according to the national Biodiversity Conservation Strategy and Action Plan, a system of protected resource sites in the south-east is being prepared.

Five sites (4 strict nature reserves and the Nemunas River Delta Regional Park) are on the Ramsar list. According to the Biodiversity Strategy, another nine sites have been identified and will be proposed to the Ramsar Convention's Bureau for designation. These areas are: the Baltic Sea coastal area at Palanga, the north-western part of the Curonian Lagoon, the Lakes of Kretuonas, Žaltytis, Meteliai Regional Park, Reiškiai Wilderness Area, Aukštasis Wilderness Area, and the marshes of Kanis and Beržalotas.

8.2 Pressures on nature

Agriculture

There are 400 000 private household plots of an average size of 2.1 ha, and 135 000 private farms, which average 8.4 hectares. Private farms account for 34 per cent of agricultural farms. On the one hand, small farms and the fragmented use of land favour less intensive land use. On the other, it makes it difficult to control the large variety of operations. Approximately one third of Lithuania's agricultural land (1.2 million ha) is farmed by agricultural companies (2 000 entities in early 1997). Changes in land ownership have a direct and indirect impact on the use of land and natural resources. Total farmland is shrinking by 14 400 ha a year.

Human activities, such as changes in land use and management, especially transforming forests, shrubbery or wetlands into agricultural land so that typical habitats disappear, are having a detrimental impact on ecosystems. For example, as land is drained and shrubs are cut, waders and passerines disappear. Felling trees and cutting back large forests directly affect the habitats of large birds of prey and the black stork.

The implementation of land drainage schemes has resulted in the loss of habitats. The natural environment has been affected by the construction of irrigation systems and dams on many rivers. However, during the transition, irrigation systems (still largely State-owned) have become redundant and are abandoned.

14-15 per cent of Lithuania's arable land is subject to erosion, resulting in a loss of valuable topsoil and productivity. The average detachment of soil particles from agriculture land is approximately 1.8-2.5 tonnes per ha. More pronounced erosion is occurring in west Lithuania: 12-15 tonnes/ha.

Aerial spraying with pesticides has been banned. The use of herbicides and pesticides has fallen sharply, as has that of mineral fertilizers (e.g. by 50 per cent in the period of 1992-1995), due to their high cost.

Organic farming is spreading slowly. The association of organic farming "Gaja" was founded in 1990. In 1994, there were two farms whose production was classified as organic. However, the movement is getting increasing support among the 200 members of "Gaja".

North Lithuania's hydro-geology is characterized by karst. The area covers 500 to 1 000 km^2 of land. Together with the area in Latvia, the karst region may cover 3 500 km^2. A sustainable agricultural programme for the North-Lithuanian Karst Region was approved by the Government and commenced in 1993. The 'Tatula' Fund was set up to (1) provide interest-free credits to farmers, agricultural partnerships, food-processing companies and others that work to make their farming sustainable and organic, and (2) create a market infrastructure for these products.

Forestry

The composition of forest tree species has remained stable: coniferous species such as pine and spruce account for some 60 per cent and deciduous tree species such as birch, black alder, grey alder and aspen for some 40 per cent. However, pine stands have shrunk over the past 30 years. This has been partly explained by the increase in the elk population, coupled with the low planting acreage (e.g. 1 194 ha in 1986-1988 instead of the 5 500-6 000 ha necessary to replace felled stands).

The Forest Monitoring Programme has shown that the proportion of damaged trees has increased over the past years. The data published jointly by UNECE and the European Commission illustrate the relatively poor state of Lithuania's trees (Table 8.2).

Table 8.2: Health of trees in Lithuania and
some neighbouring countries, 1996

	Defoliation class			
	0	1	2	3 + 4
	(healthy)	(slightly damaged)	(moderately damaged)	(severely damaged)
Lithuania	29.1	58.3	9.7	2.9
Belarus	12.9	47.4	36.9	2.8
Denmark	40.0	32.0	23.9	4.1
Estonia	50.4	35.4	13.3	0.9
Latvia	27.3	51.5	20.3	0.9
Poland	10.4	49.9	37.3	2.4

Source: Forest Condition in Europe, United Nations Economic Commission for Europe and European Commission, 1997, Technical Report, prepared by Federal Research Centre for Forestry and Forest Products, 1997, Annex II-3.

Tree felling has risen sharply in the past few years to 4 - 6 million m^3 a year, compared to previous annual totals of 2.7 - 3.3 million m^3. It is expected that 5.1 million m^3 a year will be harvested until 2003. 27 per cent of forest land is subject to conservation restrictions, e.g. aiming at conserving biodiversity. Commercial forests make up some 73 per cent of forests.

Hunting and fishing

In 1997, 18 animal species and 27 bird species were allowed to be hunted. Lithuania has a long history of keeping records of hunted species. The data go back to 1934 (Table 8.3). Hunting grounds occupy 5.6 million hectares of land. There are 29 000

Table 8.3: Population of the main hunted species, 1934-1997

Number

	1934	1943	1955	1965	1975	1985	1995	1996	1997
Elk	201	267	389	3 800	8 850	7 800	2 850	2 936	3 830
Red Deer	18	239	277	830	3 650	10 900	13 800	13 945	15 000
Roe	13 930	22 510	15 400	63 000	54 200	41 200	41 000	37 647	36 300
Muflon	-	-	-	-	-	145	100	59	..
Wild Boar	280	1 040	2 090	7 200	17 000	19 000	18 500	19 494	19 400
Beaver	-	-	..	2 400	8 800	10 950	18 500	8 443 a/	..
European Hare	84 600	87 000	87 400	240 000	207 000	71 100	66 200	86 268	..
Red Fox	5 400	14 500	12 700	11 000	13 900	8 400	12 600	13 425	..
Grey Wolf	112	564	270	..	130	290	600	543	..
Raccoon	-	-	-	8 800	13 800	4 300	6 100	6 496	..
Mallard	..	..	..	..	140 000	246 200	..	41 926	..

Sources: Adapted from "Aplinkos apsauga Lietuvoje", Vilnius, 1996;
Statistical Yearbook of Lithuania 1997;
Biodiversity Conservation Strategy and Action Plan, Vilnius, 1998.

a/ Beaver places.

hunters in the country. 5.6 per cent of the hunting grounds are used for commercial hunting, in which up to 900 foreign hunters participate annually. 96 species of fish have been recorded in Lithuania: 27 marine fish, 52 freshwater fish and 9 species of anadromous fish. Commercial fishing concentrates on five species: Baltic herring, Baltic sprat, cod, sea trout and Atlantic salmon.

Lithuania's commercial fishing dropped considerably after independence (Table 8.5), both in absolute terms and in relation to its Baltic neighbours. Previously, fish catches ranged up to 353 000 tonnes a year (in 1990). In 1995, Latvia caught a total of 149 200 tonnes, Estonia 131 600 tonnes, but Lithuania only 48 200 tonnes. Marine fishing focuses on sprat, Baltic herring and salmonids, of which Lithuania caught 4 800 tonnes, 3 700 tonnes and 5 tonnes, respectively, in 1995.

The two main reasons for the smaller catch were the break-up of the ocean fleet in 1991-1992 and the use of the Curonian Lagoon as Lithuania's main fishing ground. Commercial fishing is the biggest threat to the Lagoon's fish resources, which have declined by more than half. However, the potential fish catch in the Lagoon remains in the range of 7 000 to 12 000 kg a year. There was a considerable rise in 1996, when the catch almost doubled.

Lithuania's fishery sector employed a total of 3 510 people in 1996, down from 10 261 in 1992. Klaipėda State Seaport (main port), Nida and Šventoji are the regions that depend most on fishing. In 1996, the Baltic fleet consisted of 70 vessels and 150 smaller boats.

Extraction of mineral resources

The mined mineral resources are listed in Table 2.2. Areas where peatbogs (10 200 ha) and building material quarries (3 300 ha) have been exploited need urgent rehabilitation. Abandoned small

Table 8.4: Hunting of the main species, 1965-1996

Number killed

	1965	1975	1985	1995	1996
Elk	421	3 269	2 554	60	85
Red Deer	-	152	2 784	2 796	1 946
Roe	4 060	10 329	7 375	5 863	-
Muflon a/	..	..	..	1	2
Wild Boar	1 740	9 684	14 680	8 359	7 807
Beaver	-	547	1 866	466	1 690
European Hare	59 100	26 448	4 566	9 769	14 759
Red Fox	1 960	1 398	1 880	4 051	7 283
Grey Wolf	..	61	144	91	142
Raccoon	1 950	292	1 672	577	776
Mallard	..	16 379	21 991	12 839	12 394

Source: Adapted from "Aplinkos apsauga Lietuvoje", Vilnius, 1996;
Statistical Yearbook of Lithuania 1997.

a/ Muflon started to be hunted in 1995.

Table 8.5: Fish catch, 1991-1996

Live weight in 10^3 tonnes

	1991	1992	1993	1994	1995	1996
Total	..	190.9	120.1	50.7	48.2	56.5
Open Seas	..	175.6	108.8	38.0	33.2	33.4
Baltic Sea	12.1	9.9	7.5	10.0	12.4	20.5
Inland waters	2.0	1.5	0.9	0.9	0.9	1.0
Pond farms	..	3.9	2.9	1.9	1.7	1.5

Source: Natural resources and environmental protection 1996, Department of Statistics, 1998.

quarries are also a problem (over 3 000 ha of land is damaged in addition to the unrestored peatbogs).

Transport

The number of private cars has shot up in the past three to four years. In 1993, pollution from cars accounted for 97.4 per cent of all mobile source pollution. Transport priorities are the construction of the *Via Baltica* motorway and increasing the capacity of the seaports. According to Lithuanian tourism statistics (1997), the majority of tourists arrive in Lithuania by road (71.1 per cent). Only 2 per cent arrive by sea. It is expected that the *Via Baltica* motorway will increase road traffic considerably. In this connection, the World Tourism Organization (1997) has pointed out the need to analyse the potential increase in tourist numbers in national and regional parks alongside the motorway, in order to take it into account in park planning.

The further development of Klaipėda port (including its oil terminal) and the completion of the Butingė oil terminal will increase shipping at sea and along the coast. In 1993 Det Norske Veritas assessed the environmental impact of the Butingė development and the related activities. The environmental impact statement concluded that there were no significant obstacles associated with the construction of the terminal. Nevertheless, the environmental aspects of the project gave rise to an international dispute with Latvia.

According to the results of the Survey of Water-birds Washed Ashore (RULL) in Lithuania, the major threats to bird assemblies during migration are the transport of oil and oil products by sea and oil exploration in the region.

Recreation and tourism

Tourism presents a rich opportunity for Lithuania, both economically and environmentally. The beautiful Baltic coast and the lake region in the east provide many possibilities for further development. The World Tourism Organization carried out a special project on the prospects of Lithuania's eco-tourism in summer 1997. At present tourism is no major threat to nature management and nature conservation, but this could change.

According to Lithuanian tourism statistics, 3.5 million foreigners visited Lithuania in 1996. Most

tourists prefer to make their own travel arrangements rather than use the services of travel agencies. They spent US$ 350 million, which accounted for 4.4 per cent of GDP and 10.5 per cent of all exports. Most came by road (71.1 per cent), fewer by rail (23.7 per cent), air (3.2 per cent) and sea (2 per cent). Half the tourists hailed from the Commonwealth of Independent States (CIS) (1.7 million). In 1996 the most popular places of natural beauty outside major cities (like Vilnius, which attracted 83 per cent of the tourists) were Palanga (22 per cent), Trakai (12 per cent) and Neringa (11 per cent).

Some areas are particularly popular, such as the Baltic coast, and the lakes in the east. Tourism and recreation are concentrated on the coast (0.8 per cent of recreation area), affecting the sand dunes and pine stands on dry sandy soils. On a nice summer's day Smiltynė beach welcomes about 26 000 visitors. There are no data on visitors to national and regional parks. According to the National Tourism Development Programme, about 70 per cent of the country's natural resources for recreation are in national and regional parks and landscape reserves. In terms of landscape preferences, forests come first. It is estimated that 11 million people visit the regional parks each year. Their conservation status limits their availability for intensive recreation, but favours eco-tourism (Law on Protected Areas, Governmental Resolutions on national and regional parks).

8.3   Nature policy and management

Legal framework

According to the Biodiversity Conservation Strategy and Action Plan, 32 acts either directly or indirectly govern nature protection and the use of natural resources. The following eight form the core of the legal framework in that field:

• Law on Environmental Protection (1992)
• Law on Protected Areas (1993)
• Law on Land (1994)
• Law on Forests (1994)
• Law on Territorial Planning (1995)
• Law on Environmental Impact Assessment (1996)
• Law on Wildlife (1997)
• Law on Protected Plant, Animal and Fungi Species and Communities (1997)

Biodiversity conservation

Lithuania's Environmental Strategy, adopted by Parliament on 25 September 1996, is its main political document on environmental protection. The Action Programme was approved by the Government on 5 August 1996. It is too general and does not list the exact responsibilities of the authorities.   The Biodiversity Conservation Strategy and Action Plan was adopted on 21 January 1998. It is the main programme on biodiversity conservation. The document provides a thorough insight into Lithuania's natural richness.

Pending documents

- Biodiversity country study (scheduled to start in 1998)
- CITES implementation programme
- Access to environmental information
- Amendments to environmental permitting system to consider ecological aspects, e.g. carrying capacity of the receiving environment
- Law on genetically modified organisms (GMOs)
- Law on hunting

Forestry, hunting and fishing

Legal instruments

- Law on Forests (1994).
- Special conditions for land and forest use (1993)
- Hunting Regulations (1994)
- Rules on forest protection and use in protected areas (1996)
- Rules on the use of minor forest resources (1996)
- Rules on mushroom picking (1996)
- Draft law on fishing (is under consideration as the Law on Water has been adopted).

The Ministry of Agriculture till 1998 implemented forest policy.   Within the jurisdiction of the Ministry there were 44 forest enterprises and 3 national parks. Forest enterprises comprise 452 forest districts with an average area of 4 030 ha. The forest districts are, in turn, divided into 2-6 sectors with an average area of 1 000 ha. These sectors are looked after by forest guards. In 1990, the Union of Lithuanian Foresters was restored.

Forest managers supervise hunting. The Division of Forestry and Hunting was the State institution responsible for game husbandry.   The Hunting

Regulations of 19 December 1994 and the Hunting Rules of 15 March 1995 regulate hunting.   A hunting law was drafted in autumn 1997 and is expected to be approved by Parliament soon. The Natural Resources Division of the Biodiversity Department at the Ministry of the Environment sets annual hunting quotas, based on population estimates (see Table 8.3) for 8 environmental regions. The Regional Environmental Departments issue the hunting permits.

The annual hunting season lasts from 1 April until 15 February. For the 1996-1997 hunting season quotas were set for six species: elk – 86; red deer – 3 000; wild boar – 12 500; fallow deer - 53; muflon – 4; and beaver – 4 500. 20 species of animals and birds were hunted altogether. The hunting quota is based on the population estimates obtained from the regional hunters' organizations and foresters. According to the Natural Resources Division, the survey data are collected by different organizations using their own counting methods. Poaching is also a problem.

Lithuania's Environmental Strategy (1996) states that the number of hoofed animals is decreasing. The population of elk has more than halved since 1975, and the Action Programme specifies that the population status of hunted fauna has to be assessed and models developed. The Action Programme also foresees the need for a register of fauna and wildlife resources (incl. hunted species). A full-time specialist has been employed at the Division to computerize the data on hunted species surveys, quotas and killed individuals. These are the data that the Regional Environmental Departments report to the Division.

The top priorities for nature conservation according to the NES are: protecting the spawning grounds of rare and endangered fish species, introducing commercially valuable fish species into inland waters, improving fisheries techniques and equipment, and drawing up an inventory of fish resources. The Action Programme focuses on two issues: developing supplementary legislation to the Fisheries Law and promoting research in this field.

Two ministries manage the fisheries: the Ministry of the Environment and the Ministry of Agriculture. The Department of Fish Resources at the Ministry of the Environment reports directly to the Minister. The Department has four regional divisions: Klaipėda, Curonian Lagoon, Tauragė and Kaunas. There is a Department of Fisheries at the Ministry of Agriculture, comprising two divisions: one for freshwater fisheries, the other for sea fisheries.

The Baltic fish resources are currently managed by a joint body of the EU and Lithuania: the International Baltic Sea Fishery Commission. Lithuania has also concluded fisheries agreements with the Faeroe Islands, the United States and Canada. It has no agreement with neighbouring Latvia and Poland. Lithuania does not exchange quotas with any country.

Tourism

The National Tourism Development Programme has been completed under the leadership of the Lithuanian Tourism Board. The Programme stresses the need for incorporating tourism and recreation into land-use planning and conservation management. The Programme for tourism at national and regional parks also focuses on eco-tourism activities. The Programme and the World Tourism Organization Mission Report (1997), however, emphasize the difficulty of developing and implementing national, regional or local tourism plans because of the very complex system of ownership, administration and management of these areas. As mentioned in the World Tourism Organization Mission Report, the administration of parks and protected areas is dispersed over a number of ministries (e.g. national parks are administered by the Ministry of the Environment, the Ministry of Agriculture and the Ministry of Culture), which are relatively free to follow their own development strategies, which, in turn, may result in duplication of functions. If there were a clear system of roles and functions for each park, it would be feasible, for example, to establish a first-class outdoor education centre at one of them. Similarly, park planning would follow the primary function of the territory. The World Tourism Organization has proposed a system of regional parks based on functional differentiation: (1) recreation parks, (2) wilderness preservation parks, (3) outdoor education parks, and (4) resource-based parks. Each would have a set of standard guidelines for that particular type of development.

The law on tourism (comes into force in September 1998) does not provide for eco-tourism or sustainable tourism, although it has been estimated that about 70 per cent of the country's natural resources for recreation are in national and regional parks and in landscape reserves. Whereas the role of different authorities (Tourism Council, Lithuanian Tourism Fund, Ministry of Science and Education, local governments) in the implementation of the law has been defined, the Ministry of the Environment is not mentioned. The only article (art. 28, p.2) related to tourism in protected areas stipulates that "the use and protection of the tourism resources in protected areas shall be established by legal acts and special planning documents".

Species conservation

Legal instruments
- Law on Environmental Protection (1992)
- Law on Protected Areas (1993)
- National Environmental Strategy (1996)
- Law on Protected Animal, Plant and Fungi Species and Communities (1997)
- Law on Wildlife (1997)
- Law on Animal Protection (1997)
- Biodiversity Strategy and Action Plan (1998)

Other laws regulating land use:
- Law on Territorial Planning (1995)
- Law on Environmental Impact Assessment (1996)
- Law on Construction (1996)

Lithuania has been a party to the Bern Convention on the Conservation of European Wildlife and Natural Habitats since 1996, to the Ramsar Convention on Wetlands of International Importance Especially as Waterfowl Habitat since 1993 and to the Convention on Biological Diversity since 1995. Lithuania is in the process of acceding to the Washington Convention on International Trade in Endangered Species of Wild Fauna and Flora, and the Bonn Convention on the Conservation of Migratory Species of Wild Animals.

The institutional structures for protected area management are complicated as several ministries and their sub-organizations as well as local authorities share the same responsibilities. For example, the management of national parks is coordinated by two ministries, that of regional parks by one ministry and by local municipalities (Figure 8.4).

The Biodiversity Conservation Strategy and Action Plan draws attention to the need to protect Lithuania's genetic fund of domestic and cultural breeds: a breed of carp (Bubiai), originally introduced in Lithuania in the

Figure 8.4: Institutional structures for protected area management and biodiversity conservation

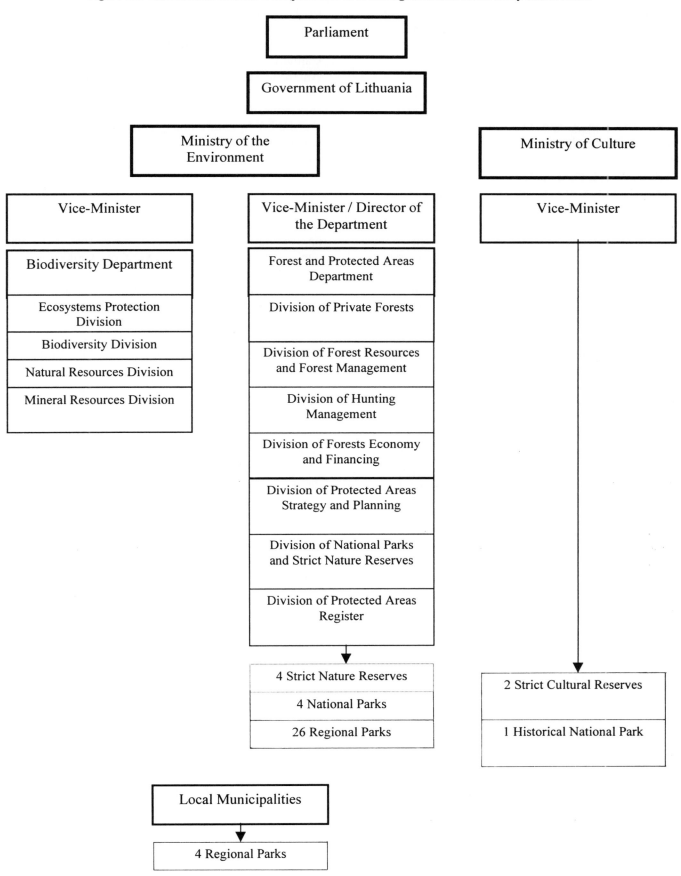

17th-18th century, a horse breed "Žemaitukai", a Lithuanian black head sheep breed, a Lithuanian hound breed, and other breeds of animals, birds, crops, vegetables, fruits and flowers.

Protected areas

The system for protected areas is very diverse as well. The names and functions of the protected areas and natural objects do not entirely coincide with the IUCN categories (IUCN Guidelines, 1994), except for those of strict nature reserves, national and regional parks and reserves. The Nature Frame system, legally adopted in 1992, was designed to strike a balance between built and natural landscapes. The Land Management Group of Vilnius University was the leading organization in the development of the concept and the drafting of the legal document. The Law states that the Nature Frame system must form the basis for national, regional and local planning. The Ministry of the Environment also admits that the task is complex, and this obligation difficult to implement. The difficulties lie in the system's focus on ecological concerns to the detriment of economic and social aspects.

The first national park was founded in 1974 (Aukštaitija). The network of regional parks was created in 1992. The regulation on the boundaries and management zones of regional parks (incl. strict nature reserves) was adopted in 1996. The two categories are analogous. The Register of Protected Areasis currently being prepared.

At present there is a map for each national and regional park to show its functional zones. These are intended to indicate the type and intensity of development, if any. It is regarded as a site-by-site segmented approach to planning. These zones are regarded as indicators of the potential and constraints for development rather than providing guidelines for management. Their borders are often arbitrary.

Approximation of EU directives in the area of nature protection

EU nature protection legislation consists of two principal directives and two regulations: the so-called Habitats Directive 92/43/EEC, which is the main mechanism for protecting European species of fauna and flora as well as their habitats; and the Birds Directive 79/409/EEC, which protects birds and sites of importance for the maintenance of populations of wild birds. One of the two

regulations, EC/338/97, guarantees the fulfilment of EU nature protection under the Washington Convention (CITES). The other, 90/3943/EEC, regulates the protection of the Antarctic under the Canberra Convention on the Conservation of Antarctic Marine Living Resources (1980).

It is difficult to evaluate to what extent Lithuania's legislation on nature management and conservation corresponds to EU legislation. According to Ministry of the Environment officials, an analysis of the compliance with and the implications of the EU directives for Lithuania's present legislation has started. The first step has been taken: nature conservation issues are part of Lithuania's EU approximation strategy. The need for such an analysis was expressed on several occasions.

Since Lithuania is not yet a party to CITES, there is no legal instrument available for controlling and monitoring trade. However, Lithuania is in the process of acceding to CITES. Two regulations - one on animal trade, the other on animal import and export - already exist.

Lithuania is a party to the Ramsar Convention, and has five Ramsar sites. The Lithuanian Ornithological Society has been a Partner Designate to Bird Life International since 1994. Lithuania is in a favourable position to comply with the Birds Directive.

Biological monitoring

The Law on Environmental Monitoring was adopted in November 1997. The new monitoring programme has been approved (June 1998). It does not explicitly include biodiversity monitoring in the list of sub-programmes, but the biota monitoring sub-programme is relevant here too. The first national monitoring programme was launched in 1989. The Ministry of the Environment developed a new Ecological Monitoring Programme in collaboration with several research institutes in 1991-1992. The programme has been State-financed since 1993.

The status of biological diversity in Lithuania is not specifically monitored. However, vegetation and wildlife are monitored at selected monitoring stations. The integrated environmental monitoring covers individual flora and fauna species, and ecosystem monitoring is generally performed at technical research level. There are three integrated ecological monitoring stations in Aukštaitija, Dzūkija and Žemaitija National Parks. According to the Biodiversity Conservation Strategy and Action Plan, the status of protected species is not monitored and there are no programmes for the conservation of biotopes, species or ecosystems.

The institution responsible for environmental monitoring is the Joint Research Centre at the Ministry of the Environment. The practical work is conducted by research institutes like the Institute of Ecology, the Institute of Botany, the Institute of Forest Research and the University of Agriculture, as well as by the staff of strict nature reserves, national and regional parks.

The longest non-stop monitoring programmes are that for the zoocenoses and fish resources of the Curonian Lagoon and the Nemunas River Delta by the Institute of Ecology, started in 1949, and that for the vegetation and zoocenoses of Lake Drūkšiai, the source of the Ignalina Nuclear Power Plant's coolant, started in 1980.

According to the Joint Research Centre, four monitoring programmes were carried out in 1997: Flora and Fauna Monitoring (10 sub-programmes), Ecosystems Monitoring (2), Semi-natural Ecosystems Monitoring (4) and Integrated Monitoring (5). The sub-programmes, 21 in total, are all extensive in scope and require substantial financial and technical assistance. However, there is a lack of both, and according to the Biodiversity Conservation Strategy and Action Plan ecological monitoring may be terminated as a result.

NGOs active in nature management

According to the Biodiversity Conservation Strategy and Action Plan, there are about 80 environmental non-governmental organizations in Lithuania. The majority are concerned with biodiversity and nature conservation. The most active in nature conservation are the Lithuanian Fund for Nature, the Lithuanian Green Movement, the Lithuanian Ornithological Society, and the Lithuanian Botanical Society. REC-Lithuania and ECAT-Lithuania are also important as funding bodies.

8.4   Conclusions and recommendations

The past 6-7 years, Lithuania has carried out much intensive work to develop legislation on nature management and integrate it into its overall legislative system, and to comply with European and other international agreements and conventions. As a result, Lithuania's legislation

generally satisfies the European Union legal framework for nature protection and management. At the same time, the pace of development of new legislation is not always matched by adequate institutional measures. Nor have all the provisions been fully implemented. For example, the actions of the Biodiversity Conservation Action Plan are too general and not supplemented by funding provisions (no estimates are given). Species conservation action plans need to be drawn up also.

The aim of Lithuania's protected area management is to enlarge rather than optimize it. The practical management of the country's protected territories is impeded by the ongoing land reform, the land and real estate restitution to former owners or their descendants, the low integration of various types of protection and management systems (e.g. national parks and regional parks) and the lack of updated management plans for each protected area (following the 1993 Law on Protected Areas). In particular, the organizational structure for nature management is very complex and responsibilities are divided among several authorities. The administration of protected areas should be consolidated. At this stage, it appears reasonable to consolidate all protected areas under the Ministry of the Environment.

The consolidation of all protected areas under the Ministry of the Environment could be expected to facilitate nature conservation, recreation and tourism development in these areas, as well as fiscal planning. The Ministry of Agriculture could continue to carry out forest management in protected areas on the basis of an agreement between the two ministries. The current system of protected areas is too expensive and difficult to manage. Implementation of nature management policies is constantly under-financed. Decisions on protected area management are taken at higher administrative levels (Government). However, the senior management of State parks together with local environmental authorities and local governments should be actively involved too. Nature conservation and management principles are insufficiently integrated into regional planning, agricultural, forestry, fisheries and tourism policies, strategies and action plans.

Recommendation 8.1:
The institutional consolidation of the administration of all protected areas under the Ministry of the Environment has started. The necessary cooperation with other ministries in managing protected areas should be assured by

way of special agreements between them, paving the way for a fuller integration of nature management issues into sectoral policies.

To be effective, the institutional consolidation of protected area management needs to be accompanied by the introduction of new instruments. A strategic plan for national and regional parks aims at defining the role and functions of each park in the overall protected area system, supplemented by outdoor training and education systems. The idea stems from the understanding that it would be too costly to maintain the system and duplications cannot be avoided if each park prepares its own management policy and action plan. In this connection, the World Tourism Organization has proposed a system of four categories of regional parks (1997) to minimize overall expenditure.

Within the strategic plan for national and regional parks, the management of protected areas should be based on a management plan, specifying the role and functions of the area, an inventory of development potential (including the rationale for present functional zones), a policy statement on the area's utilization capacity, the maximum number and type of users, in particular, and an action plan schedule and budget. The plan might be reviewed after three years and then updated and adjusted as needs change.

Recommendation 8.2:
Management plans should be drawn up as soon as possible for each protected area as the basis for its management.

Landscape and biodiversity conservation and management require strengthening. It is necessary to allocate funds both to regional departments of the Ministry of the Environment and to municipal agencies. Funds will also be required for training staff in protected areas. Such training should be targeted on general management, on biodiversity conservation and monitoring, as well as on public relations with tourists and the local population.

Strengthening the present joint councils and administrations (permanent staff) of the parks would be one step to advance the management of regional parks. A park advisory board, including representatives of local governments, local NGOs and interest groups, could support the administration of each park - as recommended by the World Tourism Organization (1997). The park director could chair the board, which would

facilitate systematic communication of the park administration with all interested groups, meet public interests and local needs, and avoid conflicts. It could also be feasible to integrate NGOs into the management of protected areas.

Recommendation 8.3:
Strengthening joint park councils or systematically creating park advisory boards should be considered. It would also be an opportunity for associating - if not integrating - NGOs and other local interests into the management of State parks. Their management should also be strengthened through training programmes.

Involving local and national initiatives, local governments and NGOs in public consultations and providing public access to environmental information are an important condition for success, particularly in nature management. Public access to environmental information has to be secured, since transparency in nature management and conservation results in better cooperation with the public. Providing access to information also means making its presentation more user-friendly.

Sources of information for dissemination exist. There is a biological monitoring system, the Lithuanian Ecological Monitoring Programme (incl. integrated monitoring stations), but it is too cumbersome and expensive to manage. A well funded biological monitoring strategy is required to make it more result-oriented and optimize the monitoring expenditures.

The Biodiversity Conservation Strategy and Action Plan proposes a new framework for biological monitoring, but further activities and financing need to be specified. The Joint Research Centre also collects environmental data, mostly in paper form. However, relatively little analysis and dissemination take place. NGOs complain that little environmental information is spread to the public and that there is no formal access to environmental data. Close cooperation between ministries, other State environmental authorities and NGOs to use environmental data banks and information systems on the implementation of environmental policy more effectively would be beneficial. In this context, State institutions would also benefit from the data collected and analysed by NGOs.

Gaps in information also exist. For example, the most popular recreation and tourism areas (e.g. seaside, national and regional parks) should carry out visitor surveys. Such surveys are also required to determine the maximum number of visitors the area could receive without adverse consequences (see also text preceding Recommendation 8.2).

Recommendation 8.4:
A systematic approach needs to be taken to the compilation, analysis and dissemination of data on nature conservation, specific species and habitats. The approach should include provisions for bridging important data gaps.

An area of major concern for nature management is territorial and land-use planning.   In the first instance, various components of the Nature Frame Action Programme, the Biodiversity Conservation Strategy and Action Plan, the National Tourism Development Programme and others need to be integrated into territorial planning and environmental protection.   Special training on strategic environmental assessment would help planners, but also local authorities. In the current land privatization and land reform, land-use planning could become an instrument for striking a balance between commercial interests and nature conservation. Present land-use planning, which is generally based on restricted versus non-restricted zones in protected areas, could be used as a framework for creating or opening up the potential of the protected areas for more diverse functions.

Recommendation 8.5:
Strategic environmental assessment, i.e. land-use and sectoral planning integrated with environmental and natural resource planning, should be introduced into Lithuania's legislation and practice.

The importance of tourism in Lithuania makes it necessary to develop close ties between tourism policy and nature management.   The obvious economic benefits of tourism need to be harvested. At the same time, the existing potential for further tourism development can best be exploited by adhering to sustainability principles from the beginning. Accordingly, local decision makers need courage and determination to apply a number of important principles:

(1) Keep tourism development within the environmental carrying capacity of the area
(2) Involve the local population in planning and decision-making
(3) Control water and air quality effectively and protect coastal ecosystems

(4) Invest in the environment when creating infrastructure
(5) Ensure effective planning of natural resources use in the coastal zone, controlling impacts on water and land.

A special eco-tourism programme would facilitate the systematic introduction of eco-tourism into territorial planning of municipalities, regions and national and regional parks. Close cooperation between municipalities, the Ministry of the Environment and State park administrations would make it possible to integrate tourism and recreation into park development and management plans. Similar cooperation is needed with entrepreneurs, local interest groups and municipalities. Sustainable tourism as a concept should be explored further, but the introduction and preservation of ethnographic values in protected areas would certainly have to be combined with the provision of services for tourists.

Involving the private sector with tourism development in State park areas will require special instruments.   For example, compensation mechanisms (e.g. land tax exemption) for the physical and legal persons based in a protected area (other than strict nature reserves) subject to land restitution do not currently exist. Also, tax breaks are not granted to national park residents, a measure that could help to preserve the ethnographic heritage of the area.

Recommendation 8.6:
A tourism development programme should be implemented at local level. It should be compatible with the objectives of nature conservation on the one hand and economic requirements on the other. Local authorities should have sufficient resources for the programme. Its implementation should involve the private sector. The programme should specify adequate implementation measures.

A number of more specific recommendations can also be made regarding special problems and/or measures in the field of natural resources. It will be necessary for Lithuania to establish a fisheries administration to manage the fish stocks, fishing, fish processing and fish trade, collecting relevant data and coordinating the necessary activities with the authorities responsible for health, hygiene and the environment.

In the Karst region, special measures are required

to integrate the management of agricultural activities and that of water resources.

The required restoration activities for abandoned mines etc. should be clearly regulated, and accompanied by legal and tax measures.

Acceding to the Washington Convention should be a priority for Lithuania. This process should be followed by the adoption of related domestic regulations and training of customs officials.

Chapter 9

WASTE MANAGEMENT

9.1 Current waste flows and waste management

General overview

The former Environmental Protection Department began the compilation of a comprehensive waste inventory in 1991, with the preparation of waste classification and a waste inventory system, which were improved in 1992 (Table 9.1). The amount of waste generated, its type and origin can be found in the waste register. The register covers about 1 600 industries. Non-hazardous wastes are broken down into 23 groups and hazardous wastes into 37 groups. A legal definition of wastes that is consistent with EU directives is included in the Law on Waste Management. Municipal waste data are obtained from waste collectors. As a result, Lithuanian waste data should be read with caution.

Table 9.1: Waste generation, 1992-1997

1 000 t

	1992	1993	1994	1995	1996	1997
Non-hazardous waste	17 700	3 624	6 368	7 956	6 134	5 312
of which:						
- Secondary raw materials waste	505	325	282	320	401	509
- Municipal waste	333	209	217	284	337	394
- Organic waste	7 648	1 739	1 386	1 978	2 158	2 080
Hazardous waste	212	215	130	153	108	131

Source: Statistical Yearbook of Lithuania, 1997;
Ministry of the Environment.

Generation of non-hazardous waste

The broad structure of the generation of waste is given in Table 9.1. Most of these wastes are organic or domestic. The organic waste is: 64 per cent manure, slurry and excrement, 30 per cent food waste, 2 per cent field and garden cultivation waste, and 4 per cent are wastes of animal origin. The raw mineral material wastes were: 92 per cent quarry waste and 8 per cent raw mineral saturation wastes.

In 1996, Lithuania generated 1 444 000 tonnes of household waste or approximately 384 kg per person. This figure is in the European range (285 kg in Portugal, 465 kg in the Netherlands). The recent changes in the composition of waste are the subject of Table 9.2. According to estimates, about 360 000 t of paper and cardboard waste, 67 000 t of glass and 42 000 t of plastic and metal wastes were disposed of at landfills - quantities which could potentially be used as secondary raw materials.

The composition of the construction waste is shown in Table 9.3. Construction waste is managed and used in many different ways, but 32 per cent of construction waste is dumped at dumping sites, together with domestic waste.

Table 9.2: Composition of domestic waste, 1992-1996

%

	1992	1993	1994	1996
Kitchen waste	60	53	26	39
Paper and cardboard	17	19	13	16
Glass	3	4	16	9
Metal	2	3	2	3
Plastic	2	4	5	7
Other flammable waste	6	8	9	14
Other non-flammable waste	10	9	30	12

Source: Waste management problems in Lithuania, Ministry of the Environment, February-March 1997.

Table 9.3: Composition of construction waste, 1992-1997

1 000 t

	1992	1993	1994	1995	1996	1997
Phosphogypsum	199.0	199.3	404.9	666.1	816.0	992.5
Chalk, lime	69.7	81.5	41.7	45.3	33.2	75.6
Building structures scrap	20.7	8.8	5.8	3.8	5.6	16.4
Concrete	26.0	11.9	12.4	5.3	7.2	6.3
Asphaltconcrete	1.3	6.4	6.6	3.2	2.3	3.0
Ceramics	18.1	4.9	5.9	3.6	2.9	2.3
Bricks	23.2	14.0	6.6	3.2	4.0	2.3
Asbestos-containing waste	8.2	3.1	2.6	2.6	1.6	1.6
Silicagel	0.6	0.6	1.4	1.6	0.0	2.3

Source: Ministry of the Environment.

Figure 9.1: Composition of non-hazardous waste, 1992-1996

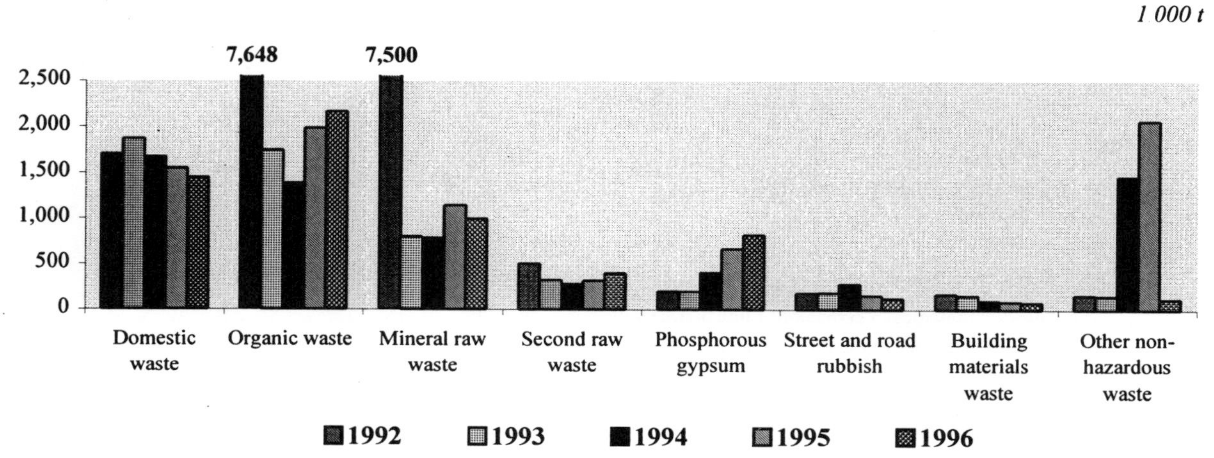

1 000 t

Source: Ministry of the Environment.

Generation of hazardous waste

The generation of hazardous waste seems to be on the decrease. A total of about 130 000 t of hazardous waste was reported to be generated in Lithuania in 1994 and 131 000 in 1997. Detailed data for 1997 indicate that roughly half the amount of hazardous wastes generated were oil/water mixtures. Most of the wastes included in this category are generated in oil traps but the group comprises other types of oil wastes as well, e.g. cutting fluids. Oil-containing wastes are also included in various other hazardous waste categories such as spent oils, storm water sewage sludge, contaminated soil, etc.

Of the 59 150 t oil/water waste generated in Lithuania in 1996, 50 000 t was generated at the Mažeikiai Oil Refinery, making the Šiauliai region an obvious leader in hazardous waste generation (see the box below on Šiauliai). Another important oil/water waste generation area (5 534 t in 1996) is the Klaipėda region, where the generation is related to the operation of the oil export terminal.

The second largest hazardous waste generator is tanneries, with an annual generation of more than 9 000 t. Two tanneries in Šiauliai generate 98.7 per cent (9 020 t) of tannery waste containing chromium and this is the second largest hazardous waste source in the Šiauliai region. Oil-containing waste and tannery waste together comprise 95 per cent of all hazardous waste generated in the Šiauliai region and 57 per cent of hazardous wastes generated in Lithuania.

Another important group of hazardous wastes is heavy metals containing waste. Its considerable

Table 9.4 : Hazardous waste generation, 1992-1997

1 000 t

	1992	1993	1994	1995	1996	1997
Medical waste	11	1 792	1 462	291	336	561
Pharmaceutical waste	6	14	2	4	3	6
Biocide and phytopharmaceutical waste	23	85	55	169	8	302
Organic solvent waste	179	71	83	691	331	12
Halogenated organic solvent waste	15	3	3	3	9	1
Oil product waste without water	12 706	2 264	48 347	65 914	1 795	2 154
Substances contaminated with oil products	2 131	1 189	890	6 853	813	5 296
Oil and water mixtures and emulsions	104 741	107 641	15 959	7 903	59 150	71 985
Waste of paints, varnish, lacquer and pigments, dyes, boiled linen seeds oil	242	148	94	72	1 514	704
Substances polluted with paints, lacquer	416	165	61	669	651	33
Waste of tar, plastificators, glues and latex	5 117	4 207	205	3 960	97	3 564
Mineral wool waste	5 154	2 432	3 036	1 062	0	7 101
Waste of unidentified chemical material	0	13	5	3	3	1
Photographic processing material wastes	3 767	35	37	1 469	493	31
Waste of animal fats, oil and soap	4 113	5 277	2 823	3 063	2 375	1 393
Non-halogenic organic substances, excluding solvents	2 131	113	0	18	339	0
Inorganic waste without heavy metals	1 998	1 229	2 119	344	1 529	1 314
Slag and ashes	14 191	20 121	2 091	380	68	1 971
Contaminated soil	11 873	36 748	12 737	14 122	4 037	8 727
Soil contaminated with oil products	846	650	3 390	23 109	1 281	3 538
Chilling salts without cyanides	57	25	19	16	4	21
Catalysts waste	114	133	157	127	172	173
Solutions and silt with heavy metals	6 812	1 040	467	514	146	66
Electrolyte from acid batteries	319	231	146	44	76	54
Electrolyte from alkaline batteries	15	22	18	17	28	12
Galvanic sludge	4 091	1 359	1 058	1 817	459	416
Tannery waste	22 676	14 846	13 426	12 506	9 136	7 113
Spent filter materials	1 480	526	219	188	481	355
Scrubber sludge	1 070	101	291	1 068	1 652	80
Decarbonization waste	2	2	1 160	2	1	0
Ion-exchange column waste	23	1	12	10	0	97
Waste from cleaning and washing equipment	53 576	3 345	4 925	3 355	4 369	393
Car wash sludge	4 412	2 421	2 329	1 094	906	528
Spent alkaline solutions for degreasing processes of fat reduction	845	21	7 140	57	161	432
Mercury-containing waste	0	3	13	0	0	0
Galvanic elements	235	117	2 450	34	13	6
Vegetable oil waste	8	118	1	10	79	119
Acid batteries	522	418	276	236	581	4 563
Alkaline batteries	147	13	8	12	30	598
Waste arising from refining, distillation and any pyrolitic treatment	36	233	215	210	3	182
Bitumen waste	29	278	1	4	1	0
Mercury-containing lamps	122	110	105	89	165	153

Source: Ministry of the Environment.

fraction is also dispersed in various categories, though the most important part is concentrated in galvanic sludge. Of the 7 678 t of wastes generated in 1996 in the category of not specified hazardous wastes, 6 543 t is abrasion sludge containing copper and zinc. Most of the organic solvent waste is generated during painting and equipment cleaning and its quantity is comparatively low. Some data in Table 9.4 on the hazardous waste generation show erratic changes from year to year. The reasons are not fully clear but a major cause is probably serious deficiencies in reporting.

Radioactive waste

At present there are three sources of radioactive waste in Lithuania:

- Ignalina nuclear power plant (INPP, in operation since 1986)
- Research medical and industrial waste (RMI)
- Illegal freight transport.

INPP is the main source of radioactive waste. The main types of waste produced at INPP are as follows: solid waste including spent fuel, bitumenized evaporation concentrates, ion-exchange resins. The main reason for the incidental occurrence of illegal freight transport is insufficient border control caused by a lack of training and equipment. Lithuania lacks international agreements enabling it to send back illegal radioactive freight.

Until 1989 there were two radioactive disposal sites in Lithuania: the Maišiagala low and intermediate level waste repository and the repository at the Ignalina site. The Maišiagala repository was filled up and closed in 1988 and sealed in 1989. RMI waste has been stored in a reinforced concrete basin. At present a long-term assessment is being carried out of the site and decisions concerning the future of the repository will be made later. There are 3 options: to keep it; to improve it; or to move it to the Ignalina site.

The radioactive waste produced at INPP is stored at its waste repository. Per year about 0.4-0.65 GBq of artificial radio-nuclides are accumulated. Waste-water sludge, containing radio-nuclides, is stored in a quarry. Solid waste is processed in a recently installed bale compactor for volume reduction and is dumped into reinforced concrete troughs with removable roofs. Evaporation concentrates are solidified in bitumen and then poured into large concrete storage basins at the site. Ion-exchange resins are used for the cleaning of the reactor water. They are stored in a tank which will soon be completely full. The radioactive waste storage facility at Ignalina serves at present for all newly produced RMI in Lithuania.

The main problems with spent fuel are:

- there are no contracts for reprocessing/disposal of spent fuel abroad;
- the lack of capacity of the repositories;

- the assessment of safety of existing storage (report pending from a Swedish company).

Temporary dry containers for the spent fuel will be built at the site in the near future. They will have a lifetime of 50 years. This facility will be extended to cover the needs of the INPP during the foreseen remaining operation time. As the reprocessing of nuclear fuel in Lithuania is forbidden, the issue of final disposal will have to be considered in the coming years.

Domestic waste collection and recovery

The Law on Environmental Protection has placed the responsibility for household waste management on municipalities. Most municipalities have established their own waste collection and management companies, though there are some private companies operating under contract with the municipalities. Waste collection is funded from the tariffs collected from the population and the industries disposing their waste in landfills. The municipalities set the tariffs on the basis of the proposals of the waste collecting companies. They should cover operating and capital costs of waste collection and transport equipment. In general, however, collected charges hardly cover operating expenses.. In many cases, the operation of waste collection companies and the purchase of equipment are subsidized by the municipalities. Landfill construction and maintenance are financed by the municipalities, usually from the municipal environmental funds.

Waste collection charges do not cover landfill costs. Municipal waste landfills are the property of the municipalities and are operated by the waste collection companies free of charge. Most municipalities have local landfill operation rules dividing the wastes into three categories: (1) waste permitted to be landfilled, (2) waste not permitted to be landfilled, and (3) waste that needs a special permit for disposal. Wastes not permitted to be landfilled include hazardous wastes and some special waste that potentially could be recycled such as used tyres, wood waste, metal scrap, etc., but the lists vary between municipalities. Wastes that need a special permit are usually certain area-specific slightly hazardous wastes. Large industries have contracts with waste collecting companies for the disposal of their waste in landfills and take their waste there themselves.

An ordinance of the Ministry of the Environment, issued in 1989, requires hazardous wastes to be stored at the site of production if they cannot be safely treated and disposed of. The ordinance does not lay down storage conditions . Some big companies have built their own hazardous waste storage facilities.

Table 9.5: Secondary raw materials from domestic waste, 1993-1996

1 000 t

	1993	1994	1995	1996
Wood waste	198.0	185.4	223.9	269.1
Ferrous metal waste	57.1	56.6	73.1	105.5
Glass waste	39.5	12.8	4.4	4.2
Paper and cardboard waste	11.2	10.6	8.2	6.4
Textile and natural fibre waste	7.2	8.2	4.2	5.1
Non-ferrous metal waste	2.1	1.6	1.2	5.3
Rubber waste	6.5	2.7	2.8	2.1
Plastics and polymer waste	2.3	1.3	1.6	2.7
Natural hide and fur waste	1.3	0.7	0.4	1.0

Source: Statistical Yearbook of Lithuania 1997.

Waste sorting has started in a number of cities and larger towns (see e.g. the box regarding the city of Kaunas below), but is hampered by the lack of investment and poor infrastructure. The collection of non-ferrous and ferrous metals is operating at a satisfactory level. There are currently seven companies interested in waste paper, with a total capacity of about 70 000 t per year, against an annual demand for secondary paper of about 25 000 t. The price of waste paper has fallen recently and does not cover the collection and transport expenses.

There are two glass companies in Lithuania, but the Panevėžys Glass company takes only white glass and sorting collected glass is too expensive. Kaunas Glass Company can process coloured glass, but currently it is in poor financial shape and does not pay for glass deliveries. The market for secondary glass is approximately 25 000 t a year. Breweries reuse beer bottles, which are collected by small retailers with the help of a deposit system. The breweries estimate that about 95 per cent of the 15 million beer bottles in circulation are being reused.

Two large and several smaller companies operate in Lithuania in conventional plastic production. The main plastic waste processing capacity is in the Vilnius-based Plasta company. The company imports considerable amounts of PE waste from Germany, and a small amount of sorted Lithuanian plastic waste (PE film) is purchased by the company for recycling, at a price of 200 Litas per t. Two smaller companies produce plastic tiles from

different plastics, bought at a price of about 300 Litas per t. It is estimated that they collected almost 2 700 t in 1996.

Other recycling relates to used tyres and to organic waste from catering establishments. Tyres are collected at a price of 200 to 300 Litas per t. A recent study suggests that tyres should be incinerated in cement kilns. Organic waste is recycled as food for farm animals.

Kaunas municipal waste management

The Kaunas Municipality has developed an advanced and successful approach to the separate collection, registration and disposal of municipal wastes. There are 2000 containers for the separate collection of glass, paper, plastic and metals. Bulky waste is also separed. At each of the 500 locations ("platforms") there are in principle 4 containers serving about 1 000 inhabitants. Each month, 80 - 100 t of glass and 130 t of paper are recovered. The weighing and registration of wastes is computerized. The main landfill has been designed and operates in accordance with EU requirements.

The remaining problems in this project are:
° There is no composting installation.
° There is no incinerator for the combustible waste components.
° Construction waste is not recycled and still goes to the landfill.
° Some city quarters resist the integration of 3 small landfills into a common one.
° The municipality does not have the authority to levy taxes and decide how to spend the municipal environmental fund.
° There is no clear-cut separation of operating, financing and control mechanisms for municipal waste management.

Recovery, treatment and recycling of industrial and hazardous wastes

The recycling of industrial and hazardous wastes in Lithuania is slowly taking off, though some specific recycling is actually decreasing. Several boilers fired by wood chips have been constructed recently with the financial assistance of the Swedish and Danish Governments. Fuel briquette production from wood waste is planned, but is hardly likely to expand much as the briquettes will be too expensive for the Lithuanian users and will be sold only in western, especially Scandinavian, markets.

The system of spent oil collection and recycling was developed in the eighties when fresh oil was sold to industries and transport enterprises only in exchange of spent oil. The volume of waste oils collected by the Lithuanian Fuel company decreased from 35 694 t in 1989 to 844 t in 1996. The collection of engine oils during the same period decreased from 14 972 t to 378 t per year. Lithuanian Fuel pays for collected waste oils and makes some profit from selling the processed product. Currently, the demand for the products exceeds the supply and the company claims that it can treat substantially higher amounts of used oils. However, the overall composition of waste oils has been changing significantly. There is a rapidly growing number of used car filters (0.5 million per year), which currently cannot be collected, treated or disposed of.

Installations for the biological treatment of oil-containing wastes operate in various parts of Lithuania. The Biocentras company, specializing in biological oil waste treatment, estimates that the total capacity of Lithuania's biological treatment installations is currently approximately 5 000 to 6 000 tonnes per year. Oil-containing sludge generated at the Mažeikiai oil refinery is collected and treated in centrifuges by the local Ekoring company. Separated oil is recycled to crude oil, the remaining sludge is dispersed in a thin layer on the soil surface. It is believed that the remaining oil is almost completely degraded by natural bacteria within one year, but no chemical analysis is performed and the site is not monitored. The refinery is building a new facility for the biological treatment of oil-containing sludge using artificially raised bacteria strains. The facility should have started operating in 1998, the planned capacity is approximately 2 000 t per year. A similar facility operates in Klaipėda for the treatment of oil sludge generated in the Klaipėda Oil Export Terminal.

In the beginning of nineties, several companies started paint and glue production using paint waste and spent solvents and it seems that some of them are still operating. However, the quality of their products is comparatively poor and they have a very limited market. Additionally, only a small fraction of wastes meeting certain criteria can be used for such production.

A system of plating sludge (galvanic sludge) recycling was developed in Lithuania in the seventies. Heavy metal containing sludge from plating effluent treatment was mixed with clay slurry for the production of keramzit (expanded clay) insulation material at the Palemonas Ceramic Plant. In the late eighties, Palemonas was turning into keramzit the bulk of plating sludges generated in Lithuania, except the sludge precipitated with lime as calcium, which was considered to undermine keramzit quality. In practice, 6 800 tonnes of galvanic sludge and 15 400 tonnes of oil waste have been mixed with clay to produce bricks. The rise in power generation and transport prices

after the collapse of the Soviet Union increased very considerably the cost of keramzit production, which is, currently, higher than the market price. Palemonas tried to survive by increasing its charges to the industries for their sludge deliveries, and now keramzit is produced only sporadically.

There are companies licensed to collect spent car batteries. The total amount of lead batteries collected in 1996 was 6 470 t, containing 3 634 t of lead and 217 t of nickel-iron batteries. The batteries are exported to Estonia in accordance with the Agreement between the Lithuanian and Estonian Environmental Protection Ministries. Estonia has ratified the Basel Convention and can export the batteries for further processing. Battery acid is taken free of charge by the Fostra chemical company in Kėdainiai to produce sulphuric acid.

A demercurization plant is being built in Vilnius by the Liuksitis company in order to recycle used luminescent lamps (about 2.5 million lamps have to be disposed of each year). The company collects spent luminescent tubes, charging 1.20 Litas per unit. The charges amount to more than 10 per cent of the price of a new tube, but Liuksitis has already collected approximately 350 000 tubes. Most of the luminescent tubes are still stored by the industries, though some of them are exported to a demercurization plant in Latvia.

The Aukštrakiai dumpsite in the vicinity of Šiauliai contains a huge amount of hazardous liquid wastes, produced over 10-20 years by the leather industries of Šiauliai city. For tanneries, waste disposal in Aukštrakiai continued for more than 10 years. The ponds containing the liquid wastes are built of clay and overflowing with highly contaminated, semi-liquid mixtures of different waste waters, predominantly from tanneries. In the event of heavy rains or melting snow, the ponds' banks could easily be washed out and many thousand tonnes of liquid waste, containing chromium, sulphides and organic matter could, by way of nearby small rivers, cause an environmental catastrophe along the Baltic coast.

A pilot test of clean-up technology has been carried out at the Aukštrakiai dumpsite by a mixed team of Danish and Lithuanian experts supported financially by Japan. The technology considerably reduced the contaminant contents in accumulated liquid wastes. The resulting processed waste water can be safely treated and commonly used in Šiauliai sewage treatment facilities. The sludge is stabilized, and heavy metal contaminants form non-soluble sediment. The processed sludge can be easily de-watered and deposited in the pits, to be recultivated later. The technical aspect of a complete clean-up of the Aukštrakiai dumpsite is now under consideration, together with plans to reduce and completely recycle tannery wastes. If the dumpsite is rehabilitated, its useful life can be extended for another 20-30 years.

Hazardous waste problems of Siauliai

In the course of the last 50 years, Siauliai has become the most heavily polluted region in Lithuania. The estimated quantities of waste generated by various activities amount to:

household waste	408 000 m³
solid waste	3 000 tonnes
liquid waste	1 100 tonnes
sewage sludge	1 400 tonnes
mercury lamps	45 000 units

The dominant industry in the city is food processing. It includes meat and milk-processing plants, Ruta and Gliukoze confectioneries, a bakery, the Gubernija brewery, and also light, machine-building and construction material industries. The biggest enterprises of the city are: the Tauras TV factory, the Vairas bicycle factory, the Nuklonas electronic devices enterprise, and the Venta furniture factory. The oldest industry in Siauliai are leather tanneries. Elnias and Stumbras are the leaders in this field in the Republic. Toxic waste from industry amounts to:

stored in plants	1 100 tonnes
converted	2 700 tonnes
deposited in the municipal landfill	300 tonnes

Industry has only limited incineration capacity. There are no recycling plants. Under the Hazardous Waste Management Programme, a plant for the treatment and one for the temporary storage of toxic waste have been designed. These plans remain uncertain until a new strategy for hazardous waste management has been approved.

Landfills

There are approximately 900 registered landfills in Lithuania. In addition, waste dumping in unreported small provincial landfills may continue to occur. Most of the municipal landfills, especially in small rural municipalities, are poorly designed and constructed. Numerous landfills are old abandoned gravel quarries, some of them already full. A landfill with plastic lining and a drainage system was recently constructed in Kaišiadorys. However, the design did not include leachate treatment facilities and the landfill was flooded by leachate and rain water. The construction of a similar landfill with plastic lining began 8 years ago in Kėdainiai but is not completed for lack of finance. According to the design, leachate will be returned to the waste in the same way as in Kaišiadorys. The Kėdainiai Municipality has no resources to design and build a leachate treatment facility. A new landfill of the same design is under construction in Panevėžys. The landfill is comparatively small and will be full after 3 to 4 years of operation. The Kaunas municipal landfill is being expanded by 1 to 1.5 ha annually. A newly constructed landfill area has a compacted clay barrier, plastic lining and two drainage layers. The construction of a leachate treatment facility should have started at the end of 1997 and be completed in 1998.

The economic potential of recovering landfill gases has not been evaluated. According to the European Renewable Energy Study - Draft country report on Lithuania, 1994, a total amount of 40 million m³/a of methane could be recoverable, corresponding to a thermal value of 150 TJ. A current pilot project in Kaunas may answer the economic questions involved. Some wastes currently dumped could be composted. Construction waste and raw mineral material waste could technically be used, respectively, in construction and in road building.

Information about the impact of dumping and other polluted sites upon the environment is insufficient, such investigations being carried out only sporadically. In 1993 the Ministry of the Environment, together with the State Geological Survey and consulting company, prepared "An Inventory of Dumping Sites and other Polluted Areas, and the Legal Basis for the Preparation of a Clean-Up Programme". This study investigated 632 polluted areas; the level of their impact was assessed, priorities were established, and clean-up plans were prepared for the 10 sites that had the worst effect on the environment. This work is expected to continue and municipalities are supposed to prepare their own clean-up plans.

Contaminated soils and sites

The Geological Survey is carrying out a survey of contaminated sites of both military and civilian origin. Pesticide waste generation has been comparatively low in recent years, but the huge quantities accumulated in unsafe storage facilities dispersed throughout Lithuania are causing considerable concern. In 1995, it was estimated that 954 storage facilities contained more than 4 000 t of pesticides, of which nearly 2 200 t were obsolete, i.e. either prohibited, outdated or unidentified. During 1989-1995, 29 pesticide storage facilities caught fire, 9 fires occurred in 1996 and one minor fire in 1997. The Programme for the Management of Obsolete Pesticides has been developed recently (see below for measures taken) and is being implemented.

The bulk of hazardous waste produced in Lithuania is stored on the production sites of enterprises. Since 1991, Lithuanian law has mandated that hazardous waste (153 000 t in 1995) should be temporarily stored at its production site, until a decision is taken on how to deal with it. Before the implementation of this law, many municipal landfills accepted hazardous wastes, which were normally mixed with domestic waste. Outside large cities, most of these dumping sites do not have monitoring programmes in place. Rainfall and runoff are creating problems to both surface and groundwater. A second source of soil contamination is solid waste landfills, which, in most cases, were not designed properly. They have often been located in geologically unsuitable places, many are too small and in a neglected state. In the past, hazardous waste disposal practices have included mixing it with industrial waste-water effluents, domestic and non-toxic industrial solid wastes for disposal in poorly designed landfills. Monitoring by the Kaunas Regional Environment Protection Agency detected chrome, cadmium, lead, nickel, manganese, and heavy ferrous metals in wells at the Kaunas municipal landfill. Higher concentrations of these metals were reported in nearby stream banks that lead to the Neris River, only 2 km away from the landfill. Similarly, the Vilnius Municipal Environmental Board has found high levels of hazardous waste in its three closed landfills as a result of subsurface monitoring, and is concerned about the hydrogeology of its present landfill.

Soil contamination exists also at former Soviet military sites and training grounds. The former military sites alone cover 67 762 ha or 1.04 per cent of the country's territory. These grounds are mainly contaminated with oil products. Heavy metals, specific chemical and radioactive substances have been found as well. Many sites suffer from soil erosion and subsidence. The state of 425 sites has been reviewed, and 27 pilot sites have been investigated in detail, with plans for remediation proposed. For the Šiauliai airport a phased remediation programme has been started. The amount of leaked or spilled oil or fuel is such that its recovery may make the operation self-financing. Total remediation of all sites would cost approximately US$ 1 billion.

9.2 Policy objectives and management instruments

Legal provisions

Article 20 (on the production and use of toxic and hazardous materials), Art. 21 (on the production and use of radioactive matter) and Article 23 (on waste management) of the Law on Environmental Protection are particularly relevant for waste management. They stipulate, for instance, that:

° Legal and natural persons using toxic and dangerous chemicals are responsible for all costs incurred for their use, storage, transport and disposal.
° Their production or import shall be permitted only following State examination.
° Lists of toxic and hazardous materials shall be approved or renewed by the Ministry of Health and the Ministry of the Environment.
° Regulations for the record-keeping, import, use, transport, storage, and dumping of radioactive matter, as well as norms of radiation safety shall be established.
° Users of natural resources must keep records of waste and must comply with regulations concerning the identification, use, storage, dumping, and treatment of waste.
° Legal and natural persons are liable for toxic, hazardous, and radioactive waste which is the result of production until it is recycled or treated in the established manner.
° Toxic, hazardous, and radioactive waste shall be stored, dumped and treated in special installations or storage facilities.
° Reprocessing of radioactive matter used for fuel elements of nuclear power plants and the reprocessing of spent nuclear fuel are prohibited.
° Sites for the containment, storage, dumping, and treatment of toxic and radioactive waste shall be allotted by the Government.
° The regulations for the transit of toxic and radioactive materials shall be established by international treaty.
° The Ministry of the Environment coordinates waste policy, management and enforcement. Hazardous waste is managed under the responsibility of the Ministry of the Economy. Non-hazardous industrial and municipal wastes are managed by local authorities.

The following legal documents were also adopted after independence: (i) the Regulation on the Site

Selection for Landfills of Solid Wastes issued by the Ministry of the Environment and the Ministry of Health, 18 March 1992, setting the basic requirements for landfill site location and distance from environmentally sensitive objects such as well-fields, water bodies, residential and recreation areas, etc.; (ii) the Regulation on the Conditions for the Selection of Hazardous Waste Storage Sites (adopted by general order of the Ministry of the Environment and the Ministry of Health, 10 June 1992); (iii) norms for the use of sewage sludge (in agreement with Council Directive 86/278/EEC on use of sewage sludge in agriculture); and (iv) environmental requirements for the establishment and maintenance of facilities for the dismantling of road vehicles (in agreement with the proposal for a council directive on end-of-life motor vehicles).

The following regulations are in preparation: (i) regulation on the construction and operation of solid waste landfill (in harmony with the proposed landfill directive); (ii) basic requirements for waste incineration (in accordance with Municipal Waste Incineration Directive 89/369/EEC and Hazardous Waste Incineration Directive 94/67/EEC); (iii) regulation for the establishment and operation of interim storage stations for hazardous waste generated in households; and regulation on licencing of the collection, transport, storage, disposal and recycling of hazardous waste.

Former Soviet regulations still valid in Lithuania until 31 December 1998 (see Chapter 1) include:
- Landfills for the disposal of toxic industrial waste. Basic design guidelines. Moscow, 1985
- Limit values for the accumulation of toxic industrial waste in industrial enterprises (organizations), Moscow, 1985
- Limit values for toxic compounds in industrial wastes causing their attribution to the categories of toxicity. Moscow, 1985
- Limit values for toxic industrial waste permitted to be disposed in landfills for solid waste. Moscow, 1985
- Rules for the accumulation, transport, treatment and disposal of toxic industrial waste. Moscow, 1985
- Temporary classifier of toxic industrial waste and recommendation on the definition of the toxicity class for industrial waste. Moscow, 1987
- Recommendations on the conditions of accepting slightly toxic industrial waste to a landfill for solid household waste. Moscow, 1977

The Soviet regulations listed above contain many technical requirements that are inconsistent with the requirements of EU legislation. For example, the *Temporary classifier of toxic industrial waste* defines four categories of waste which cannot be related to the EU waste classification. Also, not all of the former rules have actually been enforced.

The provisions of the Law on Environmental Protection are consistent with the requirements of the EU legislation except the prohibition of waste import. It is expected that the Lithuanian Parliament will take the decision to ratify the Basel Convention and to annul the prohibition late in 1998, opening the way for a gradual implementation of the requirements of Council Regulation 259/93 on the supervision and control of shipments of waste.

The Law on Waste Management was adopted in 1998. It is a framework regulation introducing the main waste management principles and incorporating the basic requirements of the EU waste directives such as permitting, duty of care, waste management priorities, etc. A number of waste management regulations will need to be issued following the adoption of the Law, so as to introduce specific requirements for specific sectors of waste management.

The Law on Nuclear Energy was adopted in 1996. The Regulation on the Safe Transport of Radioactive Materials (in accordance with relevant IAEA documents) was adopted as a ministerial order. A government decree on shipments of radioactive materials is currently in inter-ministerial consultation. The following legislation is supposed to be drafted:

- a draft law on radioactive waste (the main provisions are not yet clear, but should be in accordance with IAEA recommendations);
- a draft law on radiation protection (in accordance with IAEA Basic Safety Standards).

Objectives, action programme and institutions

The National Environmental Strategy, the objectives of the (hazardous and non-hazardous) waste management policy for industrial and domestic waste, international legal obligations and the Strategy of EU Approximation in the Waste Sector (draft report, October 1997) formulate waste

Table 9.6: Waste Management Action Programme

Actions	Timescale	Responsible organization
Domestic waste management		
- Develop rules for domestic and other non-hazardous waste management, dumping site construction and operation	1996-1997	MCUD, MIT, M, MEP
- Assess the potential for secondary raw materials recycling, make market studies for products from secondary raw materials	1996-1997	MIT, MEP, M
- Increase efforts to sort domestic wastes and secondary raw materials collection and application	1996-2000	MIT, MCUD, M
- Renaturalize closed dumping sites	continuous	M, MEP, MH, MCUD
Industrial and hazardous waste management		
- Ratify the Basel Convention, develop rules for waste import and export	1996-1997	MEP
- Render harmless banned and old pesticides	1996-1997	MEP
- Amend the Feasibility Study on Waste Management	1996-1997	MEP, MIT
- Develop and implement a programme for hospital waste management	1996-2000	MH, MIT, MEP
Radioactive contamination and safety		
- Perform an international environmental impact assessment of the radioactive waste storage in Sirvintos District and assess its elimination possibilities	1996-1998	MEP
Reduction of soil contamination in cities and industrial areas; reduction of soil pollution with heavy metals		
- Systematize data on soil contamination with heavy metals and publish information/cartographic material on levels of contamination with heavy metals, on risk levels and prevention measures	1996-2000	MEP
- Create polluted soils databases and monitoring plans per municipality	1998-2000	MEP, M
Reduction of soil contamination with oil products		
- Draft law on liability for past environmental damage	1997-1998	MEP, ME
- Compile an inventory of areas polluted with oil products, continue with studies on clean-up possibilities of these areas, including the former Soviet military sites, and develop clean-up and renaturalization programmes	1997-2000	MEP, M, LGS (MCUD)

Source: National Environmental Strategy.

M - Municipalities;
MCUD - former Ministry of Construction and Urban Development; now part of the Ministry of the Environment;
ME - Ministry of Energy;
MEP - former Ministry of Environmental Protection; now part of the Ministry of the Environment;
MH - Ministry of Health;
MIT - former Ministry of Industry and Trade; now part of the Ministry of the Economy.

management goals. The Environmental Strategy includes an Action Programme approved by the Government on 5 August 1996. The actions, time schedule and organizations involved in its waste management segment, are given in Table 9.6.

The Law on Waste Management is supposed to be complemented by the National Strategy on Waste Management, to be adopted in the course of 1998. The Strategy was submitted to the Government in June 1998. It includes provisions for the implementation of EU requirements, but also additional measures for improving Lithuania's waste management, including lists of measures implementing the Law on Waste Management. The scope of future waste management is set out, as are the instruments to be used in waste management, provisions on information, public information and participation. The strategy also sets targets for the recovery and recycling of secondary materials, organic waste, packaging materials and landfill reduction.

The Law on Waste Management requires municipalities to develop and implement territorial waste management plans. Waste management plans should include management by group of waste, indications of financial resources, responsible institutions and control bodies. State waste management plans are the responsibility of institutions appointed by the Government, whereas local authorities implement municipal waste management plans. The nuclear fuel cycle is controlled by the Nuclear Power Safety Inspectorate. All other types of radioactive wastes are controlled by the Ministry of the Environment, whereas the Ministry of Health is responsible for occupational safety. The Ministry of the Economy operates all waste installations.

Hazardous waste management

The Hazardous Waste Management Programme (HWMP) was adopted by the Government in February 1993 on the basis of a feasibility study on hazardous waste management by Danish consultants. The study proposed the establishment of a central hazardous waste treatment and disposal facility containing incineration, physical/chemical treatment and a safe landfill as well as a network of transfer and collection stations. The cost of the implementation of the system was estimated at approximately US$ 100 million.

As Lithuania's economy was in a critical state, it was not possible to find an institution ready to finance so huge a project, so alternatives had to be found. Some financing, substantially less than planned, was allocated to the Programme from the State budget and used mainly for the design of regional hazardous waste interim storage facilities. During the 1993-1996 period, using minimal State budget resources (159 000 Litas in 1993, 601 000 Litas in 1994, 500 000 Litas in 1996), sites were selected for hazardous waste handling. The collection, handling and treatment plants or grounds are foreseen in six regions: Vilnius,

Klaipėda, Šiauliai, Panevėžys, Alytus, Kaunas. The basic design of several regional facilities is completed. The construction of Klaipėda and Šiauliai storage facilities started in 1997 with the financial support of EU PHARE Cross Border Programme.

However, as the central treatment facility may never be constructed, a new concept for a partly decentralized hazardous waste management system is currently being developed. To that end, another Hazardous Waste Management Study, funded by EU PHARE (ECU 300 000), was started in 1997 and completed in February 1998. It developed four management options from both technical and economic points of view. The proposed strategy includes:

- Improvement of hazardous waste handling practices, including packaging, labelling, waste stream control and waste tracking;
- Construction of regional transfer stations for hazardous waste collection and pre-treatment;
- Construction of a permanent storage facility for the disposal of inorganic hazardous waste;
- Incineration of organic hazardous wastes in cement kilns.

The estimated costs of implementing the approach amounts to US$ 10 million, as compared to the US$ 100 million that would have been necessary for the earlier centralized strategy.

The issue of obsolete pesticides is being solved on the basis of the 1997 Government Programme for the Management of Obsolete Pesticides. The State budget (2 million Litas) and Municipal Environmental Protection Funds will finance the solution of the problem. So far,

- 2 910.5 t of pesticides initially stored in 584 storage facilities were repacked, identified, sorted, labelled and stored adequately;
- 339 old storage facilities have been emptied and cleaned;
- 297.7 t of initially unknown pesticides were identified; and
- 730.5 t of pesticides that were not banned have been used in agriculture.

Subject to the availability of sufficient funds, all the remaining 1 300 t of obsolete pesticides will be repacked and adequately stored in 1998. The identification of the approximately 2 000 t of unknown chemicals is slated for completion in

2000. It is also expected that most of the repacked and identified pesticides can be used in agriculture, leaving only 30% (or 1 300 t) for incineration. Incineration is expected to start in the second half of 1999. The implementation of the programme has apparently led to an activation of additional municipal programmes aiming at rehabilitating storage facilities.

At present a medical waste management system is under preparation. It will be part of an integrated hazardous waste management system. The pre-feasibility studies for the collection and management of medical waste were prepared for approval in 1996. The construction of a central hospital waste treatment centre is proposed in the project as well as the development and enforcement of the necessary legislation and changes in institutional structure necessary for the implementation of the project.

Strategy of EU approximation in the waste sector

A project, funded by Denmark, on strengthening the framework and administration of Lithuania's laws on waste management and on environmental management in industry started in late 1997. Specifically, the project aims at facilitating the creation of a financially, institutionally and environmentally sustainable waste management sector as well as the development of an effective public administration for that sector. It will put into practice the EU directives and regulatory measures applicable to the management of wastes, the selection of household waste and the use of secondary materials.

A five-year action plan, comprising three phases, was developed. It follows the adoption of the 1998 Law on Waste Management by Parliament. Phase 1 (implementation planned in 1998) will start with the preparation of waste management regulations for both non-hazardous and hazardous waste. It is envisaged that no new specific requirements will be imposed on waste collection, transport, treatment and disposal. The emphasis will be on the collection of reliable information. All companies involved in waste collection or management will have to register with the Ministry of the Environment, keep records of their activities and report to the Ministry. The staff of the Ministry in Vilnius and in the regional departments should be capable of checking the reliability of data presented by the companies, evaluate them and make additional inquiries if necessary. Staff will be

trained to this end. A manual with detailed waste identification procedures will be published and regional workshops organized for representatives of industries.

The preparation and adoption of two regulations covering specific wastes is also envisaged in Phase 1. One of them concerns discarded pesticides, the other the collection and treatment of waste oils. Finally, waste management plans are to be drafted in Phase 1. As required by Directive 75/442/EEC, the plans will cover type, quantity and origin of waste to be recovered/disposed of, general technical requirements, special arrangements for particular wastes, and suitable disposal sites. A plan for the closure, reclamation and aftercare of landfills will be drawn up. At the same time, a plan for the implementation of integrated and adequate waste disposal installations will be drawn up. Drafting will be in the hands of the Ministry of the Environment and the Ministry of the Economy. The draft will be distributed for comments and proposals to the regions and municipalities, where it will also serve as a basis for regional and municipal plans. The plans will be reviewed, corrected and amended each year.

Phase 2 (1999-2000) will start with the registration of waste collection, transport, recovery and disposal enterprises. Regional and national databases will contain lists of enterprises and data on their activities. These data will be correlated with the data on hazardous waste generation obtained by notification procedure. Based on collected data, the requirements for various types of waste recovery and disposal enterprises will be drawn up and a realistic time frame set for their enforcement. At the same time, the requirements for new waste recovery and disposal enterprises will be adopted and enforced. Stricter control will be imposed over the generators of hazardous waste with the introduction of a permitting system. This will stimulate the development of hazardous waste recovery and disposal activities and the establishment of an integrated system of hazardous waste management.

The reform of municipal waste collection, sorting and disposal systems is another important activity in Phase 2. Currently, most of municipal waste collection systems are subsidized, and landfill investment and maintenance costs are covered from the municipal budgets or municipal environmental funds. Total cost recovery will be gradually introduced, allowing the accumulation of funds for landfill construction and opening the way for financing from the IFI. On the other hand, increased waste disposal costs will stimulate recycling activities and the development of markets for recovered products.

A number of specific regulations will also be drafted and introduced in this phase. They include regulations on the collection, recovery and disposal of used batteries; on hazardous waste incineration; and on the use of sewage sludge in agriculture. The adoption of a national regulation on the supervision and control of shipments of waste will open the way for international cooperation in the waste management sector, especially with other Baltic States.

The activities in Phase 3 (2001-2002) are focused on strengthening the results obtained in the preceding phases and gradually achieving compliance with EU requirements. Additionally, several lower priority regulations, including a regulation on municipal waste incineration, on PCB waste collection and disposal and on titanium waste, will be adopted.

9.3   Conclusions and recommendations

Lithuania's environmental policy has advanced to a level at which it becomes clear what steps should be taken next. With regard to waste management, substantial improvements are needed urgently in all areas. As the revision of the Law on Waste Management has been completed, it is now essential to approve and implement the comprehensive waste management strategy – including hazardous waste management - without delay.

The adoption and implementation of the waste management strategy is all the more important, as it can be seen as the organizational framework for the development of the regulations and other legal instruments complementing the Law on Waste Management, including the specification of management instruments, competences at the different levels of government and public information and participation. This being a complex programme, it is of great importance that the adoption of the strategy by consensus of all involved should be vigorously pursued. The strategy should clearly indicate the relationship between goals and priorities on the one hand, and actions and projects on the other. The action plan needs to be elaborated downstream to such levels

that the budget consequences are well understood and approved by all key players. The implementation plan should contain provisions for evaluating and monitoring its execution.

Waste treatment and disposal are major concerns for waste management. There was much criticism by Lithuania's business and industry circles, who claim that the various studies and options proposed focused mainly on the most advanced western technologies and did not consider the potential existing in Lithuanian enterprises for treatment and use of industrial wastes. They refer to installations like rotation incinerators in the cement factories, boilers or physico-chemical reactors.

Recommendation 9.1:
The waste management strategy should be approved as a matter of the greatest possible urgency, and on the basis of a consensus by all levels of government and institutions concerned. Feasibility studies of waste treatment projects should regularly include a technical and economic evaluation of the technical possibilities existing in the country. Management plans need to be part of the preparation of waste treatment facilities.

The current waste management regulations cover only very narrow, separate areas of waste management activities. The implementation of the new system of such regulations following the adoption of the waste management strategy is urgent not only because all legal instruments have to be put in place as a consequence of the approximation strategy, but also because of the abolition of old GOST standards by the end of 1998. The pending final approval of the waste management strategy should not delay the start of the work on the development of a concise system of implementing regulations. Much of this work has already started, but might require additional attention and resources.

Recommendation 9.2:
The scattered regulations that are in force should be replaced as quickly as possible by a coherent set of regulations compatible with the aims and principles of the Waste Management Law.

Still in the area of legal instruments, a complete and coherent nuclear legislation package is lacking in Lithuania. From an environmental point of view as well as from the point of view of energy policy, the absence of relevant decisions on the future of Ignalina are certainly a gap that needs to be bridged urgently.

Recommendation 9.3:
A strategy for radioactive waste management, or at least a timetable for strategic decisions, is required as part of an overall waste and energy strategy.

Owing to their potentially large volume, construction wastes are problematic. Their reuse and recycling is therefore an important option, especially once construction activity picks up again. Experience shows that economic instruments are the most effective in order to promote reuse.

Recommendation 9.4:
The reuse of construction and quarry wastes should be encouraged by charging the full collection and disposal costs to the holders of these wastes.

Wastes in dumping sites should be securely disposed of, substances which leak out and affect the environment should be collected, including biogas. For air, groundwater and landscape protection from pollution, it is necessary to rehabilitate closed dumping sites. Based on the studies done so far of hazardous wastes sites, the inventory of sites, risks and legal liabilities should be finalised. Site remediation can be extremely expensive, and should be done gradually. Rapid measures are needed to prevent exposure and contain the further spread of contamination at those sites where there are demonstrated health and environmental problems. Policy priorities should be established for medium-term site remediation.

Spent oils/waste oils and oil-contaminated wastes form a challenging waste problem, threatening water and soil in Lithuania. To solve this problem, again a special and new institutional and legal framework needs to be established which takes into account new types of waste oil and which makes use of the market potential and the energy contents of the wastes.

Due to the present deficiencies in reporting, resulting in poor reliability of reported data, there is no efficient control of hazardous wastes. In view of the risk potential of hazardous wastes, it is imperative to set up a credible, water-tight system of reporting and control of hazardous wastes, to ensure the (future) enforcement of legal provisions pertaining to hazardous wastes.

Recommendation 9.5:
A legal and institutional framework needs to be established to investigate contaminated waste disposal sites, set criteria for action, and finance remedial action , as well as to solve all problems related to used oils. An efficient reporting and control system for hazardous wastes needs to be set up and implemented.

PART III: ECONOMIC AND SECTORAL INTEGRATION

Chapter 10

HUMAN HEALTH AND THE ENVIRONMENT

10.1 Health status and environmental conditions

General health status

Mortality rates and major causes of death are the subject of Table 10.1. The infant mortality rate was 10.0 per 1 000 live births in 1996, well within the range observed in other developed countries. It was slightly higher in rural than in urban areas (11.1 against 9.4 per 1 000 live births, respectively). This was the lowest rate in 10 years, after a peak of 16.5 per 1 000 live births in 1992. The total mortality rate increased by 16.0 per cent between 1986 and 1996 (from 10.0 to 10.9per 1 000 population), with a peak of 12.5 per 1 000 population in 1994.

The most important cause of death are diseases of the circulatory system (about 55 per cent of the total in 1996). Rates increased from 596.7 to 633.2 per 100 000 population between 1989 and 1996, with a peak in 1993 of 671.5 per 100 000 population. This is in contrast to the countries of the European Union, where death rates due to diseases of the circulatory system have been constantly declining over the past 25 years. In 1995, Lithuania's standardized death rate due to these diseases was twice the EU average, but lower than that of the other Baltic countries.

Malignant neoplasms are the second cause of death (17.5 per cent of the total), with rates similar to the EU average and higher than the CIS average (in 1995, the standardized death rate for malignant neoplasms was 201.1 per 100 000 population, against 195.0 in the EU and 181.3 in the CIS). The incidence of breast and skin cancer is increasing (up ca. 1 per cent a year increase for breast cancer and ca. 6-7 per cent for melanoma); the incidence of lung cancer is stable and that of stomach cancer decreasing.

The greatest increase in mortality in the past few years has been in mortality due to external causes (13.6 per cent of the total). This is the third cause of death. The rate was 157.6 per 100 000 population in 1996, almost 35 per cent higher than in 1989 and 4.1 times the EU average. In 1996 external causes were the most important cause of death for males and females under the age of 44. Suicides and traffic accidents accounted for ca. 30 per cent and 15 per cent of the deaths by external causes, respectively. Rates were about four times higher among males than females.

The suicide rate increased by 71 per cent between 1989 and 1996. This accounted for more than half the number of deaths in males aged 30 to 59. In 1995, the standardized suicide rates for males under the age of 65 were the highest in the WHO European region (80.8 per 100 000 population, 5.1 times the EU average and around 50 per cent higher than in the CIS). The reporting of suicides is known to vary across cultures. Whether the high levels

Table 10.1: Mortality rates by important causes of death, 1989-1997

	1989		1996		1997		% change
	per 100 000	%	*per 100 000*	%	*per 100 000*	%	1989-1997
All causes	1 033.5	100.0	1 095.9	100.0	1 110.3	100.0	7.4
Diseases of the circulatory system	596.7	57.7	633.2	57.8	613.9	55.3	2.9
Malignant neoplasms	179.9	17.4	204.3	18.6	196.8	17.7	9.4
External causes	117.3	11.4	157.6	14.4	146.9	13.2	25.2
Respiratory diseases	47.2	4.6	31.1	2.8	43.0	3.9	-8.9

Sources: Lithuania Statistical Yearbook, 1997;
Economic and social development in Lithuania (3 March 1998).

Table 10.2: Standardized mortality rates for the most important
causes of death, 1995

per 100 000 inhabitants

	Lithuania	EU Average	CIS Average
All causes	**1 170.3**	**726.7**	**1 405.3**
of which:			
Diseases of the circulatory system	597.4	291.2	742.4
Malignant neoplasms	201.1	195.0	181.3
External causes	181.8	43.8	177.8
- Suicides (all)	*46.9*	*11.7*	*30.7*
Suicides (males < 65)	*80.8*	*15.7*	*52.8*
Suicides (females < 65)	*13.3*	*5.0*	*8.6*
- Traffic accidents	*20.1*	*11.7*	*18.8*
Traffic accidents (males < 65)	*32.5*	*17.0*	*30.3*
Traffic accidents (females < 65)	*7.1*	*5.2*	*7.7*
Respiratory diseases	47.5	57.0	85.2
- Bronchitis, emphysema, asthma	*34.5*	*12.9*	*42.7*

Source: WHO Health for All database.

observed in Lithuania could be due to its different reporting practices is a hypothesis that has not been assessed.

Deaths by accidental alcohol poisoning increased 3.5-fold between 1989 and 1996, while newly registered cases of alcoholic psychosis increased five-fold. New cases of chronic alcoholism increased 3.5-fold. This is at least in part related to the increase in alcohol consumption following the abolition of the State monopoly.

The standardized mortality rate due to traffic accidents is one of the highest in the WHO European region and twice the EU average (20.1 per 100 000 population, see Table 10.2). 667 people died as a consequence of traffic accidents in 1996. The number of people who died per 1000 casualties (severity index) was among the highest in Europe (128). Alcohol was involved in some 19 per cent of traffic accidents. The rate has declined since 1991, and in 1996 it stood at 23.1 per 100 000 population. During the same period, the number of cars continued to rise steadily, by almost 50 per cent. Considering that most traffic-related deaths are preventable, the still relatively high level of mortality caused by accidents requires urgent attention.

In 1996, diseases of the respiratory system were the fourth cause of death (4.0 per cent of the total), with a death rate of 45.6 per 100 000 population.

Although it declined during the period 1987-1992, this cause of death has again become more prevalent during the past few years.

Morbidity due to respiratory diseases is rising, and so is the related number of hospital admissions (up about 18 per cent in the period 1992-1995). In 1996, about 80 per cent of recorded notifiable diseases were acute upper respiratory infections (9643.4 cases per 100 000 population). Enterobiasis morbidity is fairly high: in 1996, it affected about 16.5 per cent of the population. Trichinellosis is increasing, and this is thought to be due to the growing consumption of contaminated meat from uncontrolled home-slaughtered pigs.

The incidence of tick-borne encephalitis (TBE) grew from 0.2 - 0.5 cases per 100 000 population in the period 1990-1992 to 11.5 cases per 100 000 population in 1995 and 8.4 cases per 100 000 population in 1996. This rise, with a seasonal peak between May and June, has been associated with the growing number of Borellia-infected ticks, which is estimated to affect 0 – 22.5 per cent of the tick population. For the TBE virus, the so-called mean minimal infection rate (MIR) is measured and amounts, at the national level, to 1.9 infected ticks per 1 000 ticks tested. In some areas MIR affects 29 to 77 ticks per 1000 ticks tested. This problem is being overcome with a vaccination programme for forest workers and an information campaign for the general population (especially tourists and amateur gardeners).

Air pollution and environmental health

Total Suspended Particle (TSP) levels are a major health concern. Some of the main cities (totalling about 1.5 million inhabitants) would be classified by WHO as "black spots" and require corrective measures. In 1993, levels of ambient nitrogen dioxide also exceeded the yearly average limit proposed by WHO; indoor NO_2 levels are not yet monitored, but are expected to be higher than outdoor levels. It can be roughly estimated that episodes of high TSP levels cause an extra 7 to 15 deaths and an additional 15 to 30 hospital admissions for respiratory symptoms per day. High NO_2 levels can be expected to aggravate these effects. Both TSP and NO_2 have declined since the early 1990s, but current levels in some urban areas are still dangerous to human health. Levels of sulphur dioxide have declined in the last decade and are reaching levels not currently thought to affect health. Similarly, lead levels are reaching those considered safe for human health and the recent decision to allow only unleaded petrol is probably a major contribution to that. Other heavy metals (Fe, Mn, Cu, Ni, Cr, Zn, V) are also at levels considered safe. The monitoring of ozone is too limited to allow conclusions regarding health risks to be drawn. The population living in the vicinity of certain sources of pollutants has been found to suffer health effects. For example, a high prevalence of chronic bronchitis and asthma was found among residents near the Akmenė cement plant. In Kėdainiai, the high pollution from aerosols of sulphuric acid emitted by a fertilizer plant was associated with a cluster of lung cancers and with a higher incidence of acute and chronic bronchitis, pharyngitis and pneumonia than what was observed among residents in a relatively less polluted area.

The most important and increasing source of air pollution is transport (responsible for about 70 per cent of emissions), which emitted 11 000 tonnes more in 1995 than in 1992, when the contribution of mobile sources was around 60 per cent. These figures are based on estimates of vehicle exhausts, not on measured values. Vehicles are generally old and not well maintained because tools and supplies are lacking. Vehicle inspection is required every two years. It is estimated that some 30 per cent of the vehicles on the road exceed emission standards. New vehicle emission standards for carbon monoxide, fumes and hydrocarbons were introduced in 1995, with implementation starting in January 1998.

The lead content in fuel has decreased, thanks to a switch to the production of unleaded fuel. However, imported leaded petrol is frequently added to unleaded petrol. The Ministry of the Environment estimates that leaded petrol makes up about 5 per cent of total consumption. In an effort to discourage the import of obsolete and more polluting cars, there are plans to introduce three different levels of taxation based on the age of the vehicles (up to 7 years old; 7 to 10 years old and more than 10 years old). Other problems stem from the fact that there is no scheme for vehicle inspection before registration, and that the age of the vehicle is not recorded at the moment of registration.

The energy industry, manufacturing of construction material, oil processing and chemical production are the biggest industrial air polluters. Data on air quality suggest that problems are especially acute in Šiauliai, Kaunas, Klaipėda, and Vilnius, where there is a combination of emissions from industrial activity and traffic, and on certain sites of specialized industrial and energy facilities, including Elektrėnai (oil-fired thermal power plant), Jonava (fertilizer plant), Kėdainiai (biochemical and fertilizer plants) Mažeikiai (refinery) and Naujoi Akmenė (cement plant).

Sulphur dioxide does not appear to be a particular concern for the health of the Lithuanian population. SO_2 emissions have dropped sharply over the past few years. Monitoring data indicate that in 1996 the release of SO_2 in the atmosphere amounted to 63 000 tonnes, most of it from stationary sources. Neither the annual average nor the maximum concentrations in any town exceeded the country's maximum allowable concentration (MAC) of 0.05 mg/m^3 and 0.125 mg/m^3, respectively. These MACs are in line with the revised WHO Air Quality Guidelines for average annual and 24-hour exposure, respectively. Although it is difficult to separate the health effects of SO_2 from those of particulate matter, SO_2 has been associated with increased daily mortality (all causes), morbidity (including respiratory symptoms and illness) and deficits in pulmonary function tests.

Due to their association with respiratory symptoms and daily mortality fluctuations, total suspended particles (TSP) continue to be a priority concern in many Lithuanian towns, in spite of the substantial cut in emissions in recent years. In 1993 the highest levels of TSP were observed in Kaunas, Kėdainiai and Jonava, with average concentrations of 0.2

mg/m^3 (average MAC 0.15 mg/m^3). This average is above the threshold of 0.120 mg/m^3, which, according to the WHO, defines "black spots" and calls for measures to reduce population exposure. In recent years, the Ministry of the Environment has reported an overall reduction in TSP emissions, which in 1996 amounted to 10 300 tonnes, –down 40 per cent since 1993 (17 500 tonnes). However, reported data on average yearly concentrations for the period 1990-97 include only values of < 0.1, 0.1 or 0.2 mg/m^3. This raises questions about the precision of the tests being used. According to the evaluations performed in Ukraine and the Russian Federation, assessments of 24-hour average concentrations based on these data are very uncertain. The evaluation of the particulate matter measurements in Ukraine suggests a lower limit of detection of 0.25 mg/m^3. This does not make it possible to draw conclusions about actual health effects. In 1993 peak concentrations of TSP exceeding the MAC (max) of 0.5 mg/m^3 were measured in Kaunas, Kėdainiai and Šiauliai (up to 2.0 mg/m^3), Vilnius, Klaipėda and Venta (up to 1.5 mg/m^3), and Jonava (up to 0.6 mg/m^3). Concentrations exceeding the MAC (max) were observed most frequently in Kėdainiai (6 per cent of samples), while in the other cities samples above the 0.5 mg/m^3 threshold were about 1-1.5 per cent of the total.

If the reported data correspond to actual pollution levels, a very rough estimate of the health risks associated with high TSP levels could be attempted based on the conservative assumption that circa 500 000 inhabitants in Lithuanian towns (i.e. ca. 1/3 of the inhabitants of the most polluted cities) may be exposed once a year to maximum TSP concentrations of 1.0 to 2.0 mg/m^3 over a three-day period. The daily mortality fluctuations could be 7 to 15, while the increase in hospital admissions for respiratory symptoms could be 15 to 30 cases a day. The health effects of TSPs have been investigated in Kaunas, where a positive correlation between exposure to TSPs and asthma risk in children was observed. The same authors also found a correlation between levels of formaldehyde and birth defects.

Nitrogen dioxide remains an important pollutant in Lithuanian towns, due to its association with respiratory symptoms, and to its combined action with TSPs to produce health effects, although a quantitative estimate of these effects is not possible. This assessment is confirmed by the fact that: (a) although they declined significantly between 1990 and 1993, NO$_2$ emissions have stabilized at around 13 500 tonnes/year in the period 1993-1996; (b) in 1993, the concentration of NO$_2$ often exceeded both the MAC (average) of 0.04 mg/m^3 and the MAC (max.) of 0.085 mg/m^3 (the revised WHO guideline value for the NO$_2$ yearly average is 0.04 mg/m^3); and (c) in conditions of high traffic and poor air dispersion, up to 25 per cent of air samples have been found to exceed standards.

Surface ozone is not monitored regularly (except at background stations and in Vilnius). Where measured, O$_3$ levels in rural areas are relatively low. The yearly average in 1993 was 47 μg/m^3 in Preila and 36 μg/m^3 in Vilnius. Seasonal ranges are 70-80 μg/m^3 in summer and 30-40 μg/m^3 in winter. These values are generally in line with European background levels of 40-70 μg/m^3. In 1993 ozone concentrations above the WHO guideline value of 120 μg/m^3 (8-hour average) were observed only 3 per cent of the time throughout the year (in July-August). Over the period 1982-1995 there was a yearly increase in ozone concentration of about 2.5 per cent in rural areas, mostly attributed to the ozone concentration increase in Europe and to transboundary transport.

There is not enough monitoring data on ozone to estimate the health impacts. Based on the scarce data available, the levels of O$_3$ prevailing in Lithuania would not seem to be associated with health effects. However, additional data on concentrations (e.g. data on 8-hour O$_3$ concentration) and population exposure are needed to assess possible adverse health effects. These may include transient respiratory symptoms, pulmonary inflammation, increased susceptibility to pulmonary infections, and more hospital admissions and emergency room visits.

The atmospheric levels of heavy metals (Fe, Mn, Cu, Ni, Pb, Cr, Zn, V) do not exceed either the average or the maximum nationwide MAC. In general, they do not seem to pose a particular health risk to the population. The average lead concentration in air in 1992 was 0.01 g/m^3, below the WHO annual average guideline value of 0.5 g/m^3. Efforts to decrease lead in motor fuels have contributed to significantly reducing this potential health hazard, though attention still has to be paid to the issue of irregular imports of leaded fuels. Measurements of lead and other heavy metals in biomedia of 57 pregnant women and 58 children taken in Siauliai and Vilnius show that for both subjects living in risk areas and residents in relatively unpolluted areas lead blood concentration was below levels associated with adverse health effects, although subjects living in risk areas had overall higher levels than residents in unpolluted areas.

Although in the period 1988-1993 pollution with benzo(a)pyrene (BaP) tended to decline in most towns, and stabilize in Vilnius, it remains a problem in Lithuanian towns, due to its carcinogenic potential. In Kaunas and Šiauliai the average yearly concentration of BaP was of 1.5 and 1.8 ng/m^3, respectively, above the country's MAC of 1.0 ng/m^3. Peak averages reached 3.6 ng/m^3. The highest concentrations of BaP were observed during the cold time of the year (heating season) and in places with heavy traffic. Based on the relatively high levels measured and on its potential carcinogenic effect, reducing this pollutant should be as a priority.

Assuming that in Lithuania about 600 000 city dwellers are exposed to a yearly average of 1.5 - 2.0 ng BaP/m^3 and that 50 out of every million people exposed to 1 ng BaP per m^3 for 50 years are at risk of developing cancer, roughly 30 to 60 people could be at risk of developing cancer as a result of exposure to BaP (WHO Air Quality Guidelines for Europe, revision 1996). The effects of BaP on the functionality of the immune system have been investigated among residents in Trakai (with a BaP concentration of 0.5-1.0 ng/m^3) and in Širvintos (with a BaP concentration of 0.1-0.5 ng/m^3). Results showed more signs of immuno-suppression among Trakai residents than among Širvintos residents. Another study investigated exposure to BaP by measuring levels of BaP in urine samples taken from 28 children and 26 pregnant women in areas identified as at high environmental health risk compared to less polluted areas. Results indicated that the concentration for those living in the risk area was three times higher (158.33 against 52.12 ng/l for children and 33.71 against 10.68 ng/l for pregnant women).

A few studies have investigated and found environmental health effects among residents living near industrial sites, such as the cement plant in Akmenė and the fertilizer plant in Kėdainiai. In Kėdainiai, an investigation into a lung cancer cluster showed a positive correlation with the relatively high level of sulphuric acid aerosols in the area during the previous years and a higher incidence of acute and chronic bronchitis, pharyngitis and pneumonia in the study group than in a population sample in an unpolluted area. A reduction in plant emissions resulted in a lower

incidence of lung cancer than in the 1970s and 1980s, when the region had the highest cancer incidence in the country. In Akmenė, a higher prevalence of chronic bronchitis and asthma, with lower lung functionality and corresponding changes in immunology and sputum cytology, was found in subjects living around the cement plant.

In Lithuania about 52 per cent of men and 10 per cent of women currently smoke (1992 survey among 25 to 64-year-old adults). This is similar to the average figures of the WHO European region, where 46 per cent of men and 10 per cent of women smoke. Smoking is becoming more popular among young women (up from 8 per cent in 1983 to 18 per cent in 1993 for women aged 25 to 29), while it is relatively stable (around 60 per cent) among men in the same age group. Smoking was estimated to be implicated in about 6700 deaths in 1995 (i.e. 17 per cent of all deaths). It is not known how many people are exposed to environmental tobacco smoke at work or at home (especially children). Therefore, even though the effects of environmental tobacco smoke are well recognized, the burden of disease due to it cannot currently be estimated.

The recently adopted Tobacco Control Law (1996) bans tobacco advertising and sponsorship and ensures a smoke-free environment in a number of public places. It also requires mandatory health warnings on cigarette packets, sets a maximum tar level of 15 mg/cigarette, and bans the sale of cigarettes to minors under 18. Several institutions are actively involved in activities to educate the population about the dangers of smoking, among which the Kaunas Medical Academy, the Ministry of Health, the National Health Education Centre, the National Cancer Centre, the Health Association, the Kaunas Cancer Society and Kaunas Healthy Cities Project.

Drinking water, food and environmental health

According to data reported by the National Centre of Hygiene and by the Ministry of Health, 41.3 per cent of all tested samples of centralized drinking water failed to comply with hygiene norms, mostly for high iron concentrations. Deep groundwater is the main source of drinking water in Lithuania, especially in urban areas. Some two thirds of the population rely on it. Water sources in Vilnius and Kaunas are judged to be adequate over the medium term. New groundwater sources are expected to require more purification than existing ones. In

1994 the amount of water used for drinking water purposes amounted to 29.3 millions m^3, there were some 6 000 watering places and 2958 water supply plants . Overall, some 78 per cent of the population (or 3 million inhabitants) receive piped water. About 800 000 inhabitants, mostly in rural areas, use water from dug wells. There are an estimated 300 000 dug wells. In urban areas, 93.3 per cent of the housing units receive piped water . The water distribution networks are in bad condition. The pipes are old and of poor quality, and many of them leak. Water pumps are also of poor quality.

Microbial contamination of drinking water is an important problem in Lithuania. Of the shallow groundwater wells that are used by over one million people in rural areas, 77 per cent exceed the established limits for bacteriological and nutrient contamination. Of more than 39 000 samples from centralized water supplies, 6 per cent of samples from artesian wells, 10.5 per cent of samples from watering places that are replenished from open bodies of water and 56.6 per cent of samples from wells were found to be contaminated by microbes. Microbial contamination is detected in about 7-8 per cent of samples analysed at the tap, and it occurs most likely in the distribution system. It is estimated that about 20 per cent of cases of salmonella, shygella and hepatitis A (i.e. some 2 000 cases a year) may be caused by the consumption of water contaminated by microbes. Water is disinfected mainly with chlorine. Overdosing occurs occasionally. Disinfecting lamps are installed at only 0.4 per cent of watering places.

The main chemical pollutant in Lithuania's drinking water from dug wells is nitrate, most of which comes from fertilizers and organic waste (e.g. manure). It is estimated that nitrate pollution affects about 30 per cent of dug wells. This translates into approximately 300 000 inhabitants consuming water that exceeds permitted nitrate limits (national MAC: 50 mg/l, in line with WHO guidelines).

High nitrate concentrations (50 mg/litre and above) are associated with methaemoglobinemia, a condition that may even cause the death of young children (the most vulnerable group being infants aged less than 3 months). Nitrates have also been suggested to be implicated in stomach cancer, but this association has not been demonstrated. One to three cases of methaemoglobinemia are diagnosed among new-born babies each year, but this condition may be under-diagnosed. To prevent the

problem, pregnant women reporting to the Health Care system are asked to specify whether they consume dug well water. If so, the nitrate concentration of the water is analysed and, if it exceeds the limits, the woman is advised to stop drinking the contaminated water. In practice, it is difficult to enforce this recommendation, as these women may not be able to afford bottled water.

Cases of drinking water contamination by heavy metals are rare, with only 0.4 per cent of test samples exceeding the limits for Cu, Zn and Pb. Iron levels above the limits for organoleptic quality were found in 38 per cent of water samples. In 12 per cent of the samples the iron limit was exceeded threefold at least. Only 63 per cent of municipal water supplies have and use equipment for reducing the amount of iron in drinking water. 3.5 per cent of the population consumes water with a fluoride content above the 1.5 mg/litre value, sometimes even reaching levels that could cause fluorosis. Most people consume water whose fluoride guideline concentration is below optimal levels (around 1.0 mg/litre), and this raises the question of how to supplement their fluoride intake to prevent dental caries.

The Centre of Ecological Medicine of the Institute of Hygiene is responsible for setting quality standards for recreational water and for monitoring it. Due to the high level of sewage water that does not receive sufficient treatment, the microbial contamination (coliform index) on the beaches of Klaipėda, Giruliai and Palanga sometimes exceeds acceptable levels for bathing. However, since the ban on bathing in these waters is well enforced, there has been no reported incidence of disease among bathers.

In 1996, 641 tonnes of examined food were found to be unfit for consumption by the State Hygiene Inspectorate. If the established microbial norms are exceeded, the food concerned cannot be sold or served. Contamination is two to three times more frequent in places where food is sold or served than at food-processing plants. The problem of microbial contamination is growing, especially in view of the proliferation of small food kiosks. These have been identified as possibly the main source of food-borne disease outbreaks in Lithuania today. However, there is not enough monitoring data to quantify the problem. The kiosks are managed by licensed street vendors, who do not receive training on safe food storage or handling. Starting in 1998, the National Nutrition Centre plans to implement a training programme on food hygiene for newly licensed vendors. Contamination at levels exceeding the national standards was found in 6 per cent of the samples taken from food-processing sites, in 9-9.5 per cent of those from shops, in 13.5 per cent of those from State-owned catering units and in 23 per cent of those from private catering units.

Contamination is frequent in dairy produce (especially the traditional "curd") (16-23.2 per cent of analysed samples), meat (13 per cent), fish (19.5 per cent), soft drinks (16.3 per cent), fruit and vegetables (26.8 per cent). Contamination was also found in eggs (0.9 per cent) and canned food (2.2-3.4 per cent). Out of the 4 000 samples of baby food tested, 5.5 per cent showed microbial contamination.

Another source of food (especially agricultural produce) contamination comes from pesticide and fertilizer residues. Some 3 per cent of milk and dairy produce samples were found to be contaminated by lead and 6.0 per cent by cadmium, and 2.9 per cent of vegetables were found to be contaminated by pesticides and 10.2 per cent by nitrates.

The microbial contamination of drinking water and food is associated with a relatively high incidence of water- and food-borne diseases, such as outbreaks and isolated cases of hepatitis A, salmonella and other enteric infections. Lithuania is the Baltic country with the highest incidence of viral hepatitis, about 10 times the EU average. The incidence of this disease during the period 1990-1996 was between 74.2 per 100 000 population in 1991 and 164.9 in 1995. This increase is almost entirely due to the higher incidence of hepatitis A (which in 1996 amounted to 3704 cases, i.e. 86 per cent of notified hepatitis cases). In 1996, the most affected were children aged 7 to 14, suggesting that the school environment may play a role in the transmission of the infection.

In 1996 there were 1966 notified cases of salmonella , i.e. 53.0 per 100 000 population, and about 10 per cent of these cases occurred in outbreaks. Bacillary dysentery and other intestinal infections increased in the period 1990-1996, reaching a peak in 1995 with 142.5 and 193.1 cases per 100 000 population, respectively. During recent years, 60 per cent of shygella and 80 per cent of salmonella cases were associated with food. About 80 per cent of hepatitis A patients are infected through household activities. Only about 5.8 per

cent of shigella and 9.2 per cent of hepatitis A cases are associated with water.

It is estimated that 11 000 to 27 000 people visit their health centres complaining of enteric diseases. These patients are around 1 to 5 per cent of all infected people. Only half of these complaints are confirmed by laboratory examinations. Rotavirus infections cannot be diagnosed at the moment, due to a lack of appropriate equipment. During the past 10 years, dysentery has represented 30-40 per cent of acute enteric diseases, with milk and dairy produce being the most frequent causes.

Waste and environmental health

No data are available concerning either exposure, or waste-related health effects. The main general concern of the public health authorities is the risk of transmission of vector-borne (e.g. those transmitted by rats) and microbial diseases. Another, more specific, problem is that posed by the homeless who live close to or even at dumping sites, which they scavenge for a living. Though no reliable figures are available, it is estimated that this problem could affect up to a few hundred individuals country-wide. The public health authorities are also concerned about the risks related to the handling of hospital wastes. A programme for hospital waste management is being developed, but without Government funds. (For details on current waste management, the Law on Waste Management and the waste management strategy, see Chapter 9.)

Ionizing radiation and environmental health

Overall, there is an indication that the population's exposure to radioactivity from both the Ignalina Nuclear Power Plant and the consequences of the Chernobyl accident is practically insignificant at present. More recently contamination around the radioactive storage facility in Sirvintos District and levels of indoor radon in some areas of the country (especially in the Karst region) have raised concern.

The INPP came on stream in 1979. It is located in the rural region of Ignalina, which is scarcely populated (25 300 inhabitants, i.e. some 0.7 per cent of the total population), with more people aged over 65, and fewer women of child-bearing age than the national average. In 1996, the Ignalina region experienced the largest decrease in population (-12.9 per 1 000 population), with the lowest birth rate (7.3 per 1 000 population) and the highest mortality rate in the country (20.2 per 1 000 population). About 5 per cent of Lithuania's population (some 185 000 inhabitants) live within the 50 km radius that marks the observation area around the INPP.

Measurements of whole body external equivalent dose rates within 30 km from the INPP and in the "control" region of Kupiškis indicate overall comparable levels of exposure (some 0.7 mSv/year against some 0.65 mSv/year, respectively, in 1995). Also, an analysis of Sr-90 and Cs-147 in foodstuffs (milk, meat, fish, vegetables) in the period 1993-1995 showed that radionuclide concentration in food sampled within a 30 km radius of INPP was well in line with national averages and below permitted limits.

Studies investigating the cancer incidence in the period 1978-1995 in the region around INPP indicate that in the Ignalina region it exceeds the national level. The studies are continuing, to investigate whether there is a link between living near nuclear facilities and the risk of developing cancer.

Other studies investigated thyroid disorders in a cohort of children aged 8 to 9 in the regions of Zarasai and Visagina (relatively closer to the INPP). Results showed a higher prevalence of goitres among children in the "control" region Zarasai (61 per cent of 176 children) than in children in Visagina (39 per cent of 299 children). This seems to indicate that causes other than living near the INPP may be implicated in these thyroid disorders (e.g. iodine deficiency).

The National Nuclear Emergency Plan was approved in 1995. The Plan, which is coordinated by the Civil Defence Department, consists of a detailed description of the responsibilities and tasks of the institutions involved. In addition, Lithuania has started cooperating bilaterally on nuclear safety with Sweden.

A source of potential exposure to radionuclides has been identified at the radioactive storage facility in Sirvintos, a district in Vilnius province. Contamination by tritium and radon, exceeding a few thousand and about 30 times, respectively, the "normal" levels of contamination (which is in the order of tens of kBq/m^3) has been detected around the facility, where radioactive waste (mainly from hospitals and research institutions) is stored. Remedial actions are currently under evaluation with the technical support of Sweden.

In April 1986 Lithuania was hit by the plume from Chernobyl. The south and the west were most contaminated. Adults received a 9.1 mSv equivalent dose and children a 73 mSv equivalent dose as a result of iodine-131 exposure. These levels are not known to be associated with health effects. One of the consequences of the accident was the contamination of basic food products such as milk, meat, fish and vegetables with Cs-137 and Sr-90. In recent years the contamination of food has decreased and is now back to pre-Chernobyl levels. Only about 0.3 per cent out of 31 477 food samples tested between 1993 and 1995 did not comply with the hygiene standard.

A study investigating thyroid disorders among a total of 735 residents in two Lithuanian regions which suffered different degrees of radioactive pollution after the Chernobyl accident did not find any significant difference in the prevalence of these disorders between them.

Recent data indicate that indoor radon is a problem in Lithuania, though not enough date are available to map clearly the areas at risk and to identify the exposed population. Preliminary estimates suggest that some 10 000 buildings could be affected. Measurements taken in 400 detached houses show that in some "hot spots" (e.g. areas with the geological condition known as karst) the indoor radon concentration exceeds 200 Bq/m^3, and would require remedial action (which, according to WHO Air Quality Guidelines, should be considered for dwellings exceeding 100 Bq/m^3). The measurement programme is continuing in collaboration with the Swedish Radiation Protection Institute.

Noise

Noise is not routinely monitored in Lithuania and available data are very patchy, usually from ad hoc investigations conducted to assess noise levels in dwellings facing streets with heavy traffic, or near airports. One exception is Kaunas, where noise levels have been measured in different districts and it is estimated that 16 per cent of inhabitants are exposed to noise levels (mostly caused by traffic) exceeding 65 dB(A). Above this level people's quality of life deteriorates significantly.

Occupational health

The Centre of Occupational Medicine has since 1994 maintained the National Register of Occupational Diseases. Diagnoses are reported by occupational health doctors, often employed at the workplace, and as a result of periodic medical check-ups. In addition, the Centre provides training and accreditation for laboratories that assess hygiene at the workplace (including quality control of equipment used by these laboratories) and is preparing a register of dangerous workplaces.

The Centre also carries out research into occupational risks, develops norms and regulations for health and safety at work, and collaborates with Nordic countries and relevant international organizations. The Centre also organizes meetings for occupational health doctors, issues a newsletter (for trade unions, doctors and industry, not workers) and shows films on occupational health on television.

Occupational health problems are more common amongst rural workers, and about half their complaints have been linked to vibration syndrome (Table 10.3). This involves peripheral neuropathy, arthrosis and osteo-muscular disorders and is the most prevalent problem registered. The workers most affected by this syndrome are lorry drivers and drivers of agricultural vehicles.

Since the Register was set up, reporting has increased, as expected. The greatest increases were in hearing loss (four times) and poisoning (three times higher in 1996 than in 1995). It is difficult to say how much of this increase is due to better reporting only, and how much could be due to actual increases in occupational diseases. Studies comparing the severity of reported cases in the two periods could provide a clue.

The Centre of Occupational Medicine is concerned about the continued use of asbestos tiles in rural areas. Many people in rural areas refurbish their own homes with the help of friends. The Centre believes that there is a need to warn the rural population of the risks and of the need to take precautionary measures when working with those tiles, and perhaps also the need to have a hygienist check the house to be refurbished for asbestos.

10.2 Environmental health policy and management

Major legislation relevant for environmental health

One of the aims of the Law on Environmental Protection is to ensure a healthy and safe environment. The Law regulates the use of natural resources and the emissions of pollutants in terms of their impact on the environment. Although the Law does not specifically mention human health, the rules for its implementation require public health professionals to estimate the potential impact on health and check of compliance with existing hygiene norms. The amounts of pollution that an enterprise is allowed to emit, the monitoring of emissions, and any economic charges (pollution taxes) or other pollution control measures will depend on these estimates.

Table 10.3: New cases of occupational diseases, 1995 and 1996

	1995		1996		
	Number	%	Number	%	Index 1995=100
Total	**370**	**100.0**	**606**	**100.0**	**164**
Infectious and parasitic diseases	6	1.6	2	0.3	33
Diseases of the nervous system	28	7.6	31	5.1	111
Hearing loss	41	11.1	181	29.9	441
Diseases of the respiratory system	35	9.5	35	5.8	100
Diseases of the skin and subcutaneous tissue	5	1.4	5	0.8	100
Diseases of the musculo-skeletal system and connective tissue	54	14.6	85	14.0	157
Vibration disease	188	50.8	250	41.3	133
Other diseases	5	1.4	3	0.5	60
Poisoning	5	1.4	14	2.3	280
Diseases of the cardiovascular system	3	0.8	0	0.0	0

Source: Statistical Yearbook of Lithania, 1997.

Several major laws in the health sector have provisions pertaining to environmental issues, like the Health System Law (1994), the Acts on Alcohol and Tobacco Control (1995), the Law on Health Care Systems Institutions (1996), the Law on Safety at Work (1993), the Law on the Prevention and Control of Communicable Diseases (1996), and the Law on Economic Sanctions for Violation of Public Health Legal Acts (1996).

Environmental impact assessments often include health impact estimates, depending on the activity envisaged. Changes to the proposed plans may be required on the basis of the assessment results. The issuing of permits by local or national authorities for government or private activities is linked to these results.

Policy commitments

There are commitments both in health policy and in environmental policy. Since independence in March 1990, Lithuania's health policies and management structures have been completely overhauled, with the primary goal of improving the quality and cost-effectiveness of the country's health care. The introduction of the new "National Health Care Concept" in 1991 brought in the principles of primary care and the WHO "Health for All" targets, including those related to environmental health (Health for All Targets on accidents, policy on environment and health, environmental health management, water quality, air quality, food quality and safety, waste management and soil pollution, human ecology and settlements, health of people at work). Of the 13 new State Health Programmes, adopted in 1996, only one deals with an environmental health target: the programme on the prevention of trauma. It has the third largest budget of all programmes (US$ 5 million over 10 years). However, the focus is not on the prevention of accidents but on the treatment of injuries (prevention of sequelae). A new National Health Programme is currently before Parliament.

The Environmental Strategy and Action Programme (1996) defines specific environmental quality protection goals by media (water, air, soil, waste, physical pollution) and protection goals for natural resources, landscape and biodiversity. Of the actions identified by this Programme for implementation by the year 2000, several address the most important environmental health issues identified in the country, including: environmental health monitoring and control; reducing groundwater contamination, improving drinking-water quality; reducing air pollution from transport and suspended solids; preventing radioactive contamination; reducing noise in cities; industrial and hazardous waste management. An Environmental Strategy Implementation Coordination Group under the Ministry of the Environment has been set up to facilitate coordination between the different ministries and speed up the Action Programme's implementation.

National environmental health objectives are subdivided into short-term (up to the year 2000) and long-term (to be achieved by 2005) objectives. The short-term objectives are:

- Creating a legislative framework for environmental health
- Setting priorities
- Developing environmental health indicators and assessing vulnerable groups
- Facilitating intersectoral cooperation in environmental health
- Creating a network of laboratories to investigate hazards related to occupational exposure
- Establishing occupational health services at manufacturing sites
- Improving the occupational health care system
- Adopting European Union requirements to prepare hygiene norms for the workplace

The long-term objectives are:

- Creating intersectoral collaboration to improve environmental quality
- Creating an information system on environment and health (through the combination of data on environmental pollution and morbidity)
- Setting up environmental health services
- Involving society in solving environmental health problems
- Reforming occupational health management to bring it in line with international standards and ensure that it is effective.

Regulations and standards

The thresholds for the concentration of pollutants in the air and in water are based on their health effects. The existing system of standards is a legacy of the former Soviet Union, and requires monitoring an unmanageable number of regulated pollutants. This is currently being revised and standards are also being harmonized with EU directives and technical norms. All previous GOST standards will be repealed by the end of 1998, when practices will be fully harmonized with those of the EU.

Lithuania's air quality standards are based on those of the former Soviet Union (GOST), which applied to more than 800 pollutants, and envisage two levels of air pollution concentrations: (i) the average maximum allowable concentration (MAC average), defined as the concentration of periodical or constant effect on nature which has no negative impact on humans or the environment; and (ii) the maximum of maximum allowable concentration (MAC max.), defined as the highest concentration of pollutants allowed for short-term human exposure. The current MAC standards specify 30-minute and 24-hour averages. Most of the standard limit values are consistent with those of the WHO Air Quality Guidelines.

The drinking-water quality standards were also developed at the time of the former Soviet Union, and included almost 4 000 indicators. There were standards for water supplied to households, for services, for recreational use, and for use in fisheries. A number of national standards and norms, based on health risks, also exist to regulate levels of contamination of food, and exposure to X-rays, radon, noise, vibration and temperature. There are also occupational health standards and regulations on dangerous substances.

Enforcement and institutions

Several agencies, at both the national and the regional level, carry out inspections and check compliance with hygiene norms. Some of their functions overlap. The State Hygiene Inspectorate, recently established within the Ministry of Health, is responsible for inspecting consumer products and manufacturing sites. Inspections consist mostly of documentation checks for compliance with hygiene regulations and standards (e.g. by checking labels). The Hygiene Inspectorate, through its network of inspectors, has the power to issue fines for non-compliance (up to US$ 10 000).

The Hygiene Inspectorate is trying to change the role of its inspectors from a purely compliance monitoring into a more proactive "advisory" role (including negotiating functions). The objectives are to promote a change in the attitude of industry towards increased self-regulation and to move gradually towards the introduction of the liability principle. The Inspectorate also has plans to

develop a register of all licences and permits, and a framework for monitoring compliance with regulations (defining the responsibilities of different agencies with inspection functions).

The Veterinary Inspectorate (part of the Ministry of Agriculture) has food safety responsibility regarding compliance with regulations on animal products and production of food of animal origin.

The State Quality Inspectorate (part of the Service of Competition and Consumer Rights Protection within the Ministry of Finance) has responsibility for food quality. It ensures protection against fraud and controls competition and pricing.

The Ministry of Transport has been given responsibility for inspecting vehicle emissions (carbon monoxide, fumes and hydrocarbons), as of January 1998. However, at the moment there are difficulties in fulfilling this task, due to a lack of technical and financial resources (only 9 mobile units are available).

The Nuclear Power Safety Inspectorate (VATESI) is an independent agency responsible for nuclear safety and compliance with existing safety norms at the INPP.

A recent restructuring of the Ministry of Health has led to the creation of the Division of Public Health, which reports to one of the three Deputy Ministers of Health. The Division employs five staff. The public health institutional framework (Figure 10.1) also includes the following bodies relevant to environmental health:

- *State Hygiene Inspectorate* - Inspection of consumer products and manufacturing sites and enforcement of hygiene norms.
- *National Centre of Nutrition* - Management of the National Food Monitoring Programme; development of policies for healthy nutrition and for food quality and safety; development of technical standards for the quality and safety of foodstuffs, food additives, drinking water and soft drinks.
- *Radiation Protection Centre* - Development of policies and technical standards on prevention and control of exposure to ionizing radiation, and for monitoring radioactive contamination in food, and indoor (radon). Involvement in the safety and prevention programme for the Ignalina Nuclear Power Plant and in environmental monitoring of radioactive contamination. Responsible for radiological

Figure 10.1: Lithuanian Public Health Institutional Framework

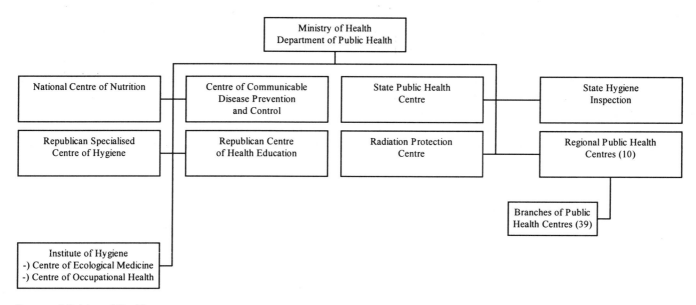

Source: Ministry of Health

safety of workers and the general population in the event of natural and man-made disasters.

- *Institute of Hygiene* - Epidemiological and toxicological research into the implications of environmental contamination (Centre of Ecological Medicine) and into occupational health, (Centre of Occupational Medicine); development of hygiene standards for recreational water, air (indoor and outdoor), noise, soil and non-ionizing radiation

- *State Public Health Centre* – Development of environmental health policies, including NEHAP, and draft legal acts, public health monitoring; generation and maintenance of the environmental health information system; health impact assessments and expertise of compliance with public health legal acts, etc.

- *Regional Public Health Centres* - There are 10 such centres, which have similar responsibilities as the national institution, though at the regional level. They are also active in the control and prevention of communicable diseases and carry out hygiene inspections at the regional level. Each Regional Public Health Centre supervises three or four local branches. The centres participate in the National Food Monitoring Programme, by collecting and analysing water and food samples.

Development of human resources for environmental health

The Faculty of Public Health, at Kaunas Medical Academy, has recently been established to develop human resources in public and environmental health. Its first 30 graduates will complete the course in 1998. The Faculty receives international support (EC TEMPUS programme) and works in cooperation with the Kaunas Healthy Cities Project, providing the students with practical experience.

Participation in international projects/networks such as EC PHARE programme and the WHO Global Environmental Epidemiology Network for Europe (GEENET) provides Lithuanian health professionals with opportunities for contacting and exchanging ideas with an international community of experts.

10.3   Integration with other sectors

Transport and health

The National Transport Development Plan (1994) incorporates a Programme on Transport and Environment Protection, based on an impact assessment of transport in Lithuanian towns carried out in 1992 by the Ministry of Transport in cooperation with the Ministry of Health. The objective of this Programme was to minimize the environmental and health impact of all modes of transport. It involved the four largest cities of Lithuania. Noise was measured, air pollutants (particles) were monitored at fixed points (hot spots, big roads) and the number of vehicles was counted. No assessment of the economic impact was incorporated. Health risks were estimated based on the frequency of limit values being exceeded. The Programme made a few recommendations, some of which have been implemented.

Traffic safety is one of the most relevant public health issues in Lithuania. The Traffic Safety Commission is attempting to promote cross-sectoral cooperation . It is chaired by the Ministry of Transport. The Ministry of Health also participates in it. The Commission has a mainly coordinating function and has no policy mandate. To improve road safety, the Traffic Safety Fund (funded by the EU PHARE programme) supports remedial action on road infrastructure and action to limit speed, perform alcohol tests, and develop rescue teams. However, it works with limited input from, or interaction with, the health sector.

There is a need to give further emphasis and support to the cooperation that has already started between the Ministry of Transport and the State Public Health Centre. Also, it would be necessary to clarify the roles and promote coordination among the actions carried out by the Ministry of Transport (road safety intervention), the Road Police (enforcement of speed limits, drink-driving, collection of road accident statistics) and the public health sector. There should be activities on accident and injury prevention, in addition to the current trauma care activities. Moreover, there is a strong need to integrate transport-related information (on accidents and exposure to transport) into the health information systems.

Agriculture and health

There is cross-sectoral cooperation, for instance in food safety, where the National Nutrition Centre regulates and monitors the level and types of pesticide residues allowed in food. The Nutrition Centre also produces standards for the Hazard Analysis Critical Chain Point system, which will be implemented by the Ministry of Agriculture. In addition, the Veterinary Inspectorate of the Ministry of Agriculture helps to control the safety of food of animal origin.

Energy and health

The existence of the Ignalina Nuclear Power Plant and the complex problems posed by the production of nuclear energy have fostered a high level of inter-sectoral cooperation. According to the Law on Nuclear Energy, 11 institutions share responsibilities for nuclear safety, radiation protection, accounting and control of nuclear material. Among these, the Radiation Protection Centre of the Ministry of Health, the Ministry of the Environment, the Nuclear Power Safety Inspectorate (VATESI) and the Civil Defence Department of the Ministry of Defence are the most closely involved in the protection of the health of personnel of nuclear facilities and of the population residing in the monitored zones.

10.4 Monitoring and information systems

National statistics on mortality, hospital admissions and outpatient morbidity, and on health care systems are collected and presented by the Health Information Centre. The Centre collects data from the various institutions involved in health monitoring and from the State Department of Statistics (death certificates). The WHO "Health for All" strategy was taken as a basis for developing health statistics.

The main responsibility for outdoor air quality monitoring and data distribution is with the Ministry of the Environment. The environmental monitoring network consists of 22 observation stations, where key air pollutants (dust, sulphur dioxide, nitrogen dioxide and carbon monoxide) are analysed three times a day. In addition, emission data are collected at approximately 200 point sources. Other pollutants being monitored include: sulphates, sulphur hydrogen, phenol, hydrogen fluoride, ammonia, formaldehyde, xylene, toluene, benzo(a)pyrene and some heavy metals (Pb, Cd, Cu, Zn, Hg).

Data collected in Kaunas, Šiauliai, Vilnius, Klaipėda, Panevėžys on NO_2, SO_2 and TSP are integrated in the Health and Environment Geographical Information System (HEGIS) developed by WHO ECEH-Bilthoven.

The National Food Monitoring Programme falls under the responsibility of the National Nutrition Centre of the Ministry of Health. The monitoring programme was tested in 1993 and started in 1994. It is part of the Global Environmental Monitoring System (GEMS/Food-Euro). Other information is collected through inspections by the State Hygiene Inspectorate, the State Quality Inspectorate, and State Veterinary Service.

The systematic monitoring of food started in 1993. It covers dairy products, meat and poultry, eggs, fish products, fresh vegetables and fruit, cereals, canned food, baby and children's food. Food samples are collected four times a year at eight fixed locations throughout the country by the local branches of the Regional Public Health Centres at various points of the food distribution chain (factories, shops, food outlets, canteens/restaurants) and analysed for the presence of microbial, radioactive and chemical contamination (i.e. pesticides, heavy metals, nitrates, mycotoxins and PCBs).

For drinking water, nitrate concentration and microbial contamination are the key parameters analysed. Data are collected through regular monitoring, occasional tests (e.g. on dug well water) and inspections. Water samples are collected by the Regional Public Health Centres, which have the additional responsibility for analysing "routine" contaminants and reporting results to the National Nutrition Centre, where more sophisticated analyses are carried out. The monitoring takes place in cooperation with the Lithuanian Geological Service. The above-mentioned monitoring system is still not considered fully satisfactory by the Nutrition Centre, which has produced a proposal for additional controls at critical points in the distribution system (HACCP system), especially in small catering services/food outlets.

Ionizing radiation

Radioactivity in the environment is monitored through two separate networks by the Ministry of the Environment (26 monitoring stations) and by the Radiation Protection Centre of the Ministry of Health (10 monitoring stations). In an effort to use their resources more efficiently, the two Ministries have recently started to consider integrating their networks.

Monitoring of radioactive contamination of food and water (Cs-137, Sr-190 and gamma contamination) is part of the National Food Monitoring Programme and is the responsibility of the Radiation Protection Centre. The Regional Departments of Radiation Protection take samples of water and foodstuffs at eight sampling points and analyse them four times a year for contamination. Time series data are available starting from 1965.

Transport accidents and injuries

In the national health statistics, information on injuries from accidents is limited to mortality for all traumas, traffic accidents, suicide and alcohol poisoning. All accident injuries and cases of poisoning are reported as one group in outpatient and hospital admission figures. There are no data on causes or other consequences of accidents. There are plans for health care facilities to collect routine data on the causes and results of accidents, the results of treatment and the causes of disability, and to classify accident and injury severity.

Traffic accidents are reported by the Road Police. Exposure data (i.e. the usual transport performance data) are collected by the Ministry of Transport and reported in the National Statistics Yearbook. There is a need for stronger links between all the information on traffic accidents and injuries collected and available through the Ministry of Health, the Ministry of Transport and the Road Police. In addition, there is a need to integrate available information on human exposure to transport into the Environmental Health Information System, giving the adequate disaggregation for public health prevention purposes.

Environmental health information

The experience with environmental health information started with a description of the status of environmental health in various areas, using the indicators requested by WHO in the project "Concern for Europe's Tomorrow" in the early 1990s. Subsequently, a study of geographical associations between air, water and soil pollution and morbidity was carried out in the four main cities.

In 1994 a plan for a national environmental health information system was developed by the National Public Health Centre. Its objective is to be able to establish links between environmental monitoring data (air - point source emissions, water, soil) and morbidity and mortality data, with the possibility of conducting analyses at micro-district level, in order to identify areas of priority environmental concern and achieve a more efficient use of resources for preventive or remedial action. This system should integrate the systems already existing in some of the biggest cities of the country (Kaunas, Vilnius, Šiauliai and Klaipeda). It should give rise to close collaboration with the Ministry of the Environment.

In Kaunas, the city administration and the Kaunas Medical Academy have created a health information system with computerized maps. Environmental monitoring data (air pollution and noise) are combined with morbidity data, disaggregated at the micro-district level. This has made it possible to identify "hot spots" in the city and to direct efforts towards priority areas.

Research on environment and health

WHO Healthy Cities Project: the example of Kaunas

The city of Kaunas has joined the WHO Healthy Cities Project, and is a member of several Multi-City Action Plans and City Networks, including those on Accident Prevention, Tobacco-free Cities, Baltic Cities and Alcohol. In addition, Kaunas coordinates the Lithuanian Healthy Cities Network, which was established in 1995 and has 11 members.

As part of its Healthy City action plan, Kaunas has recently introduced an "Environmental Council", with representatives of the municipality, of the Regional Agencies of the Ministries of Health and of the Environment, and of the Kaunas Medical Academy. This Council makes proposals both to the Political Committee of the Municipality and to the Municipal Environmental Protection Department, strengthening coordination among the different parties with responsibility for environmental health issues and cross-sectoral cooperation.

The National Scientific Committee includes the Minister and Deputy Minister of Health, and a board of medical specialists. It decides on the priorities for environmental and other public health investigations. The Committee evaluates research projects submitted by research and academic institutions and distributes the available research funds.

One of the main scientific institutions carrying out environmental health research is Kaunas Medical Academy and its institutes (for example, the Institute of Biomedical Research, the Institute of Cardiology, and others). Research into environmental health and occupational questions is carried out by the Centre of Ecological Medicine of the Institute of Hygiene. This scientific institution initiates studies on the National Scientific Committee's instruction and its priority is the health of people living in polluted areas. The Institute has access to polyclinical records and the right to carry out environmental sampling. Research relevant to environmental health is also carried out by Vilnius University Medical Faculty, the National Oncology Centre, and others.

10.5 Conclusions and recommendations

Over the past two decades, Lithuania has shared with the other countries in transition of central and eastern Europe the experience of a deterioration in key health indicators. At the same time, the environmental monitoring data of recent years indicate an overall decrease in environmental pollution compared to the period 1985-89. To a large extent, the drop in air and water pollution resulted from the decline in industrial production of the past years, rather than from the implementation of effective environmental policies. This is illustrated, for example, by the increase in transport-related air pollution that followed the steady expansion of this activity.

Trends in health indicators have worsened over the past years, further widening the gap with the health status of populations living in European Union countries. The increase in mortality and morbidity related to environmental conditions (accidents and injuries, respiratory diseases, food-borne diseases) needs to be reversed. This requires action within the health system (e.g. more effective procedures and enforcement to control food and water contamination) and more inter-sectoral action to reduce pressures on the environment that have a negative impact on health (e.g. enforcing controls on the exhaust emissions of private cars).

The high mortality rates due to preventable external causes, such as injuries, poisoning and traffic accidents, are a priority concern. In particular, death rates due to traffic accidents are among the highest in Europe. The State Health Programme on Prophylaxis of Trauma addresses only the medical care of crash victims. A much broader approach, looking upstream at a variety of strategies to prevent accidents, including through cross-sectoral cooperation (e.g. with the Ministry of Transport) is necessary to deal with the issue more effectively. Although this review did not address in detail health issues related to the psycho-social environment, the very high mortality rates due to suicide are also a cause of concern which should be investigated.

Traffic-related air pollution is a growing concern both for the quality of the environment and for the potential health risks to the exposed population. Based on available data, particulates (TSPs), nitrogen oxides and benzo(a)pyrene appear to be the pollutants of priority concern, especially in urban areas. In some cities, the average concentration of particulates is above the threshold that, according to WHO, identifies "black spots" for which remedial action is needed. However, the ambient air monitoring data are probably not very reliable. Additional reliable and precise data would be needed to assess the potential health risks.

Recommendation 10.1:
The effects of traffic on human health should be addressed as a priority environmental health concern. The enforcement of controls on vehicle exhaust and noise emissions and of measures to prevent the registration and circulation of noisier or more polluting vehicles should be top priority. Traffic in city centres should be reduced and public transport using less polluting and less noisy vehicles/fuels, cycling and walking should be promoted. Traffic accident prevention should receive more attention from the public health sector. It should be considered as an environmental health issue and managed in cooperation with other Ministries (i.e. Transport, Social Welfare and Labour, and Internal Affairs).

The high increase in water and food-borne diseases indicates the need for better microbial water and food quality. About 800 000 inhabitants drink water from dug wells. Some 30 per cent of well water samples are microbially contaminated, and around 300 000 inhabitants may drink well water with a high nitrate content. The current practice of asking pregnant women whether they drink water from wells and, if so, of testing the nitrate level of the water should be maintained. This should be accompanied by a communication strategy to inform healthcare workers and the population of the risks posed by high-nitrate drinking water to pregnant women and young children and the need to carry out the appropriate test. In the medium to long term, the possibility of supplying more dwellings with piped water is the first choice. Newly dug wells should be deeper. The protection of sources from nitrates should also be integrated with measures to better protect groundwater against the risk of contamination by inadequately treated sewage water, pesticides and leachate from dumping sites.

The required prevention programme for microbial contamination of well water should be based on: (a) the identification of risk factors for well contamination through sanitary inspections and of population groups at risk; (b) preventive action

directed at groups at risk, to be selected on the basis of its cost-effectiveness; (c) action to protect sources, using chlorine only as a second choice, and concentrating on the actual implementation of these measures (e.g. economic incentives, technical packages, education, etc.); (d) monitoring of drinking water quality limited to the extent necessary. Strategies and practical aspects of implementation should be based on the WHO Drinking Water Guidelines (volume 3, 1997).

Recommendation 10.2:
There is a need to develop and implement a strategy to prevent microbiological contamination of well water and extend the centralized artesian well drinking-water supply.

Improved hygienic standards and improved food quality controls are needed to prevent health problems. Microbial contamination is increasing, especially at the end of the distribution chain, especially owing to the proliferation of small food kiosks. These are managed by licensed street vendors, who do not receive training on safe food storage and handling. Hygiene regulations for small catering outlets are not effectively enforced. The National Nutrition Centre intends to implement a training programme on food hygiene for newly licensed vendors. The development of regulations for such establishments may bring about substantial improvements in the situation and should be encouraged. Furthermore, attention should be paid to improving sanitary facilities in public places (canteens, offices, schools, restaurants). Further measures could include, for example, the promotion of access to running water, and of hygienic food preparation and storage facilities for kiosk operators.

Recommendation 10.3:
The system of food monitoring and control should be further strengthened by introducing Hazard Analysis Critical Control Points (HACCP).

Both the Law on Environmental Protection and the Environmental Quality Action Programme specifically mention environmental health. The Law asserts the right of Lithuania's inhabitants to a healthy, secure and clean environment. The Programme puts forward priority actions to improve environmental health. The development of policies to promote environmental health is among the future priorities of the Ministry of Health. This should be given much more emphasis once the current focus on restructuring the health care system is completed. However, the current environmental monitoring system does not make it possible to assess human exposure and therefore to quantify the risks posed to the health of the population by environmental hazards.

In addition to TSP, it would be appropriate to monitor breathable particles (such as PM10 or PM2.5). Indoor exposure to NO_2 (e.g. from domestic gas appliances) and environmental tobacco smoke should also be monitored, as available data are quite patchy. This is partly due to a lack of a systematic monitoring programme for indoor pollutants, for which institutional responsibility has only recently been assigned to the Public Health Department of the Ministry of Health.

Recommendation 10.4:
Strategies to monitor and assess indoor air quality, including levels and exposure to nitrogen dioxide (NO_2) should be developed and implemented to better assess health risks. Ground-level ozone should be monitored to refine current exposure assessments.

High levels of indoor radon, which according to preliminary estimates might involve up to 10 000 dwellings, pose a threat to health, and measures should be taken to decrease the risk to those living in dwellings with high radon levels. The potential exposure to ionizing radiation from the Ignalina NPP is generally under control and does not seem to be a matter of concern. The health status of the population living within the observation area of the plant should continue to be monitored.

Recommendation 10.5:
There is a need to identify areas and dwellings with high indoor radon concentration and to develop a strategy to reduce human exposure to radon where this exceeds critical thresholds.

The lack of effective cooperation between the State Public Health Centre and the Regional Public Health Centres and their local branches entails a risk of overlaps and inefficient use of resources. In addition, the organization of the 10 Regional Public Health Centres may be difficult to integrate with the decentralized structure of the Ministry of the Environment, which operates through eight Regional Centres. Another potential source of overlap and conflict in the assignment of responsibilities is the existence within the municipal administration of Public Healthcare

Offices and Environmental Protection Departments, which are independent from the ministerial administrations.

Consequently, it appears that several of the observations and recommendations made a few years ago in the WHO/EURO "Health Sector Review Report" (1991) are still valid, in that there is room for improving the coordination and use of resources both within the structure of the Ministry of Health (e.g. central versus decentralized levels) and between the organizations of the Ministries of Health and of the Environment.

A shortage of qualified staff to manage the changes in the healthcare system has been a difficulty. The establishment of the Faculty of Public Health at Kaunas Medical Academy was a step in the right direction. However, it will be important for the health system to be able to take full advantage of the contribution that these new professionals can make in the coming years. A very positive example of cross-sectoral cooperation in environmental health at local level is the work done in Kaunas in the context of the Healthy Cities Project.

Inter-sectoral cooperation with the Ministry of the Environment (both at national and regional level) and with the municipal structures for environment and health protection should be strengthened. There should be a critical review of the current structures of both the Regional Public Health Centres (and their branches) and of the Regional Departments of the Ministry of the Environment to clarify responsibilities and use the available resources more efficiently.

Areas for potential improvement in cooperation and coordination include: (a) optimizing monitoring carried out by both institutions; (b) identifying common priorities (e.g. on air pollution, noise, drinking water, sectors of the economy, drawing up the National Environmental Health Action Plan), developing joint plans of action and coordinated strategies to achieve goals; (c) strengthening capabilities in environmental health (including the development of human resources); (d) defining more clearly the areas of responsibility of the two Ministries; (e) making better use of their respective technical competencies, for example in integrated environmental health impact assessments. The National Environmental Health Action Plan is an important tool for improving coordination between the two Ministries at both national and local levels.

Recommendation 10.6:
Within the Ministry of Health, the responsibilities and competencies of the Centres within the State Public Health Service should be better clarified (e.g. the role of the Hygiene Inspectorate, the responsibility for monitoring of noise and of indoor air). Between the Ministry of Health and the Ministry of Environment coordination and agreement on common objectives and priorities should be improved, using the National Environmental Health Action Plan as a tool, which should take the work done on the National Environmental Action Programme (NEAP) into account.

The environmental health information system should put more emphasis on the use of environmental health data for health impact assessments and, ultimately, health policy. This would require more than geographical analysis, and consider for example driving forces, stakeholder interests, available policy mechanisms, and key indicators selected to inform policy makers and monitor implementation. This could extend beyond air, soil, and water pollution to areas of human activity such as agriculture, transport, energy and their implications for the environment and health. Relevant methods and experiences are available internationally. The current project should be reviewed in order to identify a conceptual framework for the information system. This framework would be based on an analysis of Lithuania's medium- and long-term environment and health objectives and on an understanding of the processes influencing environmental pressures and human exposure to environmental hazards. The framework would guide the selection of the type of information systems to be developed, including choice of indicators, types of analyses to be carried out, and type of presentation of information and communication strategy to be chosen.

Recommendation 10.7:
There is a need to further develop and implement the National Environmental Health Information System building on the work already done, and to further expand current work on environmental health impact assessment on new economic initiatives.

Chapter 11

ENVIRONMENTAL CONCERNS IN ENERGY

11.1   Energy production and use

Primary energy supply

Lithuania has very limited energy resources. Its indigenous sources met about 7.4 per cent of its total energy demand in 1996. Peat is probably the indigenous resource with the largest potential. Total geological reserves of peat are estimated to be 19 774 million toe (9 200 PJ), half of which could profitably be exploited. Lithuania could also produce about 3.5 million m^3 per year of wood for fuel, which corresponds to 0.478 million toe (20 PJ), if it used all its forest reserves in the future. Some boiler houses in different regions were reconstructed to use fuelwood and straw. Their total capacity is around 900 MW. The construction of a geothermal plant was started in Klaipėda. Moreover, of the estimated potential of some 50 million tonnes of onshore oil reserves, about 5 million tonnes are economically recoverable at present. This amount is modest, but significant.

Lithuania's large hydropower plants have a current capacity of 706 MW (600 MW from a pumping station in Kaunas, 100 MW from the Kaunas Hydro-power station and 6 MW from several smaller stations). The potential of wind, biogas, geothermal and solar energy is only limited. The country has comparatively modest oil resources (production in 1995 was 0.115 million toe (4.8 PJ)). Oil production is forecast to reach 0.478 million toe (20 PJ/year).

However, the Lithuanian energy sector, as it stood in 1990, considerably exceeds the country's requirements. The capacity of many industrial and energy enterprises was based on the requirements of the former Soviet Union's large north-western region. Primary energy supply is dominated by inputs from one country: crude oil, natural gas, nuclear fuel and almost all the coal are imported from the Russian Federation. In 1996, Lithuania imported 55 per cent of its total primary energy requirements (TPER). The political and economic consequences of this dependence are an ongoing concern. Table 11.1 shows the structure of Lithuania's relevant energy parameters.

After Lithuania regained independence, it suffered a severe recession. GDP dropped by about 52 per cent, between 1991 and 1994. As a direct consequence, both energy production and energy demand plummeted: primary production from 4.7 Mtoe in 1991 to 2.5 Mtoe in 1994, and final demand from 9.9 Mtoe to 5.2 Mtoe over the same period. Nuclear energy represented the main primary input into the indigenous production of energy with 84 per cent of the total in 1994. The remainder was covered equally by oil, hydro and wind, with 4 per cent each, and by "others", with 8 per cent. The fall of about 53 per cent in the total supply in Lithuania was caused mainly by a decrease in exported electric power, combined with the stagnation in industry. In 1995 and 1996 the GDP grew, as did primary energy production (to 4.3 Mtoe) and gross inland consumption (to 9.6 Mtoe). However, final energy demand shrank and stabilized at 4.8 Mtoe.

Lithuania imports coal, but above all oil and gas from the CIS. These imports dropped sharply, by almost 36.5 per cent, between 1991 and 1994. At the same time, gross energy consumption fell 42.8 per cent and the energy import dependency, which stood at 73.5 per cent in 1991, declined to 67.5 per cent in 1994 and 55.2 per cent in 1996 (Table 11.2).

As imported fuels were cheap, the use of all domestic energy resources fell even more dramatically - from 46 per cent of TPER in 1960 to 2.5 per cent in 1990. Natural gas has been imported and used in Lithuania since 1961, when the gas pipeline from Ukraine was built. At present, less than 40 per cent of homes are connected to the grid. Most of the natural gas is used for cooking. In 1991, the share of natural gas in gross inland consumption (GIC) reached 23 per cent.

Since 1984, when the first unit at the Ignalina Nuclear Power Plant (INPP) was commissioned, the role of nuclear power has increased

Table 11.1: Summary energy balance, 1991-1996

Mtoe

		1991	1992	1993	1994	1995	1996
Primary Production		4.7	4.1	3.3	2.5	3.7	4.3
of which:	Oil	0.0	0.1	0.1	0.1	0.1	0.2
	Nuclear	4.4	3.8	3.0	2.1	3.1	3.6
	Other	0.3	0.2	0.2	0.3	0.5	0.6
Net Imports		13.3	6.8	5.2	5.3	5.1	5.3
of which:	Solids	0.6	0.4	0.1	0.2	0.2	0.2
	Oil	9.0	4.0	3.7	3.2	3.1	3.3
	Crude Oil	11.8	4.1	5.2	3.6	3.3	4.3
	Oil products	-2.8	-0.1	-1.5	-0.4	-0.1	-1.0
	Natural gas	4.8	2.9	1.6	1.8	2.0	2.2
	Electricity	-1.1	-0.5	-0.2	0.1	-0.2	-0.4
Gross Inland Consumption		18.2	11.2	9.1	7.8	8.8	9.6
of which:	Solids	0.7	0.3	0.3	0.2	0.7	0.8
	Oil	9.0	4.4	3.9	3.3	3.2	3.4
	Natural Gas	4.8	2.9	1.6	1.8	2.0	2.2
	Other a/	3.7	3.6	3.3	2.5	2.9	3.2
Total Final Energy Demand		9.9	7.6	5.6	5.2	4.8	4.8
of which:	Solids	0.6	0.3	0.3	0.2	0.7	0.8
	Oil	4.1	2.6	1.8	1.5	1.6	1.7
	Natural Gas	0.7	0.9	0.6	0.7	0.4	0.4
	Electricity	1.0	0.8	0.6	0.5	0.6	0.6
	Heat	3.2	2.8	2.1	2.1	1.5	1.4
	Other	0.3	0.2	0.2	0.2	0.0	0.0

Sources: Ministry of the Environment;
           Eurostat and Energy Statistics and balances of Non-OECD countries, 1994-1995, IEA/OECD.

a/ Includes nuclear, hydro and wind, net imports of electricity, and other energy resources.

Note: 0.0 = Magnitude not zero, but less than half of unit empoyed.

Table 11.2: Electricity capacity and generation, 1991-1996

	1991	1992	1993	1994	1995	1996
Generation Capacity (GW)	5.7	5.7	5.7	..	5.8	5.8
Nuclear	2.5	2.5	2.5	..	2.5	2.5
Hydro and wind	0.5	0.5	0.5	..	0.7	0.7
Thermal	2.7	2.7	2.7	..	2.6	2.6
Electricity Generation (TWh)	29.3	18.7	14.2	10.0	13.9	16.8
Nuclear	17.0	14.6	12.3	7.7	11.8	13.9
Hydro and wind	0.3	0.3	0.4	0.7	0.8	0.9
Thermal	12.0	3.8	1.5	1.6	1.3	2.0
Average Load Factor (%)	58.9	37.5	28.3	..	..	..

Sources: Ministry of the Environment;
           Eurostat and Energy Statistics and balances of Non-OECD countries, 1994-1995, IEA/OECD.

Table 11.3: Indicators describing the energy economy, 1991-1996

	1991	1992	1993	1994	1995	1996
GDP (index 1995=100)	162.7	128.2	107.3	96.8	100.0	104.7
EU GDP (index 1995=100)	85.8	86.0	100.5	105.1	100.0	107.8
Gross Inl. Consump./GDP (toe/MECU)	..	1.9	1.9	1.6	1.1	1.0
EU Gross Inl. Consump./GDP (toe/MECU)	..	0.3	0.3	0.2	0.2	0.2
Gross inl. Consump./Capita (toe/inhabitant)	4.9	3.0	2.4	2.1	2.4	2.6
EU Gross inl. Consump./Capita (toe/inhabitant)	..	3.6	3.6	3.5	3.5	3.6
Electricity Generated/Capita (KWh/inhabitant)	7,917	5,047	3,804	2,713	3,757	4,541
CO_2 Emissions* (Million t of CO_2)	34.2	20.8	16.0	15.9	..	..
CO_2 Emissions/Capita (t of CO_2/inhabitant)	9.2	5.6	4.3	4.3	..	..
Import Dependency ** (%)	73.5	61.2	56.8	67.5	58.0	55.2

Sources: Ministry of the Environment; Lithuanian National Accounts in 1990-1996;
Eurostat and Energy Statistics and balances of Non-OECD countries, 1994-1995, IEA/OECD;
European Commission for Economic and Financial Affairs, Annual Economic Report for 1997.

Note:
* From energy sector.
** Share of net imports in gross inland consumption.

significantly. Its share in electricity generation ranges from 80 to 90 per cent. In the near future, three fuel types (oil, natural gas and nuclear fuel) will dominate the country's total primary requirements. The share of nuclear power could, however, increase, if an export market for electricity is found. Some increase in the share of domestic energy resources is also expected.

Electric power and district heat supply system

The electricity generation capacity remains at about 5 800 MW (Table 11.2). By comparison, the 1996 peak load was about 2 000 MW – so the generation system is oversized for the country's needs. Electricity exports in 1996 amounted to about 5 000 GWh and could be much higher. The Lithuanian Power System includes the INPP, the Lithuanian Power Plant, the co-generation plants (CHP) of Vilnius, Kaunas and Mažeikiai, the Kruonis Pumping Station, Kaunas Hydro Power Plant and regional district heating utilities (Table 11.4.)
The role of the various types of power plants has changed over the decades. In the beginning of the electrification of the national economy, most electricity was produced by small power plants and by the Kaunas Hydro Power Plant, which was the biggest at that time. The conventional Lithuanian Thermal Power Plant dominated during the next two decades. Lately, the INPP has become much more important.

In 1991, Lithuania took over jurisdiction over the Nuclear Power Plant (two of the world's most powerful reactors of the Chernobyl type) at Ignalina. Today, 90.8 per cent of INPP shares belong to the Government. The plant produces about 90 per cent of the country's electricity in two third-generation RBMK boiling water reactors, and gives Lithuania the world's highest dependency on nuclear energy. The Government of Lithuania is committed to operating the Ignalina plant in the safest possible circumstances, and safety measures have been retrofitted. Annually, around US$ 20 million are spent on safety improvements. The transmission and distribution systems, as well as all power plants except INPP, are owned by "Lietuvos energija", a joint-stock company.

INPP was designed in the 1970s and built in the 1980s according to the safety requirements of the former Soviet Union. These are now outdated and even in the 1980s were far less stringent than those applied in western countries. The safety level of the INPP depends on the implementation of safety improvement programmes to eliminate the design faults and upgrade the operational technology. International assistance for these programmes is essential. In 1993, with the assistance of western and Russian experts, the Ignalina Safety Enhancement Programme was developed. It is expected that the update of the programme will pass Parliament in 1998. The European Bank for Reconstruction and Development (EBRD) and the

Table 11.4: Power plants in Lithuania, 1995

MW

Power plants	Installed capacity	Utilised capacity	Fuel
Total	**6,324**	**5,759**	
Ignalina nuclear power plant	3,000	2,600	Nuclear
Lithuania power plant	1,800	1,800	Oil, gas
Vilnius CHP-2	24	18	Oil, gas
Vilnius CHP-3	360	347	Oil, gas
Kaunas CHP	170	152	Oil, gas
Petrasiunai CHP	8	7	Oil, gas
Mazeikiai CHP	194	99	Oil
Klaipeda power plant	11	9	Oil, gas
Kaunas hydro power plant	101	101	
Other hydro power plants	5	5	
Kruonis hydro pumped storage plant	600	570	
Industrial power plants	51	51	Oil, gas

Source: Lituanian Energy Institute.

Government of Lithuania signed a grant agreement in February 1994 to resolve the most urgent issues. Thirteen European countries allocated ECU 33 million through the EBRD. The plant has also been made much safer thanks to bilateral Swedish assistance and funding from the G-7 Nuclear Safety Account. Nevertheless, United States experts still consider the plant to be one of the least safe in the world. The Lithuanian Government has announced that its two reactors would be shut down in 2005 and 2010, respectively, but for economic reasons the plan to decommission INPP was suspended although it is still on the agenda. The Decommission INPP Fund has been established to this end.

Lithuania took over INPP operations without having its own research and technical infrastructure, design and construction potential, or systems for training specialists and experts, or organizing public information and public relations. Therefore, building capacity and strengthening institutions in the nuclear sector are top priorities of the governmental programme. Moreover, a State nuclear regulatory system was established in the early 1990s. The State Nuclear Energy Safety Inspectorate (VATESI), created in October 1991, is Lithuania's nuclear watchdog. VATESI is responsible for supervising the nuclear energy sector and ensuring that it abides strictly by the applicable rules and guidelines and meets international safety standards. The top priority of the national nuclear safety policy is to ensure that preventive measures are taken to eliminate the chance of an accident ever occurring and getting out of hand. There were 29 unplanned reactor

shutdowns in 1990-1995, and eight nuclear events according to the IAEA scale, of which seven were of level 1 and one of level 2.

Finally, there is the problem of radioactive waste. About 1 per cent of the total amount of radioactive waste results from the use of ionizing sources in medicine, research, industry and agriculture. The remainder is produced by INPP (see also Chapter 9).

Lithuania's 330 kV electricity transmission grid is interconnected with Latvian, Belarusian and Russian high-voltage grids in the Kaliningrad region. A new interconnection with Poland is planned, possibly increasing export opportunities.

District heating started in 1947. At present, district heating systems operate in 52 towns, and approximately 80 per cent of Lithuania's housing stock and other buildings are heated by district heating systems. Their steam and water pipelines are in all 2650 km long. The existing district heating systems suffer comparatively high losses. Energy consumption is rarely metered because of a lack of control and metering equipment for small industrial and residential consumers. Therefore, in the residential sector, payments are not linked to actual energy consumption and there are no incentives to save energy. It is not possible to control or regulate consumption in buildings with their existing installations. Approximately 30 per cent of the heat is produced as combined heat and power from steam turbines at combined heat and power plants (CHP). The remaining heat is produced by heat boilers. The average efficiency is approximately 85 per cent. The marginal electricity efficiency of Lithuania's CHPs is between 35 and 65 per cent. Typical advanced CHPs have marginal electricity efficiencies of 80 to 100 per cent. Of the total heat production, 93 per cent is used and 7 per cent is lost. Major customers have been cut off.

The district heating enterprises belonged to "Lietuvos energija" until mid-1997. Since then they have been transferred into municipal ownership.

Natural gas and oil supply

Natural gas has been used since 1961, when the gas pipeline from Dashva (Ukraine) reached Lithuania. Depending on their current heating systems, new customers could be connected as direct users or via their district heating systems. There is no seasonality in pricing and hence little economic advantage in storing the gas for use when prices increase. The pipelines are considerably over-sized. The pipelines can provide up to 14 billion m^3 per year. The stored gas can supply Lithuania 15 to 40 days (average 24 days). There are four pipelines, which means that theoretically the supply is secure. All four come from a single supplier: the Russian Federation. Any interruption in supply would also affect Kaliningrad.

Both the future role of gas and the development of the oil industry will be largely influenced by the fate of the Ignalina Nuclear Power Plant. If INPP were to shut down, it is likely that a gas-powered plant would be considered, because it is quick to build. It would significantly increase demand for natural gas. Nevertheless, the presence of possibly cheaper heavy fuel oil locally, together with lax environmental requirements, would hinder the expansion of gas use, especially in power generation. Most power plants other than Ignalina can run on fuel both oil and gas.

Lithuania pays world market prices for its Russian oil supplies. Lithuania could be supplied with sufficient quantities of oil through its sole domestic oil terminal in Klaipėda. In normal circumstances, it is not profitable to use the terminal to this end. The terminal is used only for unloading limited amounts of the cheaper, but more polluting, liquid fuel bitumen emulsion.

Lithuania's main supplier of petroleum products is the Mažeikiai State Refinery "Nafta". Its total capacity is some 13.8 million tonnes of crude oil a year, but the refinery is currently operating well below capacity. All its crude oil is imported from CIS by pipeline. The refinery currently produces large volumes of high-sulphur heavy fuel oil. Its export price is low and its domestic use causes pollution. Storage facilities for white oil products in Vilnius, Alytus and other places are in poor condition and in some cases are causing environmental and possibly health problems. The National Energy Strategy has proposed that they should be replaced urgently. The storage facilities are limited, and new facilities are planned or under construction.

Indigenous energy sources

As has already been stressed, the share of indigenous energy resources in Lithuania's energy balance is rather small. During the past several years, energy production from wood, peat, hydro and other indigenous resources has remained almost constant; only the extraction of oil has increased.

Renewable resources have been neglected in the past because energy prices in the former Soviet Union were heavily subsidized and because of the centralized energy systems. More recently, energy prices have shot up, making it more attractive to develop renewable resources. On the other hand, Lithuania's energy industry already suffers from overcapacity: it was designed to supply a region substantially larger than itself, and the country's economy and that of the wider region are contracting. This overcapacity is seriously hindering the development of new energy industries.

Given Lithuania's high dependence on imports of primary energy resources, it would be desirable to increase the proportion of indigenous energy supplies. A special project funded by PHARE was carried out in 1994 to determine which indigenous resources should be promoted as being both economically and environmentally attractive. A rough estimate of the technical energy potential of new and renewable resources suggests that maximum about 15 per cent of Lithuania's energy demand could in future be covered by indigenous energy resources (peat, wood, waste, straw, biogas, hydro, geothermal). Consequently, one of the main policy objectives stated in the draft energy law is the promotion of domestic and renewable energy resources.

Final consumption and energy intensity

In 1994, gross energy consumption was 7.8 Mtoe, down 48.8 per cent on 1991 (Table 11.1). According to the most recent data, it stood at 9.6 Mtoe in 1996, up from 8.8 Mtoe in 1995, but down 50 per cent on 1990. This was due to a decrease in imports and primary energy production (natural gas imports have more than halved), a drop in energy demand for industrial purposes, and metering and energy saving.

Total final energy demand consists mainly of oil (from 41.4 per cent in 1991 to 28.8 per cent in 1994 and 35.5 in 1996) and heat (from 32.3 per cent to 40.4 per cent and 29.2 per cent over the same period). Demand for coal and electricity decreased in absolute terms over the period, as sharply as overall demand, while demand for gas and biomass remained stable at about 0.7 Mtoe and 0.2 Mtoe, respectively.

In 1996, heat production stood at 2 million toe (20 million Gcal). Heat generation was up almost 3 per cent compared to 1995, but down 58 per cent compared to 1990. The fall in heat consumption was caused by the same factors that accounted for the drop in electricity consumption. Industry and households are the largest heat consumers. Losses in the heating network continue to increase compared to total consumption: from 4.2 per cent in 1990 to 20 per cent in 1996.

In terms of energy intensity (Table 11.3), Lithuania appears to be inefficient compared to EU countries. On the other hand, gross energy consumption per capita dropped from 3.0 toe/inhabitant in 1992 to 2.1 toe/inhabitant in 1994 but then again increased to 2.6 in 1996. The indicator is lower than the EU ratio (3.6 toe/inhabitant). The difference in energy intensity can generally be explained by the continued use of highly energy-intensive industrial processes. The recent surge could be linked to the current increase in of industrial capacity utilization. The lower per capita primary energy consumption can be explained by the comparatively lower energy use in the transport and household sectors.

Energy efficiency and conservation potential in economic sectors

Large companies dominate Lithuania's industry. Studies carried out by the Energy Centre EC Vilnius in the Lithuanian furniture sector demonstrate that consumption of electricity could be cut by up to 27 per cent and heat by up to 61 per cent. Some studies also demonstrate that a total energy saving of 20-44 per cent is possible with a payback period of maximum two years. Applying EU best practices could result in energy savings of 26 to 60 per cent in all sectors.

In the household sector, energy prices are still below production costs. Utility bills are based on the size of individual flats and the number of occupants. Heating is estimated to be the most wasted resource. Many buildings do not have regulating equipment. Most people regulate the indoor temperature by opening the windows. Furthermore, many buildings are poorly insulated. The Centre in Vilnius estimates that up to 50 per cent of heat in buildings could be saved through energy efficiency improvements.

Much energy could also be saved in transport. Road transport takes up 81 per cent of the sector's total energy consumption. Passengers and goods are transported inefficiently, in terms of energy use. There is no efficient multi-modal transport system. The railway network was tailored to cover the former USSR and has not yet been reorganized to fit Lithuania's needs. Public transport does not meet the needs of the population, and individual transport is growing rapidly.

The total energy conservation potential in 1994 was 1.55 million toe/year (18 TWh/year) and the investment needed to upgrade the energy sector is estimated at ECU 7 billion. Financial support for some of the energy conservation projects may come from the Energy Efficiency Fund. Indigenous and renewable energy resources could offer a large potential at a modest production cost but would need a deliberate governmental effort, facilitating the introduction of efficient and cleaner technologies.

The emissions of pollutants in Lithuania are not as high as in other countries in transition. According to indexes, the country is, at present, in a position similar to well developed west European countries. This is due to the general recession and the fact that most electricity is produced at INPP. Thermal power plants are operated at very low capacity, as nuclear electricity is cheaper. But the introduction of a new fuel - bitumen emulsion - could cause new environmental problems. Bitumen emulsion can be burned in similar conditions as HFO. When the economy recovers, this situation could get worse. As it is, the emission levels from separate energy installations are not low enough to conform to EU standards (see Chapter 6).

Refinery installations, transport and the storage of hydrocarbons have other effects too. They pollute coastal waters, contaminate the soil and emit VOC. At the moment, the situation is being carefully monitored to identify corrective measures.

11.2 Environmental policy and management of the energy sector

Concerns and objectives

The basic concerns with the energy sector in Lithuania are typical for most transition countries. Energy was heavily subsidized in the former economic system, energy savings were therefore low, and energy production was inefficient. More typical of Lithuania are the high import dependency for primary energy, the oversized energy economy, and the small but untapped potential for indigenous energy production. Lithuania relies primarily on a mixture of structural reforms, privatization, and price and tax policies to manage this situation. A national programme for the production and use of bioenergy is scheduled for preparation in the last quarter of 1998. A draft law on energy conservation is under preparation.

Furthermore, a national programme to make energy consumption more efficient was revised and approved in 1996, and an Energy Saving Committee and an Energy Saving Programme Directorate were set up. In 1996, the Energy Conservation Fund (ECF) was created to finance efficiency, saving and renewable or indigenous energy production projects. Its initial capital endowment was US$ 2.5 million, and a PHARE grant was also negotiated. The banking operations of the Fund will be entrusted to local banks. The Ministries of Energy and Finance have representatives on the ECF Council. EU technical assistance is provided to define ECF rules and mechanisms so that the Fund can receive EU grants.

As all the sectors of the economy have picked up since 1994, pollution levels could increase if nothing is done to control them. Lithuania intends to reach the EU environmental standards. It is therefore very important to upgrade inefficient power plants or take them out of service at the end of the transition period.

The Law on Energy aims at reducing the impact of energy activities on the environment in several ways: it encourages energy conservation, fuel switching to less polluting and renewable forms of energy, and abatement technologies. Besides improving the country's general energy efficiency, the following are very important objectives:

- Keeping the INPP in good safety conditions and in operation as long as possible;
- Implementing the National Environment Protection Strategy.

These targets can be achieved by:

- Drawing up an atmosphere protection law (1998);
- Revising the tax system for pollution (1996-1997);
- Assessing the effect of bitumen emulsion combustion on the environment and preparing recommendations about its further use (1997);
- Modernizing and installing new boiler-burners, which would reduce NO_x emissions(1996-2000);
- Gradually applying modern technologies which do not require large investments (1998-2005);
- Setting up air-quality monitoring and public information systems in Lithuania's biggest cities and monitoring systems in energy and industrial enterprises (1996-2000);
- Designing, manufacturing and introducing technologies and cleaning equipment to render volatile organic compounds harmless (1996-2005);
- Assessing the condition of dust-catching equipment in industry and preparing a strategy for modernizing this equipment or installing it (1996-2005);
- Manufacturing, installing and repairing dust-abatement equipment (1998-2000).

The Government has adopted new emission standards, which are valid from 1996, as shown in Table 11.5. Additional modifications to thermal power plants are needed for the use of bitumen emulsion. The uncontrolled emissions of SO_2, NOx and particulates from burning bitumen emulsion are higher than from heavy fuel oil. Therefore, additional measures are required to reduce emissions. Filters for particulates are to be installed at thermal power plants. The joint-stock company "Lietuvos energija" will finance this installation.

Table 11.5: Emission targets

| | Boiler thermal capacity (MW) | Maximum permissible concentrations (mg/m³) | | | | | | | | | | | Content (%) |
| | | SO₂ | | | NOₓ | | | CO | | | Particulates | | | O₂ |
		1993	1998 Existing	New	1993	1998 Existing	New	1993	1998 Existing	New	1993	1998 Existing	New	
Gas:	1-50	-	-	-	400	350	350	400	400	400	20	20	20	3
Natural gas	51-300	-	-	-	450	350	350	300	300	300	20	20	10	3
LPG	>300	-	-	-	500	350	350	200	200	200	20	20	10	3
Liquid fuel:	1-50	3 400	2 700	2 700	580	450	450	500	500	500	150	110	100	3
Light fuel oil	51-300	3 400	2 700	2 700	680	450	450	400	400	400	140	100	100	3
Heavy fuel oil	>300	3 400	2 700	1 700	780	450	450	300	300	400	130	90	50	3
Solid fuel:	1-20	2 400	1 600	2 000	500	400	650	1 200	1 000	1 000	1 600	700	400	6
Coal, coke, oil-shale	21-50	2 400	1 200	2 000	650	400	650	1 000	800	1 000	1 300	500	300	6
Peat, straw, wood	>50	2 400	800	2 000	650	400	650	900	700	700	1 000	300	200	6

Source: Ministry of the Environment.

Note:

"**Existing**" refers to existing stationary sources and "**New**" refers to new stationary sources. Both standards are 1998 standard coming into force in May 1998.

A National Energy Strategy was prepared in 1993, with PHARE assistance. It was approved by Parliament in April 1994, and is currently under revision. The strategy addressed energy problems by (a) diversifying the primary sources of energy, (b) increasing energy efficiency, (c) implementing conservation measures, and (d) removing consumer price subsidies. The revision is expected to be approved by Parliament at the end of 1998. It aims at safe energy supply, increasing the efficiency of energy consumption, strengthening the market and attracting investors, reducing pollution, stimulating regional cooperation, and preparing the accession to the EU.

The economic crisis and the introduction of market forces have created some problems for Lithuania's power sector. To overcome these problems and meet the challenges, the Government has issued a detailed study - Least-Cost Sector Development Programme - which was carried out by the Lithuanian Energy Institute with assistance from the EU PHARE Programme. It formulates the requirements for modernizing and developing the sector. Its main objectives are:

- To identify least-cost power sector development programmes, until the year 2015, for the modernization and development of the sector in view of the various strategies for the possible retirement of the Ignalina NPP units.

- To determine corresponding investment programmes, setting out the financial requirements for demand-side measures and for the modernization and expansion of generation, transmission and distribution facilities.

- To assess the consequences of these retirement strategies and associated investment programmes.

Some of the most important issues are the environmental problems related with this retirement and with new environmental standards. Safe operation of the Ignalina NPP remains an important issue. The Law on Nuclear Energy of 1996 also regulates the public relations regarding the generation and use of nuclear energy.

Structural reforms and privatization

All State energy enterprises, except INPP, were transformed into stock companies in 1995. Energy sector enterprises are on the list of companies for partial privatization. At present, all enterprises continue to be controlled by the State, but their management enjoy more independence. The Government plans to demonopolize and decentralize the energy sector in its 1997 – 2000 action programme.

Energy prices, tariffs, costs and taxes

Energy supply costs and prices of final energy have changed since 1990. The prices of petroleum and other oil products were deregulated in 1993. Consequently, prices of energy supplied to industrial consumers (electricity, gas and district heating) were raised sharply to cover costs. Table 11.6 shows that the prices of crude oil, heavy fuel oil, petrol, diesel, industrial and residential electricity have all increased, but the price of residential heat has increased much more. A comparison of residential and industrial energy shows that the prices of residential and industrial electricity have increased equally, but the remaining residential energy prices have risen 100-400 times as fast as the prices of industrial energy in the past six years. On the other hand, a comparison of industrial heat shows a difference of a factor of 60 during that time. Within the residential sector, the difference in the increase in prices between gas and heat is of a factor of 200. The prices of heat from district heating have increased much more than that of gas within both the industrial and the residential sector.

The whole pricing and tariff system was characterized by a complicated mixture of subsidies and cross-subsidies, late payments and arrears, metering problems, and unexplained losses from the system, all of which have an adverse impact on the current performance of Lithuania's energy sector. In June 1997, Parliament amended and supplemented the Law on Energy and related laws. The changes included new pricing principles and mechanisms. In principle, suppliers determine prices in coordination with the Price Commission – except those coming under municipal jurisdiction (i.e. heating plants). While it is recognized that the new energy prices should cover all production and distribution costs, their level also has social implications.

The low exchange rates of Lithuania's currency means high energy prices (relative to other production costs or income) for consumers, as energy is purchased on the world market and consumer prices are cost-based. Subsidies to energy consumers by means of "socially acceptable" low energy tariffs are a huge market distortion and undermine any incentive to save energy and make structural changes that would render the economy more efficient. The opening-up of energy markets at a time when artificially low energy tariffs are in

Table 11.6 Consumer prices and tariffs, 1990-1996

Litas, at current prices

	1990 a/	1991 a/	Jan-92 b/	Jan-93	Jan-94	Jan-95	Jan-96
Fuel or Energy							
Crude oil *(per tonne)*	0.30	0.84	13.20	37.50	..	..	..
Heavy fuel oil *(per tonne)*	0.38	0.83	12.67	33.80	65.00	102.00	105.00
Petrol *(per litre)*	0.00	0.01	0.04	0.70	1.10	1.30	1.40
Diesel *(per litre)*	0.00	0.00	0.03	0.55	0.80	1.10	1.30
Industry							
Electricity *(per MWh)*	0.30	0.80	4.00	58.00	80.00	125.00	140.00
Heat *(per MWh)*	7.00	50.00	1.80	76.00	65.00	65.00	65.00
Gas *(per 1 000 m³)*	27.50	75.00	1,051.00	350.00	3.60	4.00	4.20
Residential							
Electricity *(per MWh)*	0.40	0.60	3.50	54.00	80.00	160.00	200.00
Heat *(per MWh)*	0.02	0.10	0.40	3.00	16.00	37.00	72.00
Gas *(per 1 000 m³)*	35.00	75.00	1,051.00	231.00	382.00	512.00	600.00
Gas for heating *(per 1 000 m³)*	35.00	75.00	302.00	18.20	50.00	222.00	500.00

Source: Lithuanian Energy Institute.

a/ 1990, 1991: - in roubles.
b/ 1992: - in talonas.
  Prices were recalculated by using the exchange rates: - 1 talonas = 1 rouble,
  - 1 litas = 100 talonas.

effect may lead to large deficits for the country and its energy sector and serious financial problems for the future.

The new prices are increasing for all consumers. As the VAT exemption for energy was abolished on 1 July 1997, prices are increasing. A VAT of 18 per cent is levied on oil products, electricity and heat. The Government has promised to compensate energy suppliers for VAT as of 1 January 1997. The second main tax on energy linked to energy consumption is excise duties. In addition, there may be stamp duties, resources taxes, contributions to the Road Fund, and charges for pollution (see Chapter 2).

The new pricing procedure and the structural reforms in district heat supply have increased the local variation in heat prices (Table 11.7). Prices for residential heat increased between 10.5 per cent and 41.5 per cent, and for other consumers between 21.5 per cent and 55.6 per cent (both excluding VAT). Some forecasters believe that electricity price increases from 20 to 40 ct/KWh and heat price increases from 6 to 20 ct/KWh between 1995 and 2005 would be compatible with a maximum annual growth of 2.5 per cent.

Table 11.7: Energy prices for the 1997 heating period by producing enterprise

	Heating	Hot water
	ct/kWh	Lt/m³
Viniaus heating network	11.26	15.04
"Kauno energija"	12.26	17.14
"Klaipedos energija"	13.00	10.87
Panevezio heating network	12.42	14.02
"□iauliai energija"	14.40	13.05
Alytaus heating network	12.53	11.50
Lietuvos power station	8.20	7.44
Mazeikiai power station	8.61	-

Source: Lithuanian Energy Institute.

Energy utilities have to pay economic and environmental taxes. Economic taxes include: taxes on land use, on road use, on the use of natural resources and on property, social insurance tax, profit tax, value-added tax and excise tax. Environmental taxes include taxes on emissions such as SO_2, NO_x and other pollutants. Since 1996, stricter environmental requirements have been enforced in Lithuania. In the future those enforcements may be even more stringent to conform with those of western Europe.

11.3 Conclusions and recommendations

Lithuania's energy sector, which is now having to face the rigours of the market, entered the transition process in poor shape. The energy strategies developed to cope with the situation were in general well adapted to the situation and have enjoyed a number of successes. The focus on energy conservation and improved energy efficiency in relevant laws and programmes is evident. One of the worst aspects of the 'energy legacy' was inefficient use. The excessive use of energy resources was caused by:

- Very low energy prices compared to world market prices;
- Inadequate or non-existent metering and management of energy use;
- Lack of incentives to encourage energy efficiency;
- Poor insulation of buildings;
- Lack of incentives to develop renewable energies.

The situation was aggravated by cash shortages, limiting the scope for rapid improvements at all relevant levels. Therefore, the main goal of Lithuania's energy policy is to provide an efficient, reliable and safe energy supply to households. To reach this goal, urgent measures have to be taken: institutional reform of the energy sector, diversification of energy supply, active energy-saving policy and integration of Lithuania's energy systems into Europe's. Regional and international cooperation is necessary for Lithuania's energy and economic development. Lithuania's major energy policy objectives are to:

- Significantly reduce the share of energy costs in GDP (currently at 19 per cent, compared to the EU average of 2.5 per cent);
- Decrease the dependency on the Russian Federation as supplier of primary energy resources and increase the security of supply (mainly through the construction of the Būtingė oil and gas terminal and the reconstruction of the Klaipėda terminal);
- Restrict the rise in air emissions caused by the economic recovery.

The main challenges for both the oil and gas supply are very similar. Supply security and the lowest possible import prices for gas and oil are sought through long-term supply agreements with a higher number of suppliers. The aim is to establish a connection to the west European gas network to ensure an alternative supply of gas at world market prices. Similar plans exist for a connection to the west European oil network or alternative sources of oil supply through the oil terminal in Klaipėda, in order to ensure a fair oil price.

International involvement is crucial to reduce capital scarcity and the lack of technical and business experience in Lithuania. One of its major policy goals is to join the European Union. It became an associate member of EU in June 1995, but there are differences in Lithuania's economy as well as in its legal system when compared with EU that need to be bridged. There are some important legal and economic obstacles to foreign investment, as the debts of energy companies compromise their profitability. Debts have mounted mainly because some consumers are not able to pay their energy bills.

Energy prices for heat and natural gas used for heating purposes do not always cover investment costs. Revenues from energy sales are often not sufficient to keep the working capital at a necessary level. This makes investments obviously very problematic. Usually, investments, when made, are financed with loans. However, loans are already used for the necessary increase of the working capital.

Increasing energy efficiency is a strategic target of prime importance. Initiatives appear to be urgently required in three directions. Industrial energy use suffers from the absence of institutional and financial frameworks that permit a clear focus on energy efficiency as a key factor for competitiveness. Along with labour and capital, energy is an important factor of production. The introduction of political and economic reforms and institutional and legal changes are stimulating the implementation of market and cost-based pricing and increasing the market's efficiency. Improvements must be made, both in the intensive energy structure and low efficiency of production, in order to be able to compete internationally and to generate sufficient economic growth and welfare. The existing initiatives in energy efficiency centres, by the Energy Saving Programme Directorate, through the Energy Saving Fund, and the efficiency programmes of the Transport Ministry might have a stronger impact, if they could be fully coordinated.

The potential for energy savings in buildings appears to be considerable. In 1994, households became the biggest heat consumers. Together with

the service sector they consumed 70 per cent of final heat, compared to 45 per cent in 1990. The restructuring of the building materials industry and its technical modernization as well as the renovation of existing buildings and the construction of new energy efficient buildings are included in the National Energy Efficiency Programme. The total heat energy saving potential by modernizing heat supply and use in buildings until the year 2000 is estimated to be 0.94 million toe (10.98 TWh). Finally, more energy efficient and more environment-friendly solutions are needed in the transport sector.

Recommendation 11.1:
A financial framework is required to help industries in their drive toward increased energy efficiency. A programme to reduce energy use in public buildings should be implemented as a matter of priority, and efforts should be made to reach the same goal in private buildings through educational campaigns. Fuels should be priced so as to stimulate more energy-efficient transport. Measures should be taken to make public transport more attractive.

The future of the Ignalina Nuclear Power Plant is addressed in the National Energy Strategy. However, it appears that the environmental concerns about the station do not receive appropriate attention in the Strategy. This is all the more unfortunate, as there are a number of both national and international aspects that will have a bearing also on Lithuania's energy economy.

Recommendation 11.2:

The current National Energy Strategy should give appropriate attention to the environmental risks connected with the operation of the Ignalina Nuclear Power Plant in all its national and international ramifications.

Another issue central to the implementation of a successful energy efficiency policy is research and development (R&D). Old and inefficient energy end-use equipment should be improved or replaced. In general, this decision should be carried out after technical and economic feasibility studies. The major part of R&D programmes in the energy sector were coordinated by the former Ministry of Energy (now by the Ministry of the Economy). All research is carried out in oil, gas, power and other sectors and financed from the State budget. The current poor economic status of the country is the main obstacle to large studies. Technology and

R&D programmes should also be very useful for solving problems related to new environmental standards.

R&D programmes can be made more successful by promoting the development of advisory services to energy end-users (e.g. Energy Saving Company Operator - ESCO Services providing the so-called "Third Party Financing"). The required business and management training should also incorporate economic assessment methods, identification of bankable conservation projects, etc. Research and support programmes should give priority to possible conservation activities and measures, taking into account any technical efficiency gap, to reducing energy intensity, and to realizing existing energy saving potentials.

Recommendation 11.3:
A wide-ranging R&D programme is required to ensure energy efficiency and environmental improvements. Such a programme should be drawn up jointly by the Ministries of the Environment and of the Economy and should be accompanied by measures that increase the managerial capacity of industry to improve energy efficiency and protect the environment. High priority in R&D programmes should be attached to solving the environmental problems caused by the burning of bitumen emulsion for energy purposes.

The development of an energy efficiency policy obviously needs to be supplemented by the promotion of domestic and renewable energy resources. Lithuania's indigenous and renewable resources are not negligible, but require active governmental efforts to be developed. The Kaunas Hydro Plant (100 MW) is currently the only major plant in that category, accompanied only by several mini hydro plants (with a total capacity of about 5 MW). Another possible renewable energy resource in the electricity sub-sector could be wood waste and wood chips burned in new CHP, where there are heat grids supplied by heat-only boilers. Renewable energy resources are virtually unused in Lithuania, although they are estimated to have potential, especially hydro, geothermal, wood waste, solar, wind, solid municipal waste, and waste incineration.

The centralized energy systems and heavily subsidized energy prices provided little incentive to evaluate the potential for renewable energy. Therefore, renewable resources play a minor role in the country's energy balance. More sophisticated energy policy instruments are needed to promote

legislation on purchasing electricity from independent suppliers and to introduce differentiated tariffs for electricity with higher prices at peak times.. Subsidies, improving technologies and research and development support and demonstration projects are the surest policy instruments for the near future.

Recommendation 11.4:
The Energy Efficiency Fund should finance projects aiming at increasing the use of domestic resources, as well as selected energy conservation projects. Realistic energy efficiency standards should be developed and used to label consumer appliances and equipment according to their energy efficiency.

The Government has incorporated environmental concerns in its energy policy by establishing strategic environmental protection objectives, such as energy-efficiency in the construction of new installations, by including safeguards and requiring permits before they are commissioned, and in the operation of installations by setting fines and making anti-pollution equipment compulsory where necessary. The emission of CO_2, NOx and SO_2 per capita in Lithuania is below the EU average. However, this is primarily the result of the recession, and the situation is likely to worsen when the economy recovers, unless measures are taken. That is why reducing the rise in air emissions is the energy policy's major environmental objective. Its success will require different measures, depending on the duration of the phase-out of Ignalina NPP. If it is phased out fast, measures to increase the generation of electricity in Lithuania's thermal power plants and make them meet environmental standards applied in western countries would become urgent.

Power and heat supply are of key importance to environmental concerns with energy. Here, the most urgent requirement appears to be the preparation of a timetable for the possible phasing-out of the Ignalina Nuclear Power Plant. Setting this timetable will require supply options to be selected for the post-Ignalina era, but it does not obviate the need to develop a comprehensive strategy to which all power producers could adapt.

Recommendation 11.5:
The electricity efficiency of combined heat and power plants should be improved, also in anticipation of the phasing-out of the Ignalina Nuclear Power Plant. A substantial reduction in the losses in the production and distribution of electricity and district heat should help to make

district heating competitive compared with decentralized oil and gas boilers.

The post-Ignalina power supply also requires the development and implementation of a conservation policy. It should aim to improve the efficiency with which electricity is generated in combined heat and power plants. However, efficiency gains will also have to be realized in other energy processes, such as district heating. Here, reducing losses (which are currently at 7 per cent of heat generated) should improve the market position of district heating plants.

Recommendation 11.6:
The establishment of a robust and diversified structure of electricity supply requires the setting-up of an institutional and financial framework for small independent power producers.

Lithuania would like to connect to the west European power grid (UCPTE). This is achievable by 2010. The first step will be the planned connection to the Polish power grid. Other options are: connecting to the Scandinavian power grid (NORDEL) or joining the powerful Smolensk-Frankfurt connection. A similar gas connection - the Baltic gas ring - is also under consideration. These connections are important for (electricity) exports, and would contribute to the effective consolidation of the country's energy market and the optimization of air protection and technological safety standards in power plants. These connections should therefore be made according to the existing plans.

Recommendation 11.6:
The connection of the Lithuanian power system to the west European power grid should go ahead as planned, subject to any arrangements that may be necessary regarding electricity export. Connection to the Baltic gas ring should be given serious consideration.

Chapter 12

ENVIRONMENTAL CONCERNS IN AGRICULTURE AND FOOD PROCESSING

12.1   The present situation of agriculture

Natural conditions

Lithuania's climate is transitional between maritime and continental. Its proximity to the Baltic Sea gives it a much milder climate than that of other countries lying at the same latitude. The average temperature in January is -4.9°C, in July +17.2°C. The amount of precipitation varies from 320 to 470 mm during the growing season; 390 - 420 mm evaporate. During wintertime the soil is, on average, frozen to a depth of 40 to 70 cm.

Roughly one third of the population lives in rural areas, where farming is the main source of livelihood. Agriculture uses 54 per cent of the land (Figure I.1), two thirds of which is arable. Bogs and marshlands, a significant feature of Lithuania's landscape, now cover 7 per cent of its territory. Over the last few decades the intensification of large-scale agriculture, the cutting of forests and the draining of bogs have contributed to erosion and loss of soil productivity. At present, about 15 per cent of the country's farmland is severely eroded.

Soil quality varies considerably. Good quality agricultural soil is found on only 34 per cent of the agricultural area. Three main regions can be identified by soil productivity: the lowlands in central Lithuania have the most productive soils, followed by the low, deeply washed carbonate soils in west Lithuania. The wooded moraine hills and interspersed sandy plains in east Lithuania have a relatively low agricultural productivity. The most characteristic soils are turfy podzolic loam and gley.

Lithuania's climate is comparatively favourable for the cultivation of perennial legumes and cereal grasses. Almost half the land used for agricultural production is under perennial grasses, in the form of cultivated meadows and natural grassland and pastures. Lithuania cultivates over one million ha of cereals, 40 per cent of them are winter wheat and rye.

Agriculture and food processing in transition

The implementation of land reform and the privatization of assets of State and collective farms as well as the establishment of new price and income support systems for agricultural producers were set as the main objectives of the agricultural policy promoted by the Lithuanian Government during the transition period.

The process of land reform started in 1989, when the Seimas passed the Law on Peasant Farms. Under this Law applicants could apply for farms with 50 hectares of agricultural land. The leaseholders did not acquire the right to sell the land.

After the proclamation of independence in March 1990, agrarian reform was decided upon. The restitution of ownership rights or the payment of compensation in cash or in kind were the basic options, with compensation in kind largely prevailing. Subsequently, a series of laws and regulations was enacted to assist the implementation of land reform, including the Law on Personal Farm Development (1990), the Law on Land Reform, the Law on the Procedure and Conditions for the Restitution of the Rights of Ownership and Conditions for the Restoration of the Rights to Existing Property (1991), and the Law on the Privatization of Property of Agricultural Enterprises (1991).

The first reference to the issue of restitution was made in the Decree of the Supreme Council of 3 July 1990. The Law on the Procedure and Conditions for the Restitution of the Rights of Ownership and Conditions for the Restoration of the Rights to Existing Property covered agricultural land and forests on the types of property for which ownership rights were to be restored.

Compensation in cash for agricultural land and forests acquired in the State's interests (construction of roads, human settlements, schools, etc.) has to be provided by the State within 15 years, or within 10 years if residential property is involved.

The fundamental legal framework for privatization was set up in the Law on the Initial Privatization of State Property and in the Law on Price Liberalization adopted in 1991. The initial application of these laws has demonstrated the need for several amendments, which were made to accelerate the reforms and the restoration of property to former owners. The amendments to the Law on Land Reform were made in summer 1993. They included some environmental protection measures. At that time the National Programme for the Development of Agriculture was drawn up and approved and the Agricultural Support Fund was set up to stabilize the market for agricultural products and develop the agricultural and rural infrastructure. The objective was to modernize the technologies in the agro-food processing industry to create a market-oriented and internationally competitive agro-food sector.

The Law on Land, establishing operational conditions for a land market, was developed and approved in April 1994. It defines the rights and obligations of landowners (private individuals, groups of individuals and the State), authorizes the sale, lease, mortgage and other operations accessible to landowners. The Government, in turn, is responsible for "... formulations and special provisions on land use, restrictions on certain activities and land use or changes to the initial land use". Private individuals can own land, which can be acquired in two ways: by purchasing it from the State, or through restitution of their former property rights if they are currently citizens of Lithuania. The maximum area of a privately owned plot was set at 150 ha, including 25 ha of forests.

The annual land tax levied on State and privately owned land is payable by individuals and legal entities. The tax is a percentage of the land's nominal value: State-owned land 3.0 per cent; agricultural land 1.5 per cent; privately owned land 1.0 per cent.

To improve the coordination of all activities related to the land reform, the Government established the National Land Survey of Lithuania in 1995. The constitutional ban on foreign landownership was lifted in June 1996. Now, foreigners can own non-agricultural land.

The restructuring and the privatization in the agro-food sector in Lithuania started in 1992, in accordance with the Law on Privatization of Property of Agricultural Enterprises and the Law on the Initial Privatization of State Property. In the wake of these two laws, a decree on the privatization of agro-service and food-processing enterprises was adopted. The process of privatization in the sector proceeded slowly. The governmental decree of April 1994, which set the price of shares at 2.5 per cent of their nominal value if agricultural producers paid for them in cash, accelerated the privatization process. In 1994, the average rate of privatization among food-processing enterprises was 50-60 per cent. By 1996 it stood at 90 per cent: 94 per cent in the grain-processing industry, 91 per cent in the sugar industry, 72 per cent in the milk-processing industry, and 82 per cent in the meat-processing industry. The biggest problem in the sector is the weak financial situation, which prevented the timely modernization of obsolete equipment and technologies and created difficulties not only in adjusting to the new market but in meeting environmental requirements too.

Sectoral structure and production

The collapse of the common market of the former USSR drastically affected Lithuania's economy. In 1983, Lithuania produced 2.3 per cent of mineral fertilizers, 2.8 per cent of meat and 2.8 per cent of milk of the former USSR gross social product. In the pre-reform period, agriculture and food production was the second largest sector of Lithuania's economy. In 1990, agriculture constituted 28 per cent of GDP, but in the beginning of the transition period that share fell dramatically. In 1994, agriculture contributed 10.7 per cent to GDP. In 1997, that contribution increased to 12.7 per cent. Partially, the decline is attributed to the revised methodology adopted for calculating national accounts from 1992 onwards. Despite the decline, the agricultural sector maintains an important position in the country's economy. The share of employment in agriculture is around 24 per cent, including employment on household plots.

Lithuania's agriculture is now characterized by three different types of farms (Figure 12.1):

- Successor companies to the former kolkhozes and sovkhozes (380 ha on average)
- Household plots (2-3 ha on average),
- Private farms (8.5 ha on average).

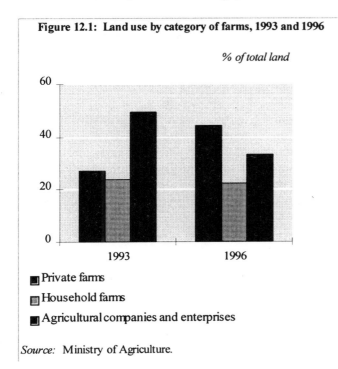

Figure 12.1: Land use by category of farms, 1993 and 1996

% of total land

■ Private farms

▦ Household farms

■ Agricultural companies and enterprises

Source: Ministry of Agriculture.

Animal husbandry and crop production have undergone the biggest changes during the transition period. Livestock was always the most important sector of Lithuania's agriculture, accounting for 52 per cent of total agricultural output before independence. Since domestic animal feed production did not cover Lithuania's needs, feed had been imported from other Soviet republics, where the surplus of Lithuania's animal products

was marketed. The disruption of these economic relations has significantly affected the sector during the transition period and reduced livestock production by over 50 per cent.

The fall in crop production by more than 40 per cent during this period was partially due to the adverse weather conditions in 1992 and 1994 as well as to the fact that arable lands have been taken out of production because of unclear ownership titles. The biggest part of agricultural output is produced by private farms and household farms (1996): grain 68.4 per cent; technical crops 45.7 per cent; potatoes 98.1 per cent; vegetables 99 per cent; meat 54.5 per cent; milk 83.6 per cent.

Agricultural and food products continue to account for a large share of Lithuania's total exports. In 1994 exports of agricultural and food products made up almost one quarter of total exports and 10 per cent of total imports. In 1996, its share in exports diminished to 17.1 per cent, while the share in imports increased to 13.1 per cent.

As well as raising expectations, land privatization and property restitution have brought numerous problems. Farmers face rising prices for energy, fuel, agricultural chemicals, machinery, etc. A survey (carried out by the Department of Statistics in the spring of 1996 among farmers, specialists and managers of agricultural partnerships and enterprises) shows that the main factors slowing down the development of agriculture are the high prices of inputs, the low food prices, the shortage of working capital and arrears in payments for sold produce.

Figure 12.2: Agricultural production by producer group, 1990-1996

%

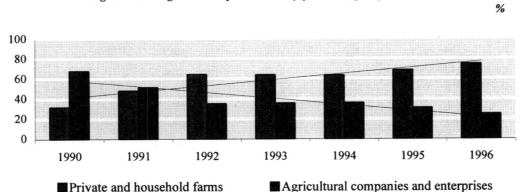

■ Private and household farms   ■ Agricultural companies and enterprises

Source: Statistical Yearbook of Lithuania, 1997.

12.2 Production techniques and environmental consequences

Use of fertilizers and pesticides

In Lithuania, the production of mineral fertilizers started in 1963 at the Kėdainiai Chemical Plant and in 1965 at the Jonava Fertilizer Plant. The stock company 'Achema' in Jonava, which produces nitrogen fertilizers, has a production capacity of 450 000 tonnes of ammonium nitrate and 170 000 tonnes of carbamide a year. The annual production of the Kėdainiai Chemical Plant comes to 200 000 tonnes of granulated superphosphate and to 280 000 tonnes of ammophos. Their technology requires the import of sulphur and apatites, while ammonia, lime and limestone are available in Lithuania. The use of fertilizers and pesticides fell sharply between 1991 and 1995. On average fertilizer applications fell to 99 kg per ha in 1997. In 1991, 196 kg of fertilizer was applied per ha. Before the agricultural reform, average pesticide use stood at some 2.0 kg per ha. After 1990, pesticide use decreased by about 30 per cent a year till 1994. Recently, its average use has remained below 0.5 kg per ha (0.363 kg in 1995 and 0.477 kg in 1996 per ha). Generally, the economic recession and the financial difficulties of farmers explain this reduction.

Mineral fertilizers are one of the most important sources of soil contamination with heavy metals. The data from the Agrochemical Research Centre show that superphosphate produced at the Kėdainiai Chemical Plant contains: cadmium (2.75 mg/kg); lead (14.5 mg/kg); chromium (7.50 mg/kg); nickel (12.50 mg/kg); copper (26.25 mg/kg); zinc (18.25 mg/kg); manganese (130 mg/kg). Assuming mean fertilization rates, the following amounts of heavy metals are introduced into the soil every year: cadmium 1.1 –to 1.8 g/ha; chromium 2.0 to 3.2 g/ha; lead 5.9 to 10.3 g/ha; nickel 5.0 to 8.5 g/ha; copper 5.7 –to 8.7 g/ha; zinc 6.4 to 10.2 g/ha; manganese 27.8 to 42.3 g/ha. Due to the accumulative property of heavy metals, these comparatively unimportant quantities represent a potential danger. The concentration of heavy metals in soils throughout the country in places distant from bigger towns does not, in general, exceed the maximum allowable concentration (MAC). Given the lack of investigation data, the applicable background (natural) limits for heavy metals are those of the former Soviet Union, for example for lead it stands at 12 mg/kg in soil.

Studies carried out between 1981 and 1991 on pesticide residues in the soils of Lithuania showed that residues of simazine and atrazine were found in 47 per cent and 85 per cent of samples analysed, respectively. However, the permissible simazine concentration (0.20 mg/kg) was exceeded only in 3.6 per cent of the soil samples and that of atrazine (0.50 mg) in only 3.3 per cent.

Surface and groundwater quality

Pollution of surface water and groundwater is a major environmental issue related to agriculture. The problem of water pollution is particularly acute because only about 2 million people receive water from a centralized water supply system in 26 major towns. The widespread pollution of surface waters

Figure 12.3: Use of mineral fertilizers, 1988-1997

1 000 tonnes

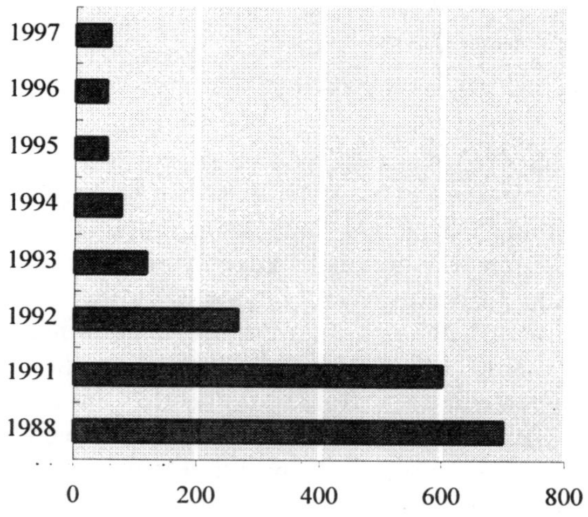

Source: Ministry of Agriculture.

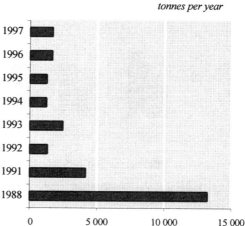

Figure 12.4: Use of pesticides, 1988-1997

tonnes per year

Source: Ministry of Agriculture.

Table 12.1: Heavy metals in the humus layer of soils in various Lithuanian regions

							Average amount mg/kg of soil
	Cr	**Cd**	**Pb**	**Ni**	**Cu**	**Zn**	**Fe**
Western	10.2	0.48	14.1	9.4	5.3	37.2	7 331
Central	11.4	0.63	13.7	10.9	7.0	31.0	7 754
Eastern	7.9	0.49	10.9	7.4	5.0	23.5	5 687

Source: Lithuania's Environment, Status, Processes, Trends, Vilnius, 1995.

and shallow groundwater by point and non-point sources has resulted in the almost exclusive use of deep groundwater as the source of drinking water supply in urban areas.

Severe pollution of surface and groundwater by nutrients from large-scale pig breeding units and livestock production is the most common and problematic in rural areas. Approximately 0.7 million people in rural areas use water from individual wells and about half of all rural drinking-water wells have a high level of nutrient contamination. This problem results primarily from inadequate waste storage facilities and poor application technology.

One of the aspects of this problem is linked to Lithuania's location in the catchment area of the Baltic Sea. Leakage and surface run-off of nitrogen and phosphorus as well as emissions of nitrogen compounds contribute to the general eutrophication of the Baltic Sea. It is estimated that agricultural sources account for about 30-35 per cent of the total nitrogen load and about 10 per cent of the total phosphorus load to the Baltic Sea (see Chapter 7). In addition, significant quantities of pesticides and herbicides are causing problems. The Nemunas River Basin is one of 132 hot spots in the Baltic Sea region because of agricultural run-off.

Soil erosion

Another major concern is soil erosion, which is especially severe in the north-western, eastern and southern parts of the country, due to the peculiarities of the relief and changes in the landscape caused by competition between agriculture and forestry. It is estimated that almost 20 per cent of agricultural land in Lithuania is subject to some degree of erosion. The measures taken to combat soil erosion such as reducing crop cultivation on eroded areas, sowing perennial grasses on fragile soils and planting trees on the

steeper slopes are not sufficient to solve the problem.

Soil compaction, drainage and irrigation

The problem of soil compaction was associated with large-scale farming using heavy agricultural machines and inappropriate technologies. With the transition to a system of small farms, this problem has become less acute. With its high rate of precipitation, Lithuania has surplus soil moisture and land drainage is consequently a big issue. Its bogs and marshlands are principally located in the centre of the country and on the coastal plains. An intensive drainage programme has been implemented over the last 30 years. It has converted about 77 per cent of Lithuania's wetlands to agricultural use.

The total drainage area is estimated at 3 million hectares, of which 2.6 million have a functioning drainage system. Since the current average cost for conversion-rehabilitation and new drainage reclamation exceeds the agricultural value of the land, this represents the main constraint on promoting sustainable farming and developing the land market. The rehabilitation and maintenance depend on the landowners' willingness to consolidate land management and share the cost of necessary works. Research into the contribution from drained areas to agriculture's impact on the environment has, in recent years, stressed the negative effects. Severe changes have occurred in the landscape structure, such as the change in soil and groundwater regime, soil moisture regime, physical, chemical and biological characteristics of the soil. Run-off of potassium, calcium, sulphates and chlorine is particularly high. Substantial changes like the disappearance of ponds and bogs and subsequent threats to biological diversity should also be mentioned.

According to the Law on Drainage (1993), the

responsibility for land melioration is vested with the State. It is expected that the responsibility for drainage will be transferred to users' associations only during the second phase of land reform (after the year 2000).

The natural environment has also been affected by the construction of irrigation systems and dams on many rivers. The irrigation systems cover almost 8,000 ha of farmland. Almost 50 per cent of the irrigation systems were intended to use liquid manure filtrate from pig-breeding units. During the transition period, the drainage and irrigation systems remained under State ownership. The restructuring of agriculture made some irrigation systems redundant, and they were abandoned. About 60 per cent of irrigation systems continue to function.

12.3 Policy formulation and implementation

Legal instruments and institutions

An important law promoting environmental aspects in agricultural activities was developed and approved in 1994 - the Law on Land. It regulates territorial distribution, protection and improvement of the environment and land use. It specifies that the land's user has to protect its quality and prevent soil deterioration and loss of fertility. The Law states also that, if land is withdrawn from agricultural activity, the resources received as compensation should be used to finance the conversion of other land designated for agricultural purposes into farmland and improve its quality.

The Law on Plant Protection (1995) established the framework for plant protection, including procedures for the registration, manufacturing, import, trade, storage and State supervision of chemical and biological means for plant protection. Responsibility for the State administration of plant protection is shared between the Ministry of Agriculture, the Ministry of the Environment and the Ministry of Health, as well as the agricultural departments in local authorities. The use of plant protection means and materials has to meet primarily hygiene and environmental protection requirements.

The drawing-up of the draft soil protection law is under way. A government decree on afforestation on private agricultural land has been in force since March 1998.

According to Government Resolution 456 (1997), the list of proposed agricultural activities and projects that are subject to a full EIA (see Chapter 1) includes:

- Agricultural service enterprises
- Livestock farms with more than 200 places
- Menageries with more than 1 000 places
- Poultry farms with more than 10 000 places
- Fish farms if the surface of the ponds exceeds 100 hectares
- Land reclamation if the surface of the land exceeds 50 hectares

Food products, beverages and pharmaceuticals, unlike fertilizers and chemical materials, are among the product groups that can be considered for eco-labelling.

Institutions and organizations directly or indirectly concerned with the management of environmental concerns in agriculture are:

- The Ministry of the Environment
- The Ministry of Agriculture
- Scientific institutions
- Associations of Agricultural Producers
- NGOs.

The Law on Land defines the direct obligations of the Ministry of Agriculture as follows:

- supervising the institutions involved in maintaining and updating the Land Register and preparing land-use plans and maps;
- monitoring the use of land designated for particular purposes, and in conformity with the Law on Environmental Protection (1992).

Being in charge of land reform and privatization, the Ministry of Agriculture determined what agricultural land had to be removed from the privatization process. In this way some recreational zones and zones with restricted agricultural practices have been established. Through its regional offices, the Ministry tries to identify environment-related problems and provide technical assistance and information to prevent and solve problems related to mismanagement.

Throughout the country the implementation of laws and decisions on environmental protection is carried out by local authorities, which can also adopt decisions, plans and projects concerning the use of natural resources and environmental protection. Local governments can also, in agreement with the Government and the Ministry of the Environment, establish norms on their own territory that are stricter than State standards, but no local government has so far done this. Local authorities administrate land use and local environmental protection funds.

The Institute of Land is in charge of the Land Register and carrying out regional agricultural development schemes.

The interests of large-scale agricultural producers (agricultural enterprises) are represented by the Lithuanian Union of Agricultural Workers. The Union was established in 1991 and has taken a leading role in agrarian reform. In 1992 the Lithuanian Association of Agricultural Enterprises was set up. The Association represents the interests of agricultural enterprises in their relations with the Seimas, ministries and other institutions. Among its main functions are developing markets agricultural input materials as well as for agricultural produce and assisting its members in promoting investment projects and finding domestic and foreign investors.

The interests of small-scale agricultural producers are represented by the Lithuanian Union of Farmers and the Lithuanian Association of Landowners, which have played an important role in the process of restitution of land to former owners during the early stage of land reform.

Policy objectives

The major responsibility for agricultural policy formulation rests with the Ministry of Agriculture. The Ministry of the Environment is mandated to take initiatives related to the environmental aspects of this policy. The major policy goals are:

- Achieving self-sufficiency in agricultural produce, with the priority given to cereals, sugar, oil-seed crops, milk and meat production;
- Making agricultural products competitive on foreign markets;
- Developing the export of agricultural products;
- Ensuring employment and a decent standard of living in rural areas;
- Developing land management and economic means for rural development;

- Supporting farm development;
- Developing agricultural research and education;
- Protecting and conserving natural resources.

The Ministry of Agriculture concentrates its attention on the funding of priority programmes. Concerning environmentally sensitive areas, the Government approved, in 1993, the Target Programme on Groundwater Protection and Sustainable Agricultural Development in the Intensive Karst Zone (Biržai and Pasvalys districts, Northern Lithuania). The Karst Zone, one of the most environmentally vulnerable areas of Lithuania, is known for both its water pollution and soil erosion problems (see Chapter 8). The Programme focuses on measures to stop both non-point and point source pollution. The 'Tatula' fund was created in 1993 to support the implementation of the Programme's objectives. The fund is a cooperative. It provides interest-free credits to farmers, agricultural partnerships, food-processing companies and enterprises implementing measures planned in the Programme or introducing sustainable and organic farming principles. As a contracting organization, the 'Tatula' fund finances the construction of waste-water treatment plants and other environmental facilities. It also funds ecological education and training, consultancies and scientific research as well as environmental monitoring systems.

Certification and control of organic farming are considered an important issue in Programme implementation. During the first years of the Karst Programme a contract was signed with the Lithuanian Agricultural Academy to assist in preparing the certification and control system. The 'Tatula' fund also supports the establishment market infrastructures for ecological products. Credits are provided on the basis of tenders. Long-term, interest-free credits were allocated to more than 40 farmers developing sustainable and organic farming (every farmer received an average of 60 000 Litas or about US$ 15 000). Two farmers received credits for the establishment of agro-services (151 000 and 223 000 Litas or US$ 38 000 and 58 000, respectively). Many long-term credits were also provided to food-processing enterprises.

Some objectives of the Programme have already been met: several scientific articles on organic farming were published, seminars and consultations were organized, a system of organic farming control and certification system was set up, and environmental monitoring was initiated. Moreover, the construction of four waste-water treatment plants has been started. In 1993, the 'Tatula' fund developed environmental activities estimated at 1 million Litas. In 1994, 3.5 million Litas was assigned for Programme implementation. At present the development capacity of the 'Tatula' fund's activities is estimated at 4 million Litas per year (or about US$ 1 million). The financing of the Programme is allotted from the State budget and from the fund members' contributions. Some Danish and American agricultural organizations have also lent a hand, and negotiations with the Netherlands and Sweden about assistance are promising.

The Lithuanian NES promotes the sustainable use of natural resources. Its priorities in agriculture are related to the implementation of sustainability principles by improving land use, preserving soil fertility, promoting clean agricultural production, and the sound use of plant protection measures and fertilizers. Among its main environmental protection goals are reducing non-point source pollution, soil pollution with organic and mineral fertilizers and other agricultural chemicals, oil products and heavy metals.

Efforts are being made to implement relevant HELCOM recommendations. They relate, among other things, to the reduction in nutrient discharges and ammonia evaporation, in nitrogen and phosphorus leaching from agricultural land, and in farm waste discharges.

Education, training and advisory services

Lithuania has two higher education establishments with an agricultural curriculum - the University of Agriculture and the Academy of Veterinary Science - eleven agricultural colleges and forty-one senior agricultural schools. Eight research institutes and the two above-mentioned higher education establishments carry out research into agriculture and food processing. The largest research centre is the Lithuanian Institute of Agriculture in Kėdainiai. Research work on methodologies for environmentally safe land improvement and water regime control, on water protection against pollution from fertilizer application, and on operating and modernizing land reclamation systems is carried out by the Institute of Land Reclamation. The Food Institute in Kaunas is engaged in investigating and developing efficient food technologies, certifying food products and

promoting ecologically clean food production technologies.

The changes in the structure of agriculture, in particular the development of small farms, have demonstrated the need for new education and training programmes, especially in agricultural economics and business management. The Agricultural Advisory Service was established in 1993. It is in strong demand, especially among young private farmers, and plays an increasing role in facilitating the adjustment of agriculture to a more sustainable, competitive and market-oriented sector. The State, with the help of foreign donors, funds all advisory services, which are provided free to farmers.

A survey carried out among 2 600 farmers showed that their level of education is as follows: 25 per cent have primary education; 24 per cent secondary general; 34 per cent secondary agricultural; and 17 per cent higher education. This means that nearly half the farmers have no formal agricultural education or other training in farming.

Foreign support

Lithuania receives foreign assistance to develop its capacity to manage environmental problems at the national as well as regional level. So far, several programmes and projects relating to the restructuring of agriculture and to solving its environmental problems have been conducted.

The Baltic Sea Joint Comprehensive Environmental Action Programme, adopted at the Conference of Ministers of the Environment in April 1992, is aimed at restoring the ecological balance of the Baltic Sea. Eight of the 132 'hot spots' it lists are related to agriculture in the former Soviet Union. Therefore, the Swedish Institute of Agricultural Engineering and the Swedish University of Agricultural Sciences carried out Agricultural Run-off Management Studies in the Baltic States and the Russian Federation during 1993 as part of this Programme. The main objective was to identify both immediate actions and a more long-term strategy to reduce the level of agricultural pollution to the Baltic Sea. The project for Lithuania was financed to the tune of SKr 2 millions by the Swedish Ministry of the Environment.

On the basis of the recommendations from these studies, the Baltic Agricultural Run-off Action Programme was drawn up. It has been operational since 1994. Its main challenge was to develop and implement a code of good agricultural practice introducing new managerial and technical solutions in farming. The Lithuanian partners in its implementation are the Lithuanian Farmers Union and the Lithuanian Agricultural Advisory and Training Centre.

The EU project 'Incentives and Obstacles to the Implementation of more Sustainable Methods in Agriculture' was carried out by the South Jutland University Centre in 1994-1996 in Lithuania and two other Baltic countries. Among other goals, the project aimed at analysing the attitude of farmers towards environmentally friendly farming, and developing an advisory system and sustainable production methods.

EU PHARE support to Lithuania's agricultural sector began in 1992. The main attention focused on the development of an overall strategy for the sector, the establishment of a land information system and the development of advisory services for private farmers. To address these issues a Programme Implementation Unit has been established within the Ministry of Agriculture.

PHARE started another three-year agricultural programme in February 1996 at a total cost of ECU 4.5 million as part of a Country Operational Programme. The strategic goal is to assist the Ministry of Agriculture and other public and private sector organizations in translating the Government's policies and reforms into practical market restructuring activities.

Baltic 21, launched at the Visby summit, Sweden, in May 1996, defined agriculture as a priority sector, which particularly needs to integrate environmental concerns. The Baltic 21 document has been adopted at the meeting of the Ministers of Foreign Affairs of the Baltic Sea States in Nyborg (Denmark) in June 1998. It focuses on good agricultural practices to reduce substantially the leakage and emission of nutrients and the use of pesticides, and on promoting less intensive farming methods.

Data of January 1997 show that 5.3 per cent of all foreign loans to Lithuania went into agriculture, while the food-processing and beverages industry obtained 1.6 per cent.

12.4 Conclusions and recommendations

The shift from the centrally planned economic system of the former Soviet Union towards a market system forced the Lithuanian Government to take measures to reorganize the agricultural sector. Despite all the problems of the transition period, Lithuania's agriculture remains one of the main economic sectors and continues to be one of the most important factors influencing environmental quality.

The priority of Lithuania's agrarian policy was to halt the decline of agriculture. The policy aimed in a very pragmatic way to stabilize the sector and to create favourable conditions for its further development. However, some measures were adopted ad hoc or borrowed from foreign experience without sufficient adaptation to the country's specifics and did not yield the desired results.

Since independence, considerable progress has been achieved in preparing the legal framework and in increasing the institutional capacity for agricultural reform. However, it is still to be seen how the implementation of the new legislation will contribute to the development of an environmentally friendly agricultural sector. Existing strategies and programmes in agriculture and the environment have limited conceptual interaction and there is still no environmentally sound agricultural policy. Lithuania's new environmental policy and strategy could support the drawing-up of a sustainable agricultural policy.

Recommendation 12.1:
A national environmental policy for the agricultural sector should be developed and approved. Its emphasis should be on sustainable development principles. The policy should pay particular attention to the problems of nitrate and pesticide concentrations in groundwater that can be attributed to agricultural practices.

The Law on EIA foresees procedures for agricultural activities. The annually valid legal provisions have so far not led to many impact assessments. It is therefore doubtful that the legal foundations for such assessments are sufficient to respond to the needs in view of agriculture's pollution potential. Furthermore, the possibilities of the EIA Division to supervise EIA procedures in agriculture are limited. The Division does not have an agricultural EIA expert, so that its staff would need special training in assessing the environmental impact of agricultural activities.

Recommendation 12.2:
The legal framework for environmental impact assessment of agricultural activities should be further developed. Its wider application is justified by the potential environmental effects of agriculture. Implementation of agricultural environmental impact assessment on a larger scale requires the specific qualifications to be available to the Environmental Impact Assessment Division of the Ministry of the Environment.

The emergence of a large number of new farmers with insufficient training creates special concerns regarding their awareness of the environmental implications of their activities. The Advisory Service should develop special training programmes to improve their knowledge of related issues over time. The programmes should include basic training in organic farming, in cooperation with the recently created Committee on Organic Farming.

Recommendation 12.3:
Training programmes for farmers should be developed and implemented by the Advisory Service, together with the Chamber of Agriculture and educational institutions, in order to improve the knowledge of farmers about the environmental consequences of · agricultural production techniques.

Some difficulties in policy implementation stem from the sector's complicated organizational infrastructure. Besides the Ministry of Agriculture, several other ministries, councils and associations are indirectly involved in policy implementation. The resulting needs for cooperation and coordination within the sector are not always satisfied, but very encouraging institutional cooperation seems to have been established recently between the Ministries of the Environment and of Agriculture, where a Land Reclamation and Environmental Protection Division was created in January 1997. However, cooperation is presently still confined to the mutual endorsement of legislative acts. Several working groups and commissions exist only on paper. For example, a Coordination Committee for Environmental

Protection in Agriculture was established in accordance with HELCOM recommendations under the authority of the Ministry of Agriculture in 1994, but there are still no significant outputs from its activity. Nevertheless, on the basis of what has already been achieved, progress in the joint management of agro-environmental schemes appears possible.

Recommendation 12.4:
The agricultural and environmental institutions should strengthen their joint management and implementation of issues of common concern by all feasible means.

The problems of agricultural waste management should be solved by concentrating more on reduction at the source. Biogas production from animal waste could contribute to such a strategy, as was suggested in a recent feasibility study.

The waste problems of the food-processing industry also need solving. Given Lithuania's economic development and prospects, probably the best strategy would be to strengthen the introduction of cleaner technologies.

Recommendation 12.5:
The Ministry of Agriculture, together with the other ministries concerned, should promote new and environmentally friendly technologies and solve any existing waste problems from food processing, in cooperation with the food-processing industry.
See also Recommendation 3.4.

Successfully implementing an environmentally oriented agricultural policy requires data support. Information on water pollution, soil pollution and erosion, and waste management is needed in particular. It is necessary to improve water quality monitoring to detect and control the agricultural sources of pollution. A study on the influence of agricultural activities on human health would be desirable. Scientific centres and laboratories in the institutes and universities hold valuable scientific data on agriculture's impact on the environment. It is necessary to process and mobilize these data to provide the relevant support to decision makers for ongoing policy formulation and the initiation of activities to improve management practices. The information exchange between the Ministry of the Environment and the Ministry of Agriculture should be improved to increase staff awareness about environmental problems in the Ministry of Agriculture.

Recommendation 12.6:
A comprehensive information system on environmental issues in agriculture should be reflected in the agricultural information system that the Ministry of Agriculture is preparing.

ANNEXES

I.   **Selected economic and environmental data**

II.   **Selected multilateral agreements**

III. **Chronology of selected environmental events**

Annex I

SELECTED ECONOMIC AND ENVIRONMENTAL DATA

Selected economic data

	Lithuania
TOTAL AREA (1 000 km^2)	65.3
POPULATION	
Total population, 1997 (100 000 inh.)	37.0
- % change (1980-1997)	8.3
Population density, 1997 (inh./km^2)	56.7
GROSS DOMESTIC PRODUCT	
GDP, 1997 (US$ 1 000 000)	9,550
- % change (1992-1997)	-25.0
per capita, 1997 (US$/cap.)	2,578
INDUSTRY	
Value added in industry, 1996 (% of GDP)	29.0
Industrial output	
- % change (1992-1996)	-41.3
AGRICULTURE	
Value added in agriculture, 1996 (% of GD	15.3
Agricultural output	
- % change (1992-1996)	39.4
ENERGY SUPPLY	
Total supply, 1996 (Mtoe)	9.6
- % change (1990-1996)	-14.3
Energy intensity 1996 (toe/US$ 1 000)	1.2
Structure of energy supply, 1996 (%)	
- Solid fuels	7.8
- Oil	33.8
- Gas	21.7
- Nuclear	36.4
- Hydro, etc.	0.3
ROAD TRANSPORT	
Road traffic volumes, 1997	
- billion veh.-km	..
- % change (1990-1997)	..
- per capita (1 000 veh.-km/cap.)	..
Road vehicle stock, 1997	
- 10 000 vehicles	102
- % change (1990-1997)	40.9
- private cars per capita (veh./1 000 inh.)	226

Sources:
Statistical Yearbook of Lithuania, 1997
Lietuvos Energetika'95

* GDP at current prices.

Selected environmental data

	Lithuania
LAND	
Total area (1 000 km^2)	65.3
Major protected areas (% of total area)	11.2
Nitrogenous fertilizer use, 1996 (tonne/km^2 arable la	0.99
FOREST	
Forest area (% of land area)	30.3
Use of forest resources (harvest/growth)	0.47
THREATENED SPECIES	
Mammals (% of known species)	5.9
Birds (% of known species)	14.7
Fish (% of known species)	3.0
WATER	
Water withdrawal (% of gross annual availability)	4.9
Fish catches (% of world catches)	0.05
Public waste water treatment (% of population served)	78
AIR	
Emissions of sulphur dioxide, 1996 (kg/cap.)	22.7
Emissions of sulphur dioxide, 1996 (kg/US$ 1 000 G	8.8
Emissions of nitrogen oxides, 1996 (kg/cap.)	7.0
Emissions of nitrogen oxides, 1996 (kg/US$ 1 000 GD	2.7
Emissions of carbon oxide (kg/cap.)	25.4
Emissions of carbon oxide (kg/US$ 1 000 GDP)	9.8
WASTE GENERATED	
Industrial waste (kg/US$ 1 000 GDP)	600.9
Municipal waste (kg/cap.)	389.6
Nuclear waste (tonne/Mtoe of TPES)	..
NOISE	
Population exposed to leq > 65 dB (A) (million inh.)	..

Sources:

Statistical Yearbook of Lithuania, 1997

Natural Resources and Environmental Protection, 1998

* GDP at current prices.

Annex II

SELECTED BILATERAL AND MULTILATERAL AGREEMENTS

Selected multilateral agreements

Worldwide agreements		Lithuania
As of 29 September 1998		
1949 (GENEVA) Convention on Road Traffic	y	
1957 (BRUSSELS) Int. Conv. Relating to Limitation of Liability of Owners of Sea-going Ships	y	
1958 (GENEVA) Conv. Fishing and Conserv. Living Resources of High Seas	y	
1963 (VIENNA) Convention on Civil Liability for Nuclear Damage	y	R
1988 (VIENNA) Enforcement and the Common Protocol	y	R
1969 (BRUSSELS) Intern. Convention on Civil Liability for Oil Pollution Damage	y	
1976 (LONDON) Protocol	y	
1969 (BRUSSELS) Conv. Intervention on the High Seas in Case of Oil Pollution Casualties	y	
1971 (RAMSAR) Conv.- Wetlands of International Importance	y	R
1982 (PARIS) Amendment	y	R
1987 (REGINA) Amendments	y	R
1971 (GENEVA) Conv. on Protection against Hazards from Benzene (ILO 136)	y	
1971 (BRUSSELS) Conv. Establishment of an International Fund for Compensation of Oil Pollution Damage	y	
1972 (PARIS) Conv. Protection of the World Cultural and Natural Heritage	y	
1972 (LONDON) Conv. on the Prevention of Marine Poll. by Dumping of Wastes and other Matter	y	
1973 (WASHINGTON) Conv.-International Trade End. Species	y	
1983 (GABORONE) Amendment		
1973 (LONDON) Internat. Conv. for the Prevention of Pollution from Ships (MARPOL)	y	
1978 (LONDON) Protocol (segregated balast)	y	
1978 (LONDON) Annex III on Hazardous Substances	y	
1978 (LONDON) Annex IV on Sewage		
1978 (LONDON) Annex V on Garbage	y	
1974 (GENEVA) Conv. on Prot. against Hazards from Carcinogenic Subst. (ILO 139)	y	
1977 (GENEVA) Conv. on Prot. against Hazards from Air Poll., Noise and Vibration (ILO 148)	y	
1979 (VIENNA) Convention on Physical Protection of Nuclear Materials	y	R
1979 (BONN) Conv.-Conservation Migratory Species of Wild Animals	y	
1991(LONDON) Agr. Conservation of Bats in Europe	y	
1992 (NEW YORK) Agreement ASCOBANS	y	
1982 (MONTEGO BAY) Conv. on the Law of the Sea	y	
1985 (VIENNA) Conv.-Protection of the Ozone Layer	y	R
1987 (MONTREAL) Prot.-Subst. that Deplete the Ozone Layer	y	R
1990 (LONDON) Amendment to Protocol	y	R
1992 (COPENHAGEN) Amendment to Protocol	y	R
1986 (VIENNA) Conv. on Early Notification of Nuclear Accidents	y	R
1986 (VIENNA) Conv. on Assistance in the Case of Nuclear Accident	y	
1989 (BASEL) Conv.-Control of Transbound. Movts of Hazard. Wastes	y	
1990 (LONDON) Conv. Oil Pollution Preparedness, Response and Cooperation	y	
1992 (RIO) Conv.-Biological Diversity	y	R
1992 (NEW YORK) Framework Conv.-Climate Change	y	R
1994 (VIENNA) International Nuclear Safety Convention		R
1994 (PARIS) Convention to Combat Desertification		

Source: UNECE and Ministry of Environment of the Republic of Lithuania
   y = in force; **S** = signed; **R** = ratified, acceded, approved

Regional and subregional agreements		Lithuania
As of 29 September 1998		
1950 (PARIS) Intern. Conv. for the Protection of Birds	y	
1957 (GENEVA) European Agreement-Intern. Carriage Dangerous Goods by Road (ADR)	y	
1958 (GENEVA) Agreem.-Adoption Uniform Cond. of Approval and Recognition for Motor Vehicles Equipment and Parts	y	
1968 (PARIS) European Conv.- Protection of Animals during Intern. Transport	y	
1979 (STRASBOURG) Additional Protocol	y	
1969 (LONDON) European Conv. -Protection of Archeological Heritage	y	
1973 (GDANSK) Conv.- Fishing and Conserv.of Living Resources in Baltic Sea and Belts	y	R
1982 (WARSAW) Amendments	y	
1974 (HELSINKI) Conv.Prot. Marine Env. Baltic Sea	y	R
1976 (BARCELONA) Conv. Prot. Mediterranean Sea against Pollution	y	
1976 (BARCELONA) Prot. Dumping	y	
1976 (BARCELONA) Prot. Co-operation in Case of Emergency	y	
1980 (ATHENS) Prot. Land-based Sources Pollution	y	
1982 (GENEVA) Prot. Spec. Protected Areas	y	
1994 (MADRID) Prot. against poll. from exploration/exploitation		
1978 (OTTAWA) Convention on Multilateral Cooperation in North-West Atlantic Fisheries	y	R
1979 (BERN) Conv.-Conservation European Wildlife & Natural Habitats	y	R
1979 (GENEVA) Conv.-Long Range Transboundary Air Pollution	y	R
1984 (GENEVA) Prot.-Financing of Co-op Programme (EMEP)	y	
1985 (HELSINKI) Prot.-Reduction of Sulphur Emissions by 30%	y	
1988 (SOFIA) Prot.-Control of Emissions of Nitrogen Oxides	y	
1991 (GENEVA) Prot.-Volatile Organic Compounds	y	
1994 (OSLO) Prot.-Further Reduction of Sulphur Emissions		
1991 (ESPOO) Conv. Env. Impact Ass. in a Transboundary Context	y	
1992 (HELSINKI) Conv. Protection and Use of Transboundary Waters and Intern. Lakes	y	S
1992 (HELSINKI) Conv. Transboundary Effects of Industrial Accidents		S
1992 (HELSINKI) Conv. Protection Marine Env. Baltic Sea (2nd)	y	S
1992 (BUCHAREST) Conv. Protection Black Sea Against Pollution	y	
1992 (PARIS) Conv. Protection Marine Env. North-East Atlantic		
1993 (LUGANO) Conv.- Civil Liability for Damage from Activities Dangerous for the Environment		
1994 (LISBON) Energy Charter Treaty		
1994 (LISBON) Prot. on Energy Efficiency and Related Aspects		

Source: UNECE and Ministry of Environment of the Republic of Lithuania

    y = in force;   S = signed; R = ratified, acceded, approved

Annex III

CHRONOLOGY OF SELECTED ENVIRONMENTAL EVENTS

1529	The First Lithuanian Statute includes articles regulating the hunting of wild animals in domestic forests and the prohibition fishing in foreign waters
1921	J.Tumas-Vaižgantas establishes the first association for the environment
1946	The first reserve Žuvintas is legally established (operated since 1937)
1957	The Environmental Protection Committee is established under the Council of Ministers
1958	The list of 194 protected parks is officially announced
1959	The first Lithuanian law on nature protection is adopted
1960	The Water Resources Use and Protection Council is established under the Council of Ministers The list of 513 trees- nature monuments is officially announced The Nature Protection Association is established
1967	The first biological waste-water treatment plant is built in Šiauliai. Surface waters and air are regularly and systematically monitored.
1968	The list of 108 geological nature monuments is officially announced.
1974	The first national park is established (currently Aukštaitijos National Park).
1975	Čepkelių Reserve is established.
1976	The Lithuanian Red Book is issued
1979	Kamanų Reserve is established
1981	The Law on Clean Air is adopted The Law on Wildlife Protection and Use is adopted
1982	The State Air Protection Inspection is established
1988	The State Environmental Protection Committee is entrusted with new functions on water, air, land and forest use and protection that formerly were carried out by other ministries and institutions
1989	The beginning of integrated ecological monitoring
1990	The State Environmental Protection Committee is reorganized into the Environmental Protection Department accountable directly to the Supreme Council
1991	New Viešvilės reserve, Trakai historical park and Dzūkijos, Kuršių Nerijos and Žemaitijos national parks are established
1992	The Law on Environmental Protection is adopted 30 regional parks and 100 protected areas are established
1993	The Law on Protected Territories is adopted
1994	The Environmental Protection Department is reorganized into the Environmental Protection Ministry The National Strategy for the UN Convention on Climate Change is adopted

1996   The National Environmental Strategy is adopted.
The Law on Environmental Impact Assessment is adopted

1997   The Environmental Protection Ministry controls the use of forest resources
The Biodiversity Conservation Strategy and Action Plan are approved.

1998   The Environmental Education Strategy and Action Plan are approved
The Biodiversity Conservation Strategy and Action Plan are adopted.

SOURCES

Personal authors

1.   *Augliené, E., Bilkis, M.* Emission of pollutants into the atmosphere. Lithuania's Environment, Vilnius, 1995, p. 18-20.
2.   *Bluffstone R.*, Achieving Environmental and Fiscal Goals in Lithuania Using Pollution Charges, Harvard Institute for International Development, International Environment Program, Central and Eastern Europe Environmental Economics and Policy Project, Lithuania Program, working paper #1, February 1995
3.   *Bluffstone R.*, Methodology and Anticipated Data Requirements for Re-Calculating Pollution Charges in Lithuania, Harvard Institute for International Development, International Environment Program, Central and Eastern Europe Environmental Economics and Policy Project, Lithuania Program, working paper #4, March 1995
4.   *Bluffstone R., Seméniené D., Čekanavičius L.*, The Lithuanian Pollution Charge System: Evaluation and Prospects for the Future, Harvard Institute for International Development, International Environment Program, Central and Eastern Europe Environmental Economics and Policy Project, Lithuania Program, working paper #8, January 1996
5.   *Čekanavičius L.*, Feasibility of a Tradable Pollution Permit Regime in Panavežys, Harvard Institute for International Development, International Environment Program, Central and Eastern Europe Environmental Economics and Policy Project, Lithuania Program, working paper #9, July 1996
6.   *Deacon R.T.*, Economic Aspects of Forest Policy in Lithuania, Harvard Institute for International Development, International Environment Program, Central and Eastern Europe Environmental Economics and Policy Project, Lithuania Program, working paper #6, October 1995
7.   *Deacon R.T.*, A Proposed Tax on Harvests by Lithuanian State Forest Enterprises, Harvard Institute for International Development, International Environment Program, Central and Eastern Europe Environmental Economics and Policy Project, Lithuania Program, working paper #7, October 1995
8.   *Dumbrauskas A., Larsson R.*, Effects of Changes in Land Use on Runoff in the Nevežis Basin.
9.   *Gaižutis A.., Mizaras S.*, Environmental problems and Policy Instruments in Lithuanian Forestry and Agriculture. Comparing Nordic and Baltic Countries - Environmental Problems and Policies in Agriculture and Forestry, Nordic Council of Ministers, 1994, Copenhagen, TemaNord 1994:572, p. 166-189.
10. *Gutkauskas A.*, Agricultural and Environmental Protection Strategies in Lithuania. NATO/CCMS Pilot Study "New Agricultural Technologies", The Scientific and Technical Research Council of Turkey, 24-25 March, 1997
11. *Jaakson R.*, Eco-tourism Development Project, WTO Mission Report. UNDP World Tourism Organisation Technical Assistance Mission to the Republic of Lithuania, Madrid, 1997, 31 pp.
12. *Juknys R.*, Trends of Lithuanian Environment during Transitional Period. Aplinkos tyrimai, inžinerija ir vadyba, No.1, 1995, Kaunas, Technologija
13. *Kritkausky R.*, Lithuania, Environmental Resources and Constraints in the Former Soviet Republics, Westview Press, Oxford, 1995
14. *Lazauskas P., Rutkoviené V.M.*, Development of organic agriculture in Lithuania. Proceedings of the international conference on Land use changes and nature conservation in Central and Eastern Europe, 5-8 June, 1995, Palanga, Lithuania. Lithuanian Fund for Nature, Vilnius, 1995, p. 30-31.
15. *Mardiste P.*, Sustainable transports systems in Eastern and Central Europe. Tallinn, 1997
16. *Seméniené D., Varneckiené J.*, Possibilities to Introduce Product Charges in Lithuaia: Waste Generation and Use, Harvard Institute for International Development, International Environment Program, Central and Eastern Europe Environmental Economics and Policy Project, Lithuania Program, working paper #11, September 1997
17. *Staniškis J., Vincevičiené V.*, Application of Models for the Nemunas River Water Quality Management. Environmental research, engineering and management, Technologija No. 1(2), Kaunas, 1996
18. *Staniškis J.*, Systems approach to the environmental problems, Aplinkos tyrimai, inžinerija ir vadyba, Technologija No.1, Kaunas 1995
19. *Šileika A.S.*, Agriculture Nitrogen's Impact on Water Quality in Lithuanian Rivers. Environmental research, engineering and management, Technologija No. 1(2), Kaunas, 1996
20. *Taminskas J., Dilys K.*, Lithuanian-Latvian Karst Region: Optimum Land use and nature conservation. In: Proceedings of the international conference on Land use changes and nature conservation in Central and Eastern Europe, 5-8 June, 1995, Palanga, Lithuania. Lithuanian Fund for Nature, Vilnius, 1995, p. 50-51.
21. *Tumas R., Povilaitis A.*, Erosion and Nutrient Transport Prediction: an Evaluation of Agricultural Non-point Pollution Models. Environmental research, engineering and management, Technologija No. 2(3), Kaunas, 1996
22. *Vaičys M., Armolaitis K. et al.* Physical, chemical and biological consequences of soil contamination, land usage under current socio-economic conditions. Ecological Sustainability of Lithuania, Lithuanian Academy of Sciences, International Centre for Scientific Cultures - World Laboratory Lithuanian Branch, Vilnius, 1997, p. 38-44.
23. *Varneckiené J.*, Summary of the International Experience with Product Charges for Environmental Protection, Harvard Institute for International Development, International Environment Program, Central and Eastern Europe Environmental Economics and Policy Project, Lithuania Program, working paper #11, October 1996

24. *Varneckienė J.,* Catalytic Converters for Vehicles, Harvard Institute for International Development, International Environment Program, Central and Eastern Europe Environmental Economics and Policy Project, Lithuania Program, working paper #12, October 1995

25. *Vazgilevičius A.,* Regional point of view and priority projects ensuring fuel supply security. Proceedings of the International Conference on Oil terminals, shipping and off-shore activities in the Eastern-Baltic: present situation, future prospects, economic and technological appraisal and environmental risk. SEI-Tallinn, p. 109-116.

Lithuanian materials

26. Action Programme of the Government of the Republic of Lithuania for 1997-2000, Lithuanian Government.
27. Aplinkos tyrimai, inžinerija ir vadyba, Technologija No.1, Kaunas, 1995
28. Biodiversity Conservation: Strategy and Action Plan. Ministry of Environment, Vilnius, 1998
29. Cancer Registration and the role of Cancer Registry in Lithuania, 1995
30. Chemical and Microbiological Contamination of Drinking Water and Food Products used by Lithuanian Population, National Centre of Hygiene, Ministry of Health, Republic of Lithuania, 1997
31. Critical Levels of surface ozone and its concentrations in Lithuania; Sveikata ir aplinka, 1996 pp 93-100
32. Ecological Problems of Šiauliai, Šiauliai Municipality Environmental Unit, Žaliasis pasaulis, 1994
33. Ecological Sustainability of Lithuania, 1995 Annual Report (abstract), Litnuanian Academy of Sciences, International Centre for Scientific Culture - World Laboratory Lithuanian Branch, Vilnius, 1996
34. Environmental Protection of the Republic of Lithuania, Vilnius, 1996
35. Environment Concerns in Energy, Ministry of Environmental Protection, 1996
36. Groundwater Monitoring in Lithuania (1994), Bulletin, Lithuanian Geology Service, Vilnius, 1995
37. Forests of Lithuania, Ministry of Forestry, Republic of Lithuania, Vilnius, 1996, 10 pp.
38. Health in the Baltic Countries, Estonian Medical Statistics Bureau/Latvian Medical Statistics Bureau/Lithuanian Health Information Centre, 3-rd edition, 1995
39. Health Statistics of Lithuania, Vilnius, 1996
40. Ignalinos Atomines Elektrinės Poveikis Gamtai ir Visuomenei, Vilnius, 1995 pp 256-261
41. Kaunas Healthy City Profile, Kaunas, 1997 - Unpublished report
42. Lietuvos Medicina, Vilnius, 1996, pp 7-10.
43. Lietuvos žemes ūkis (Agriculture of Lithuania), Vastybinis Leidybos Centras, Vilnius, 1995
44. Lithuanian Environmental Strategy: Action Programme, Ministries of Health and the Environment: Objectives: document prepared by the State Public Health Centre, 1997 - Unpublished
45. Lithuania's Environment: Status, Processes, Trends, the Environmental Protection Ministry of the Republic of Lithuania, Vilnius, 1995.
46. Lithuanian HFA Targets Evaluation Forms, document prepared by the State Public Health Centre, 1997 - unpublished
47. Lithuanian Forestry and Timber Industry. Ministry of Forestry, Republic of Lithuania, Vilnius, 1992.
48. Lithuanian National Tourism Development Programme. Lithuanian Tourism Board, Vilnius, 1996, p. 24-33.
49. "Lithuania Today - Politics & Economics", Lithuanian European Institute, September 1995.
50. Lithuanian Tourism Statistics 1996. Lithuanian Tourist Board, Vilnius, 1997
51. Lithuanian Spa Resort Development and Spa Hotel Model Project, Lithuanian Tourist Board, Vilnius, 1997
52. National Energy Efficiency Programme, Lithuanian Ministry of Energy, Vilnius, 1996.
53. National Environmental Finance Strategy, Ministry of Environment/OECD/HIID, draft, August 1997
54. National Implementation Strategy of the UNFCCC in Lithuania, 1996,
55. National Report: Lithuania, national report to the United Nations Conference on Environment and Development, Environmental Protection Department, Vilnius, 1992
56. Aplinkos Monitoringas 1993-1995 (Monitoring data), Annual Report, 1996
57. Privatisation in Lithuania, 1997-1998, Ministry of European Affairs of the Republic of Lithuania, London, June 1997
58. Republic of Lithuania: Least Cost Power Sector Development Programme, Lithuanian Energy Institute with assistance of the EU PHARE Programme, Kaunas, February 1996
59. Selected Laws Relating to Environmental Protection, Ministry of Environmental Protection, Vilnius, 1997
60. Statistical Yearbook of Lithuania, Department of Statistics to the Government of the Republic of Lithuania, Vilnius 1995
61. Statistical Yearbook of Lithuania, Department of Statistics to the Government of the Republic of Lithuania, Vilnius 1997
62. Survey of Lithuanian Economy, Department of Statistics to the Government of the Republic of Lithuania, November 1996
63. Survey of Lithuanian Economy, Department of Statistics to the Government of the Republic of Lithuania, May 1997
64. The Environmental Protection in the Republic of Lithuania, Information bulletin No 1, Environmental Protection Department of the Republic of Lithuania, Lithuanian Information Institute, Vilnius, 1992
65. The Baltic States. Comparative Statistics 1996, Riga 1997
66. Transport and Environment: A comprehensive strategy, Lithuania, PHARE, 1997
67. REC Annual Report, REC Vilnius Office, 1995
68. Waste Management Problems in Lithuania, the Ministry of Environment, February - March 1997

Corporate authors

69. Acta Medica Lituanica, No. 2, 1997, pp 73-76
70. Air Quality Guidelines for Europe - WHO Regional Publications, European Series, No 23, 1987

71. Baltic Sea Environment Proceedings, No. 65, Overview on activities 1996, Helsinki Commission, Baltic Marine Environment Protection Commission, 1997

72. Collection and Treatment System for Hospital Waste in Lithuania, project by Danwaste A/S, July 1994

73. Concerns for Europe's tomorrow - Health and the Environment in the WHO European Region", WHO European Centre for Environment and Health, 1995

74. Country Strategy Document for Lithuania-PHARE Multi-Country Energy Programme, Project on Convergence of Energy Policies, November 1996

75. Ecological Sustainability of Lithuania, 1996 Annual Report (abstract), Lithuanian Academy of Sciences, International Centre for Scientific Culture, World Laboratory Lithuanian Branch, Vilnius, 1997

76. Economic Review Lithuania, International Monetary Fund, Washington, DC, 1993-1995.

77. Energy in Europe - 1996 Annual Energy Review, European Commission DGVII, 1997

78. Environmental Protection and Use of Natural Resources in Latvia 1991-1995, A Collection of Statistical Data, Central Statistical Bureau of Latvia, Riga, 1996

79. Environment and Health in Central and Eastern Europe, a report for the Environmental Action Programme for Central and Eastern Europe, 1995

80. Environment and Health - Overview and Main European Issues - WHO, EEA; WHO Regional publications, European Series, No.68, 1996

81. Environments in transition, the Environmental Bulletin of the EBRD, Spring 1996

82. EPR Country Profiles-LITHUANIA-UN ECE ENHS Internal Papers, May 1997

83. European Commission, Agenda 2000, Lithuania, 1997 (EC Agenda 2000)

84. Exposure of Urban Population in the WHO European Region to Major Air Pollutants, Summary of the WHO-ECEH air pollution data base, WHO European Office for Europe, 1997 (EUR/ICP/TRNS 02 01 02)

85. First Meeting of a Network of Cleaner Production/Pollution Prevention/Energy Efficiency Centres in Central and Eastern Europe, report from the meeting, 23-25 April, Kaunas, Lithuania, OECD, 1997

86. Health effects of Ozone and Nitrogen Oxides in an Integrated Assessment of Air Pollution, UN ECE, WHO proceedings of an international workshop Eastbourne, UK, 10-12-June 1996, Published by the Institute for Environment and Health, 1997

87. Health for All - Health Statistics Database, Data Presentation System, 1997 WHO Regional Office for Europe, 1997

88. Highlights on Health in Lithuania, WHO EURO, 1992 - unpublished report

89. Investments in Environmental Infrastructure, Environments in Transition, EBRD, the environmental bulletin of the EBRD, Autumn 1995.

90. Guidelines for Drinking Water Quality, second edition WHO Geneva, 1993

91. Guidelines for Protected Area Management Categories. IUCN, Gland, 1994, p.17-24.

92. National Environmental Reporting Needs and Capabilities in Baltic States: the Roles of Information Networks, Information centres and GIS (with assessment reports for Estonia, Latvia and Lithuania), UNEP meeting report; Janeda, Estonia, March 23-24, 1995

93. Linkage Methods for Environment and Health Analysis, general guidelines, a report of the health and environment analysis for decision-making (HEADLAMP) project - Office of Global and Integrated Environmental Health , WHO Geneva, 1996

94. Lithuania - Case Study on National Planning for Sustainable Development, Final Report,, WHO Regional office for Europe, 1994 (EUR/LTU/RUD 199; EHE/H11/370/4)

95. Lithuania Energy Emergency Planning, the European Bank for Reconstruction and Development, January 1996

96. Lithuania: Petroleum Supply Study and Training, sectoral report on petroleum marketing, EBRD, September 1996.

97. Lithuania: the Transition to a Market Economy, the World Bank country study, Washington DC, 1993

98. Lithuania - the Transition to a Market Economy, the World Bank country study, Washington DC, 1995

99. Lithuania, 1st and 2nd quarterly reports, WHO Liaison Office, Lithuania, 1997 (unpublished reports)

100. Management of the Vilnius Energy Centre - General Sector - Related Analysis, European Commission, DG XVII - Energy Co-operation with Third countries (SYNERGY), November 1996.

101. Review of Agricultural Policies, Lithuania, OECD, Paris, 1996

102. National Energy Strategy, UN ECE, July 1995

103. Norwegian-Lithuanian Cleaner Production Training Programme, Institute of Environmental Engineering, report April –December 1996

104. Quantification of Health Effects Related to SO2, NO2, O3 and Particulate Matter Exposure, report from the Nordic expert meeting, Oslo, 15-17 October, 1995 WHO (document EUR/ICP/EHAZ 94 04/DT01)

105. Profesinės Ligos Lietuvoje 1995 Metais, Vilnius, 1996

106. Study on Impact of the EU's Future Enlargement to the East on the EU's Natural Gas Sector, Gasunie Engineeering, PARTEX-IIEL

107. Strategies of EU Approximation in the Waste Sector, Draft Report, COWI Consultant, October 1997

108. Šiauliai Environment Project, the World Bank, staff appraisal report No. 14981-LT, Natural Resources Management Division, Country Department IV, Washington DC, 1994

109. TERES II Consultation Report – Lithuania, European Commission, DG XVII, 1997

110. The European Renewable Energy Study, country report-Lithuania, January 1994

111. The Bulletin, quarterly newsletter of the Regional Environmental Center for Central and Eastern Europe, volume 6, number 3, Autumn 1996

112. Tobacco or Health, a Global Status report, WHO Geneva, 1997, pp 342-345

113. Update and Revision of the Air Quality Guidelines for Europe, meeting of the working group "Classical" Air Pollutants, Bilthoven, the Netherlands, 11-14 October 1994, WHO, 1995 (document EUR/ICP/EHAZ 94 05/PB01)

114. 1996 Statistics of Road Traffic Accidents in Europe and North America, UN ECE Geneva, 1996

WWW sites concerning Lithuania

115. Lithuanian Environment Ministry Homepage (http://www.gamta.lt/default.htm)
116. General info on Environmental Protection (http://www.ktl.mii.lt/aa/index.html)
117. Baltic Environmental Forum (http://neris.mii.lt/aa/js/js.html)
118. BALLERINA: Baltic Sea Region Online Environmental Information Resources for Internet Access (http://www.baltic-region.net/)
119. Lithuanian Laws, Governmental Resolutions, and other Legislative Acts, on-line database from Parliament (http://www.lrs.lt/DPaieska.html)
120. Department of Statistics (http://www.std.lt)
121. Lithuanian News Agency (http://www.elta.lt/)